PUBLICPRIVATE

Joe and Gail working at home in 1985, an era before
computers, the internet, cell phones, and email.
Barbra Walz © Estate of Barbra Walz

PUBLICPRIVATE

MY LIFE with JOE PAPP at THE PUBLIC THEATER

Gail Merrifield Papp

APPLAUSE
THEATRE & CINEMA BOOKS
Essex, Connecticut

For Celia Mitchell

APPLAUSE
THEATRE & CINEMA BOOKS

An imprint of Globe Pequot, the trade division of
The Rowman & Littlefield Publishing Group, Inc.
4501 Forbes Blvd., Ste. 200
Lanham, MD 20706
www.rowman.com

Distributed by NATIONAL BOOK NETWORK

Library of Congress Cataloging-in-Publication Data

ISBN 978-1-4930-7486-0 (cloth: alk. paper)
ISBN 978-1-4930-7487-7 (electronic)

Printed in India

Contents

"While Memory Holds a Seat"

Theater doesn't exist independently of life. In my world, there's always a connection between the front page and the theater page.

There's a very specific reference in Hamlet that I've always taken to heart and that is when Hamlet meets the Ghost of his father and the Ghost says, *"Remember me."*

And Hamlet says, *"While memory holds a seat in this distracted globe"*—that's how long he'll remember him.

Now that's a triple metaphor.

"This distracted globe" was Shakespeare's Globe Playhouse where all the distracted audiences gathered; the "distracted globe" was the world; and the "distracted globe" was Hamlet's head, the more literal meaning of the line.

I believe in that: my head, the theater, and the world. The interconnection has to be constant.

Joe Papp

Author's Note

Why does someone start a theater? What is its purpose? Who is it for? Who creates it? How is it kept afloat? Why should anyone care? Also, why am I alive? What is the meaning of existence?

These were the kinds of questions that Joe Papp, who founded New York City's free New York Shakespeare Festival and the Public Theater, asked himself throughout his career as a theatrical producer. Such questions were basic to his fiercely democratic viewpoint that not only changed American theater in the way that it staged Shakespeare but also brought into major focus the voices of new American playwrights who had been previously minimized or ignored due to their ethnicity and gender.

During the twenty-six years that I worked with Joe in the theater, we were immersed in these ideas and questions. Many of the social issues he confronted still reflect urgent concerns in the twenty-first century. Such matters are an important counterpoint to my story, which is, I freely admit, first of all about the connection of mind and heart that Joe and I unexpectedly discovered in each other. In the currently destabilized world of a devastating pandemic and the toxic undermining of our country's fragile democratic experiment, it seems the right time for me to remember Joe's fighting words and large perspective—and to share with others the humor and humanity of a sorely missed pragmatic radical touched with public genius.

Gail Merrifield Papp
New York City, January 2023

1

Greenwich Village, 1991

When Joseph Papp died at home in New York City on October 31, 1991, his memorial service, in accordance with traditional Jewish practice, had to be held the very next day. Arrangements were swiftly made for it to take place at the Public Theater, the theatrical complex that he had founded in Greenwich Village, four blocks from our apartment.

When I arrived for the service on November 1, people in the crowded lobby were just beginning to file into the Newman Theater on the first floor. It seemed quite natural to join them because for nearly three decades I had followed audiences into this theater with Joe to see the plays that he produced on its stage. It was a familiar place, a precinct in my theatrical home. Entering its audience area, I wouldn't have been surprised to see Joe waiting there a few steps ahead of me. Instead I saw a casket on the empty stage.

In future years I did remember that music had been playing at that heartbreaking moment, and that Joe's theatrical colleagues had spoken most movingly about him from the stage. But I couldn't recall the details. I couldn't even recall who had come with me from home to the theater. And because the memorial service had to be put together so quickly, there had been no time to create a printed program from which I might have refreshed my memory.

For a while my impaired recollection of Joe's memorial service haunted me, but faced with so many daunting challenges, I put it aside.

Fast forward twenty-seven years, to 2018. In that year I learned quite by accident that there was a video of Joe's memorial service in the film archives of Lincoln Center's Library for the Performing Arts. I was amazed. I'd had no idea that it existed. I called Patrick Hoffman, Director of the Library's Theater on Film and Tape Archive. He confirmed that they had the video and very kindly arranged a viewing of it for me at Lincoln Center.

I asked the actress Kathryn Grody to come with me. She and her husband, actor-singer Mandy Patinkin, had been our friends for many years. Both of them had been in plays at the Public Theater and in Central Park, and Joe had produced *A Mom's Life*, a solo performance piece that Kathryn had written.

Settled in a viewing cubicle at Lincoln Center Library, Kathryn and I now watched the video of Joe's memorial service more than two decades after it had taken place.

The first person to speak was Rabbi Arthur Schneier, the leader of Park East Synagogue. A good friend of Joe's, he was a human rights activist internationally known for his leadership on behalf of religious freedom and tolerance.

Rabbi Schneier opened the memorial service from the stage of the Newman Theater by reading the 15th Psalm of David, which asks, "Who will sojourn in the Lord's tent?" The answer follows: "He who walks uprightly and works righteousness, and speaks the truth in his heart"—virtues that Joe aspired to.

Next up was Mayor David Dinkins, New York City's first Black mayor. Mentioning that his own father had just died, Mayor Dinkins said that Joe had been "a beacon who enabled us to see things we've never seen." His calm and elegant manner reminded me of how he always celebrated the "gorgeous mosaic" of the city, just as Joe did, and of the unusual private dinner he had invited Joe and me to at Gracie Mansion with just him and his wife Joyce. I also remembered the handwritten note he sent me a few days after the memorial service, saying "Remember the good times," which I had taken to heart like a person hugging a lifebuoy ring in a stormy sea.

Elizabeth Swados followed the mayor. She was the extraordinary composer-lyricist-director of many productions, including the Tony Award–winning musical *Runaways*. I think it's correct to call her a protégé of Joe's because he had remained committed to her work in an era that had sometimes failed to properly value her distinctive talent. Liz talked about Joe's openness to new forms of music, as well as her working visits to our country place and the feeling of warmth and acceptance she felt there from us.

The next speaker was the director-playwright James Lapine, Stephen Sondheim's collaborator and the director of *Sunday in the Park with George*. For Joe he'd staged his own haunting play *Twelve Dreams* at the Public and an enchanting *A Midsummer Night's Dream* in Central Park. Jim recalled his initial awe on meeting Joe for the first time, but said that later, after seeing how modestly Joe and I lived, he had come to the conclusion that "Joe was far more *haimish* than formidable."

I was so happy to see our friend and colleague, Robin Wagner, appear next. His unassuming manner belied his masterful achievements as scenic designer of *A Chorus Line, Hair, Angels in America*, as well as operas and ballets. Robin read these moving lines from *Cymbeline*:

> Fear no more the heat o' the sun
> Nor the furious winter's rages;
> Thou thy worldly task hast done,
> Home art gone, and ta'en thy wages.

The actor and indefatigable social justice activist Martin Sheen then took the stage. When Martin was still in his twenties—long before he became famous for his film roles in *Badlands* and *Apocalypse Now*, Joe had cast him as Hamlet in a crazy-quilt adaptation of the play that Joe directed at the Public Theater. Like others who came under Joe's influence, Martin had subsequently appeared in other Shakespearean roles. This day, he spoke with feeling about his bond with Joe and afterward kissed the casket.

Actress Meryl Streep now appeared in the video. From the time that she first arrived in New York City, she had been in Joe's stage, film, and television productions of plays by Shakespeare, Chekhov, Lewis Carroll, and contemporary writers such as Thomas Babe and David Hare. Meryl told an anecdote about her young children—Henry age eleven, Mamie eight, Gracie five (and there was the new baby Louisa). When they asked her who Joe was, Meryl said she had told them, "He's the only boss I ever had that I loved, and he's my hero."

The Puerto Rican actor Raúl Juliá followed Meryl on the Newman stage. He had been an incorrigibly macho Petruchio to Meryl's fiercely defiant Kate in an unforgettable *The Taming of the Shrew* that Joe produced in

Central Park. He had played many major roles in Joe's productions, including *Othello*, *Macbeth*, and Mac the Knife in the musical *The Threepenny Opera*.

Raúl recalled that he had once done a rousing rendition for Joe of a famous speech by Theodore Roosevelt:

> The credit belongs to the man who is actually in the arena, whose face is marred by dust and sweat and blood, who strives valiantly, who errs and comes up short again and again, because there is no effort without error or shortcoming, but who knows the great enthusiasms, the great devotions, who spends himself in a worthy cause; who, at the best, knows, in the end, the triumph of high achievement, and who, at the worst, if he fails, at least he fails while daring greatly, so that his place shall never be with those cold and timid souls who knew neither victory nor defeat.

Raúl, who obviously associated Joe with the "man who is actually in the arena," said that Joe responded to Teddy Roosevelt's heroic speech by quietly observing that, "He was accurate, but simplistic."

The new leadership of the Public Theater followed. Its recently appointed artistic director was JoAnne Akalaitis, an experimental director and the co-founder with composer Philip Glass of Mabou Mines. She said she was committed to the Public's unique legacy and mentioned how deeply she herself had been affected by "Joe's passion for theater."

Kathryn Grody and I then watched her husband Mandy Patinkin come on stage. Famous for his musical performances in *Evita* as Che Guevara and in *Sunday in the Park with George* as George Seurat, Mandy had played a range of parts in Joe's productions from Hotspur in *Henry IV, Part 1* in Central Park to a new musical called *The Knife* on the same Newman Theater stage. Mandy spoke of Joe's important early support for his singing career and for his wife Kathryn's vocation as a writer. He concluded with a refrain from the song "Yossel, Yossel" ("Joseph, Joseph") in Yiddish.

The stage and film actor Kevin Kline followed. "Like Mandy," he said, "Joe was my adopted artistic father." Kevin had played most of the major roles in Joe's Shakespeare productions, as well the Pirate King in Joe's stage and film productions of *The Pirates of Penzance*. Kevin told the audience that just the previous week he and his wife, actress Phoebe Cates, had brought their new-born son, named Owen Joseph, for Joe to see.

The next speaker was Bernard Gersten, then the executive producer of Lincoln Center Theater, and formerly the Public's associate producer. Bernie had been Joe's closest colleague in the creation of the Public Theater in the 1960s and was in a unique position to give an eloquent summation of its amazing history, of which he had been such an important part.

Gerald Freedman, a consummate director and mentor to distinguished actors, spoke last. He had staged many of the acclaimed Shakespeare productions in Central Park before becoming the first artistic director of the Public Theater, which had opened with his famous production of *Hair*. Jerry recalled the two kosher kitchens that used to be where the Newman Theater would later stand, dating to when the building had housed the Hebrew Immigrant Aid Society. Watching Jerry, who trained as a cantor, I remembered how beautifully he had sung at our wedding.

The video now showed several speakers coming back on stage and gathering around Joe's casket as they wheeled it through an upstage curtain.

In the next footage it reappeared on the sidewalk in front of the theater, with Al Pacino and Robert De Niro among the pallbearers.

In the early days Al Pacino had done a workshop of Brecht's *The Resistible Rise of Arturo Ui* that Joe sponsored and had played Marc Antony in *Julius Caesar* in the Newman Theater. Robert De Niro had returned to the stage after a long absence in a new play at the Public Theater called *Cuba and His Teddy Bear*.

The video then cut back to the interior of the Newman Theater with a long shot of the audience exiting the memorial service. Among the last people to leave the theater I spotted the shoulders and unmistakable long curls of my mother, Gladys Merrifield, who died ten months after Joe. It's the only film that exists of her.

***

Before Kathryn and I began watching the video of Joe's memorial service, Patrick Hoffman had graciously welcomed us and set up the playback machine, kindly returning a few minutes later with a box of Kleenex.

It wasn't necessary in my case, however, because tears had long since been surmounted by the love and everlasting connection I still feel with Joe and what he stood for.

What follows is the story of how that happened.

2

Greenwich Village, 1965

In 1965 I had rented a small room above Whelan's Drugstore at the lively corner of 8th Street and Sixth Avenue in the heart of New York City's Greenwich Village. It was on a block of shops that sold handmade leather sandals, Turkish water pipes, and psychedelic posters to the hippies, folkies, and students who bustled around the neighborhood.

My second-floor window faced an all-night White Castle Diner where I went for morning coffee.

At the age of twenty-nine, I had decided to leave the publishing field where I had been previously employed and look instead for a job in the theater.

My sole inspiration for this course correction was the fact that in the nineteenth and early twentieth centuries, five generations of women in my family had been actors—my aunt, great-aunt, grandmother, great-grandmother, and great-great-grandmother.

Although I wasn't an actor myself, I felt that identifying in some way with their theatrical profession might restore my spirits after the past traumatic year when I had been divorced by the young man I had fallen in love with and married in college. Although I had been consumed by the hurt and sense of betrayal I felt when my husband left me, I still couldn't help remembering Bruce as the bright, lanky boy I once knew with whom only ten years ago I rode across the country on a Harley-Davidson Hummer Motorcycle, camping in cornfields under the stars, bedding on pine needles in national parks, and cooking meals on a Primus stove no bigger than a child's shoe.

My great-grandmother Rita Booth as
Billy Piper in *The Danites* in 1882.
Courtesy of Gail Merrifield Papp

Grandmother Izola Henderson as the
Middy in *HMS Pinafore* in 1890.
Courtesy of Gail Merrifield Papp

Great-aunt Beatrice Henderson
in *Señorita Tabasco* in 1912.
Courtesy of Gail Merrifield Papp

When I met him at New York University, I had been captivated by his youthful angst and disillusionment, seeing in him a kindred spirit to Holden Caulfield, the teenage protagonist of J. D. Salinger's recently published *Catcher in the Rye*. In those early days, our dual scholarship paths had been enriched as protégés of a brilliant professor, Dr. Charles T. Davis, and we had edited the short-lived campus literary magazine together. We got married as teenagers while still at NYU and afterward found employment with publishing companies in New York City and Mexico City. After ten years, however, the marriage succumbed to its difficulties and the relationship was over. By the time I rented that room above the drugstore in Greenwich Village, my former husband had become the head of a foreign news bureau in Italy and planned to remarry.

I was now living alone for the first time in my adult life, an unfamiliar condition that afflicted my waking hours like a dull toothache. The one thing that made me feel hopeful again was the decision to rebuild my life by looking for work, not at a publishing company again but at a theatrical organization. Blissfully unaware how difficult it was to find such employment in New York City, I pursued this goal in high spirits and, with beginner's luck, managed to land a full-time position with the exciting new Repertory Theater of Lincoln Center that was due to open in 1965.

The charismatic founding leaders of Lincoln Center Theater were Producer Robert Whitehead and Director Elia Kazan. They oversaw a Repertory Company which performed in a large 1,158-seat temporary playhouse that had been built for them at 40 West 4th Street near Washington Square while the uptown theater for them was under construction.

My new job was at their temporary midtown office, where I worked for Hugh Southern, Robert Whitehead's suave and diplomatic associate. Elia Kazan occasionally walked in, practicing his swing with a baseball bat for an upcoming softball game with the Broadway Theatre League. Because I had been a freelance playreader for the Theatre Guild and Brandt & Brandt Dramatic Agency, I was assigned to read plays for the experimental Forum Theater, which, like the Beaumont Theater being built above it, was still under construction. I could hardly believe my incredible good fortune in getting this job and took my responsibility of evaluating new plays very seriously. I had passes to see everything down at the West 4th Street playhouse, which included the premieres of Arthur Miller's *After the Fall* and *Incident at Vichy*—the latter directed by Group Theater Co-founder Harold Clurman, who enlisted my services as an assistant on the production.

Around this time I met an engaging young man in the reading room of my neighborhood library. Arthur was a tall Yale Law School intellectual who wrote speeches for politicians. I mention him now because he plays a role later in my story. Built like a football player but with the wit and élan of a courtier, Arthur was always the life of a party, attracting women as moths to flame. In my case, however, he claimed to have suffered the "calamity" of becoming fond of me, even going so far as to introduce me to his parents in suburban Riverdale—where his mother discreetly inquired, in her soft-spoken French-Canadian Yiddish accent, about our life together *("So . . . how is your life together?")* and his jovial father from Odesa toasted me with a glass of vodka.

I had been working at Lincoln Center Theater for a year when one day, out of the blue, I learned that the theater's board had decided in its corporate wisdom to replace Whitehead and Kazan with the co-directors of the San Francisco Actor's Workshop, Herbert Blau and Jules Irving. Not only were Whitehead and Kazan unceremoniously fired, but nearly the entire staff of the theater was let go, including myself.

The next morning I sat in my usual spot at the counter of the White Castle, sunk in glum reflection about my life: jobless, ignominiously fired, and recently alone again after the sudden termination of my relationship with Arthur. Apparently, his parents' welcoming embrace of me had rattled Arthur's professional bachelorhood, and he'd retreated from the possibility of its disruption.

I now had to face the fact that the two most important aspects of my bravely reinvented post-married life—a job in the theater and a new relation-ship—had evaporated into nothing. They had become as fleeting as the steam rising from my cup of coffee.

3

The Great Northern Hotel

I had to find a new job as soon as possible because unemployment insurance certainly wasn't going to cover my rent, utilities, and food, and I had no savings to fall back on. Neither of my parents, who had divorced when I was sixteen years old, were in a position to help me. My mother Gladys Merrifield, who lived in New York City, and my father Richard Merrifield, who lived in Keene, New Hampshire, barely made enough at their jobs to get by from payday to payday.

I knew very well how to scramble for and get a paying job because I'd had to do that when I was younger, mostly horrible jobs like typing bills of lading for the United Parcel Service.

But it was different now, and I hung on to the idea of working in the theater again despite the fast-approaching date when I would really and truly run out of money and be flat broke. Although my situation wasn't at all conducive to a well-planned search for probably nonexistent work in a theatrical producer's office, I nevertheless took crazily precious time to write a job-seeking letter to everyone listed under "Theatrical Producers" in the Yellow Pages volume of the New York City phonebook.

There were eighty names, including the Broadway impresario David Merrick, and I wrote to all of them, typing in this pre-computer age the same letter eighty times on my diminutive Olivetti manual portable which I placed on the only table in my small one-room apartment.

As I approached the completion of this exhausting and time-consuming labor, I worried that the résumé I planned to attach to my letters looked rather thin in theatrical experience. All I had to show was my recently terminated year of employment at Lincoln Center Theater and some freelance script reading.

I decided therefore to add a "credit" to my résumé, claiming that I had been employed as a technical assistant to the producer of the Keene Summer Theater in New Hampshire—which was sort of true although I had been only a thirteen-year-old summer apprentice there in 1947 and the "producer" had been my great-aunt, a turn-of-the-century vaudevillian who had converted the red barn on her husband's property into a summer theater in the 1930s.

I attached the embellished résumé to my brief cover letter to producers, which I'd ended with a droll non sequitur about my ability to make good coffee—and then mailed them off. I had no choice but to simply wait and hope that something good would happen.

A few days later the phone rang. I answered it on the wall of the kitchenette.

"Is this Miss Gail?" a man's voice with a Southern accent asked at the other end.

"Yes."

"Good morning! This is Hilmar Sallee of the New York Shakespeare Festival. We put on the free Shakespeare plays at the Delacorte Theater in Central Park."

"Oh yes," I said offhandedly, although I was secretly puzzled because there had been no "New York Shakespeare Festival" in the Yellow Pages of the phonebook and therefore I hadn't sent a letter to the Festival. In fact, I had never heard of the Festival.

"Come and see us," Mr. Sallee said. "We'll talk."

When I arrived for my appointment, I discovered that the New York Shakespeare Festival operated from a modest suite of rooms in the Great Northern Hotel at 118 West 57th Street on the same grimy block as Carnegie Hall. Its threadbare lobby bore few signs of its former glory when it had been advertised in 1910 as "an abode of luxury."

By 1965 the Great Northern Hotel had become a favorite hostelry for foreign students whose duffel bags littered the lobby floor as they lined up at the reception desk.

When I started working at Joe Papp's New York Shakespeare Festival
in 1965, its headquarters were at the Great Northern Hotel.
Nicole DiMella for Papp Estate

Hilmar Sallee, snappily dressed in a blue-and-white seersucker suit and a
red bowtie, greeted me at the Festival's hotel-suite door, identifying himself as
the general manager of the organization. He was courteous and boisterously
cheerful. We took to each other right away.

He introduced me to the associate producer, Bernard Gersten, to whom
my Olivetti-typed letter had been forwarded by the David Merrick office,
apparently because someone there had been amused by my coffee-making
non sequitur. Bernard Gersten had then passed my letter on to Hilmar Sallee.

Joseph Papp—who, Mr. Sallee informed me, was the founder-producer of
the New York Shakespeare Festival—wasn't in.

"You'll have a chance to meet him later on," he said.

With little preamble, Hilmar Sallee hired me to write the program biogra-
phies of dancers in the Rebekah Harkness Dance Festival that was to follow
the Shakespeare season in Central Park.

"They change their program every night," he said in his Arkansas drawl, "so you'll have to deliver your copy to the printer every day."

I didn't mind. I was glad to have this job at the New York Shakespeare Festival even though it was only temporary summer employment at the low end of the clerical totem pole, because it would pay the rent for my room above Whelan's Drugstore and tide me over until I could find another full-time job in the theater. I regarded this chance to work at the Festival as a piece of random good luck in an otherwise discouraging year.

On my first day, which was April 1, I was given a desk facing Joseph Papp's red-haired executive assistant, Ann Kingsbury. She was a theater professional in her thirties who had been with him for several years. Super-competent, and in fact overqualified, she'd taught, she'd acted, and she functioned in a truly executive fashion.

Ann was very kind to me, but I could see that she had a tense relationship with Mr. Sallee, a former actor and stage manager who had been a key associate of Joe Papp's since 1954, throughout the first decade of the Festival. Now he was the Festival's general manager, in charge of its daily operations, budgets, schedules, and personnel.

On Monday mornings, Mr. Sallee would arrive at the hotel office with a towering bunch of fresh gladioli that he unwrapped and arranged in a vase on Papp's desk. It seemed obvious to me that he simply wanted to brighten the drab atmosphere of the hotel office. However, Ann seemed to regard this as fawning behavior. She told me that she hated gladioli. She thought they were ugly and suspected her boss did too, though he'd never said so.

I didn't meet Joe Papp until later that month because he was in rehearsal with the season's third show at the Delacorte Theater.

In the meantime, since my summer job of writing the Harkness dance bios wouldn't start until August, Mr. Sallee kept me busy with other tasks. One that was very important to him involved clipping articles about the Festival from the city's then-numerous daily newspapers. Throughout the early years he had personally maintained giant-size scrapbooks of reviews, news, and interviews about the Festival, and they now comprised a valuable archive of its early history. My task was to keep them up to date by clipping relevant stories from the newspapers and magazines that he stacked on my desk each morning.

Although President John Kennedy's assassination two years earlier still hovered in the air, in April 1965 when I started clipping newspapers for the Festival, it was President Lyndon Johnson's deployment of U.S. combat troops for offensive action in Vietnam that dominated the headlines.

On April 14, however, a different kind of headline jumped out from the stack of newspapers on my desk. The lead story on the front page of the *New York Times* was "100 Years Ago Tonight: The Tragedy at Ford's Theater. *Parallels Are Noted in Lincoln's Death and Kennedy's*" by the prize-winning journalist Homer Bigart. It wrapped around an illustration showing actor John Wilkes Booth in the Presidential box at Ford's Theater in Washington, D.C. in 1865 aiming his single-shot derringer at the back of President Lincoln's head. April 14, 1965, was the hundredth anniversary of Lincoln's assassination.

Arriving early that morning, Joe Papp, to whom I had been briefly introduced, stopped at my desk for a moment to look at the assassination story and joked that it was probably only the second time in a hundred years that an actor had made it onto the front page of the *Times*. Soon after, he left for rehearsals. With the warmer weather in May, Ann Kingbury and I began taking our brown bag lunches to a bench in nearby Central Park. It was there she told me one day that she was in love with a man who lived in Vermont and was worried that unless she found a job within a fifty-mile radius of him, the relationship might dissipate.

"I've got to relocate," she said, "but I dread telling Joe I'm leaving because I know he's going to be angry."

Ann offered to recommend me for her job. I thanked her but said that I didn't want to do office work anymore. I said that since working at Lincoln Center, I had become more interested in reading plays. She waved that aside, saying, "I think you'd find it stimulating to work for Joe. There's no one else like him."

I really couldn't tell because so far my only interaction with the Festival's founder-producer had been to return his brisk "Good morning" as he walked past my desk. I was sure that he had no idea who I was or what I was doing there, but that changed one day when I wore my hair down instead of swept up.

Pausing at my desk for a nanosecond, Joe Papp said, "The Juliet look. You should always wear it that way," and strode into his office.

"What was that about?" I wrote in my diary at home that night. Whatever it was, I began to wear my hair down.

When Ann finally gave her notice, Joe Papp called me into his office. I thought he wanted to interview me, but all he said was, "Do you think you can do the job?"

I said yes.

"Fine," he said. "You're hired."

4

A Manifesto

I was hired the way that Joe Papp hired almost everybody who worked at the early New York Shakespeare Festival. His appraisals of people and situations, though not perfect, tended to be uncannily sound and shrewd. I thought they might possibly be psychic.

Unlike most men in their forties, he wore Bermuda shorts and T-shirts to work in the summer instead of suits and ties. Dark-haired and handsome, he moved around the hotel suite with athletic grace, pausing at our desks to chat in a breezy manner that struck me as facetious yet purposeful, edgy yet good-natured, invasive yet polite. His contradictions kept you on your toes.

Although he had a casual and friendly personality, he frowned on unmerited verbal familiarity, and I winced when someone presumed to call him "Joe" on too-brief acquaintance. Papp's curt rejoinder had been "*Mr.* Papp to you."

As for myself, I didn't dream of calling him "Joe" at this early stage of my employment at the Festival. But "Mr. Papp" was too formal so, since I couldn't think of anything else to call him, I called him nothing. The only exceptions to this nameless impasse were the office memos that I wrote addressed "To JP From GM." In this era, long before emails and text messages had been invented, these memos became my daily form of communication with him since he was mostly in rehearsals.

I must pause here to mention the significant fact that my parents, who were writers, used to wear tortoise-shell glasses when they wrote at home, giving them in my child's eyes an enthralling look of concentration. They also smoked cigarettes as they worked, thus smoke in my child's mind became associated with their lifelong pursuit of fulfillment as authors. Luckily I didn't become a smoker myself, but to this day the sight of anyone engaged in the act of writing who smokes and wears tortoise-shell glasses stirs an irrepressible beat of fondness and respect in my heart. I have no doubt that this childhood association influenced my positive first impressions of Joe Papp, who wore tortoise-shell glasses and smoked as he wrote at his desk.

And he wrote constantly: letters to editors, critics, mayors, presidents (of our country and others), politicians, mental health professionals, funders, children, writers, and actors. He wrote letters of introduction and letters of recommendation. He wrote forewords to books, prefaces to plays, and speeches. He would write them in longhand on lined pads or type them as rough drafts on the Remington typewriter that sat on a small table beside his desk.

Also, almost every day, Papp wrote notes to himself as a way to craft his ideas, set goals, and explore his feelings. He'd read them aloud to anyone who happened to be around. Most of the time that was me.

I liked the axiomatic brevity of some of them—"Theater is as personal as a garden. You have to cultivate it yourself"—as well as the radical fervor that resonated in others:

"A REVOLUTION!! A total political event!" one began. "ART becomes a weapon—by striking a blow against the wishy-washy tokenism, concepts and assimilation in the liberal guise of integration."

I often came across Papp's notes on the brink of being discarded, either carelessly buried under mounds of correspondence on his desk or tossed into his wastebasket. Since they struck me as a fascinating record of his ideas as a creative producer—someone who played many parts in his role as mentor, innovator, director, fundraiser, friend, foe, dramaturg, enabler, political gad-fly, and mover-of-all-things—I began to save them.

During my previous employment at publishing companies I had occasion-ally met famous people, such as former President Harry S. Truman, whose unsorted boxes of writing fragments, published by Bernard Geis Associates as *Mr. Citizen*, I had worked on. And I'd met the Irish playwright Brendan Behan, who used to position himself precariously on the corner of my edito-rial desk tilting a bottle of champagne to his lips as if it was a bottle of Coke.

But somehow I'd never experienced the personal curiosity about them that I felt now about Joe Papp. One reason is that I didn't know anything about him or his Shakespeare Festival because I had been living in Mexico with my then-husband during the time that Papp had become a public figure.

I made up for my ignorance by looking through General Manager Sallee's giant scrapbooks of clippings about the Festival's beginnings.

From them I learned that Papp had begun free performances of Shakespeare in 1954 at the Emmanuel Presbyterian Church in the East Village and later at the East River Amphitheater in 1956, when reviews of his productions made it into the city's newspapers for the first time. I would arrive early at the office, not so much to read the reviews of those plays in the scrapbooks, but to read the unusual stories I found there about Papp's constantly endangered early enterprise.

Since this was long before any books had been written about him or the Festival, it was from Mr. Sallee's scrapbooks that I became aware of Papp's legendary fight with Robert Moses, New York City's powerful, multi-hatted Parks Commissioner. Admired and feared as the master builder of tri-state bridges, tunnels, housing works, highways, and expressways, Robert Moses had long possessed the authority to demolish large swathes of urban real estate and uproot established neighborhoods and businesses for the furtherance of his multi-million dollar projects. Mayors, governors, city, state and federal representatives, builders, and unions all seemed to be within the purview and influence of this one man.

In 1957 Moses had granted Papp permission to present free performances of Shakespeare on a temporary stage in Central Park, but after two summers he ruled in 1959 that Papp would have to charge admission so that he would be able to reimburse the Parks Department for its services to the Festival. Papp was willing to raise the money, but when he refused on principle to do so by charging admission, Moses revoked the Festival's permit to perform in Central Park.

Incensed, Papp took his protest to the city's newspapers, setting off a journalistic tempest dubbed "Moses vs. The Bard" that dominated New York City's cultural news for most of the year. At first Moses seemed to regard the dispute as an annoying disturbance in the land of Lilliput, misjudging Papp's deep-seated dedication to free Shakespeare in Central Park as well as the tremendous popular support it had attracted during the past two years. Soon that support began to be expressed in the city's then numerous newspapers with a steady flow of Letters to the Editor, articles, editorials, and cartoons reframing the issue as a David vs. Goliath contest.

Devouring these stories in the scrapbooks on my furtive morning time before anyone arrived at the office, I avidly followed the uproar of public sympathy for Papp's egalitarian stance during this cause célèbre. Its cliff-hanging developments seemed to unfold on a daily basis, with arresting headlines such as "No Free Shakespeare in Park, Moses Rules," and "Moses Sends Out Unsigned Attack on Park Producer," and "Park Play Talks Break Up in Huff."

In May 1959, however, Papp's back was against the wall, and there appeared little hope that his planned production of *Julius Caesar* would take place in Central Park.

But then on May 19 Papp filed a show-cause order in New York State's Supreme Court that directed Moses to show in court why he should not be compelled to grant a permit allowing Shakespeare to return to Central Park that summer. Presiding Judge Samuel M. Gold offered to mediate the case, but Moses rejected the offer and counterfiled an affidavit defending his position. Justice Gold then "reluctantly" dismissed Papp's petition, finding that Moses had "full discretion" over "cultural activity . . . in any specified area of the public parks."

"Moses Wins Case on Plays in Park" was the headline on June 3. But on June 9 Papp filed an appeal of his case to the Appellate Division of the New York State Supreme Court with a request for immediate action.

All of these events had a dramatic immediacy for me because they had taken place less than five years before the time that I was reading them. Their drama was in no way diminished for me by the fact that their imperiled protagonist, Joe Papp, would soon resume working at his desk in an adjoining room in the hotel office suite.

On June 10, 1959, the judges of the Appellate Division had agreed to review Papp's appeal before their summer recess, and on June 18, they ruled unanimously in favor of the Festival's admission-free presence in Central Park, finding that the actions of Parks Commissioner Moses had been "clearly arbitrary, capricious and unreasonable." The headline: "Court Bids Moses Retreat on Bard."

Good for him! I thought to myself, cheering Joe Papp's populist victory six years earlier.

In future years the Papp-Moses story took on near-mythic significance, with Robert Caro devoting an entire chapter to it in his biography, *The Power Broker: Robert Moses and the Fall of New York,* as did *New York Times* Managing Editor Arthur Gelb in his memoir *City Room.* The story has also been vividly retold in *Joe Papp: An American Life* by Helen Epstein (Little, Brown and Company, 1994) and in *Free for All: Joe Papp, The Public, and the Greatest Theater Story Ever Told* by Kenneth Turan and Joseph Papp (Doubleday, 2009). These books chronicle many of the underlying issues that fueled the dispute, such as red-baiting and anti-Semitism.

Curious now about Joe Papp's personal background, I looked him up in *Who's Who in America.* The entry about him, in tiny hard-to-read type, summarized the following facts:

Joseph Papp had been born in Brooklyn in 1921 to Shmuel and Yetta Papirofsky, Jewish immigrants from Poland and Lithuania. He had graduated from Eastern District High School in Brooklyn and served in the navy during World War II. In the late 1940s he became managing director of the Actor's Lab in Los Angeles. After it closed in 1950, he moved back to New York City and worked as a stage manager at CBS Television. In 1954 he founded the Shakespearean Theater Workshop, later called the New York Shakespeare Festival.

After this dry-as-dust summary, *Who's Who* had a column listing all of the Shakespeare plays that Papp had produced with their dates and the venues where they were staged, including at the permanent Delacorte Amphitheater in Central Park which, in an amazing reversal of fortune, had been built for him by the previously hostile City in 1962.

I skimmed the next section about his numerous awards and professional affiliations, skipping to the last paragraph that said Joseph Papp was married and had two children.

Still curious, I looked around and found reprints of his published articles stacked on a shelf in the hotel office. The one that caught my attention was an "Open Letter" to Walter Kerr, the influential drama critic at the *New York Herald-Tribune,* who had sided with Robert Moses in opposing Joe Papp's free admission to his Shakespeare plays in Central Park.

Kerr had argued in his *Herald-Tribune* column that free admission was a bad idea because it encouraged "wholesale free-loading . . . A man must pay for what he gets. If he doesn't, there's something wrong with him, or something wrong with it."

Papp's published reply read like a manifesto because he compared his idea of free access to theater with free access to books at the public library. That hit home with me because during my childhood in Berkeley, California, my parents never had enough money to buy books at bookstores, so there were many I could never have read if I hadn't been able to borrow them free of charge from Berkeley's Public Library. A trip to the library with my mother and father then was always an exciting occasion because we'd return home with stacks of books for each of us to read.

Joe Papp's answer to Kerr therefore rang the bells of freedom and access, which I immediately understood when he wrote, "In a city the size of New York, it is of the utmost importance to have a public theater—a theater for everybody—yes, everybody: for those who can afford it and for those who cannot."

Well, I liked that! It made me feel I had arrived at the right place: a theater led by a charismatic founder-producer motivated by social as well as artistic goals.

5

"Tell Pandarus to Say It to the Audience"

In perusing the scrapbooks, I saw that during Joe Papp's first years of producing Shakespeare he'd favored popular plays like *A Midsummer Night's Dream* and *Julius Caesar*. But when I joined the Festival in 1965, he had decided to produce the so-called problem plays for the first time at the Delacorte Theater in Central Park, and to direct one of them, *Troilus and Cressida*, himself.

So far I had been kept busy with numerous tasks that Hilmar Sallee lined up for me to do, and the Festival's new focus on these plays was of marginal interest. But that suddenly changed one Friday when Joe Papp asked me to take his director's notes during the previews of *Troilus and Cressida*—which were due to start the following Tuesday.

This was a completely unexpected development, and I was panic-stricken. Why on earth had he asked me? I had no academic or theatrical background in Shakespeare, let alone any experience in taking a director's notes.

Since I was aware that Joe Papp had personally directed such famous actors as Frank Silvera, George C. Scott, Colleen Dewhurst, James Earl Jones, and Julie Harris, I trembled now at the prospect of being under his directorial scrutiny as an unqualified notetaker who had never even read *Troilus and Cressida*.

Taking his notes would also mean extra evening hours, but how could I say no? I saw that everyone on the Festival's small staff pitched in to help with whatever was needed because everyone believed in what Joe Papp was doing. Art for the people. Free admission. The morale on the staff was high.

It was not, for example, beneath the dignity of the general manager to shuttle important messages between our hotel office and a backstage communications desk at the Delacorte Theater in Central Park whenever squirrels had chewed on a telephone line there and brought it down.

Since Joe Papp hadn't included me in his rehearsals of *Troilus and Cressida*, I had no practical knowledge of this vexatious play other than what I could achieve by reading it for the first time in my life and consulting the editor's footnotes. Trying to catch up quickly on my own in only three days, I discovered that *Troilus* had a supersize cast of forty-six Greeks and Trojans comprising a veritable stable of mythological personages such as Agamemnon, Achilles, Hector, Ajax, Aeneas, and Ulysses. Not to mention Cassandra, Andromache, and Helen of Troy.

By the time I began my anxious note-taking at the first preview of *Troilus and Cressida*, I had crash-read the play and got some of the basics straight in my head, such as that the Greeks were the sea-faring attackers and the Trojans were hunkered down on home ground defending their walled city.

I saw the 2,000-seat Delacorte Theater for the very first time at the first preview. I had been visualizing something like the Greek amphitheater in my home city of Berkeley which had an upstage wall, but here in Central Park the audience faced an open landscape with a view of trees and a lake beyond the stage.

I caught sight of this sylvan vista as I reached the top step of the roofed entryway through which I was following Joe into the theater and was about to say how marvelous it was, when he suddenly turned around and snapped, "Why are there so many bottlenecks at the gates?"

His sharp words startled me. *Good grief,* was he holding me responsible for the congested traffic pattern at the ticket-taking gate? Could that responsibility conceivably be part of my new job? This blind-sided criticism stung me to the quick, until, after five seconds had passed, I realized that Joe had simply given me a "note" for the house manager, and I wrote it down. From then on I understood that Joe's tone of voice wasn't meant for me but for the note's intended recipient.

Finally seated next to Joe in the last row of the steeply raked Delacorte amphitheater, I watched the moon rise over Manhattan and residential lights begin to turn on in the tall apartment buildings on either side of Central Park, as the audience—which had waited for the distribution of free tickets in a long line snaking around Sheep's Meadow—rushed in to occupy their seats before the action began on the open-air stage.

I wasn't sure what to expect next, but as soon as the play started, Joe began whispering notes to me *molto presto* and I began writing them down pell-mell in the dark with a lighted pen (luckily someone at the office had suggested that I buy one). Stealing a glance to my right, I saw Joe's profile trained on the stage with the intensity of Sherlock Holmes studying evidence through a spy glass.

"Why was the trumpet fanfare late?" he whispered impatiently. I made a note of it, remembering that his questions weren't necessarily addressed to me personally.

"Cressida's breaking up her lines again," he muttered, twitching with displeasure during the first scene of the play. I scribbled it down.

His *sotto voce* comments continued to the end of the first half of the evening at which point Joe was whispering a note about how the actor playing Pandarus should say,

"And Cupid grant all tongue-tied maidens here

Bed, chamber, Pandar to provide this gear . . ."

But Joe's note was interrupted by the intermission. This being precious time for him to speak to the stage manager, he bolted from his seat, doublestepping up the bleachers to reach the control booth. Halfway there, however, he turned to face me and shouted, "TELL PANDARUS TO SAY THAT TO THE *AUDIENCE!*" I wrote it down.

On some nights I tried to gauge whether I dared set aside my lighted pen to pull a sweater on when the evening grew chilly. I had learned to accomplish this in a quick maneuver and was able to concentrate again on Joe's rapid comments without missing a beat.

Watching the previews of *Troilus and Cressida* with Joe became a crash course for me in Shakespearean performance, as well as in practical matters concerning costumes, scenery, lighting, and especially sound design. In the past, microphones had to be concealed inside set pieces on the Delacorte stage, often in low squat objects like benches or fake boulders, and the play directed in relationship to them.

However, in 1965 the Festival had changed over to wireless radio mikes attached to the actors' costumes. It was a significant improvement, Joe told me, except when signals from police cars cruising in the park interfered with the radio frequency of an actor's mike, drowning out lines like "Wherefore art thou Romeo?" with "Patrol Car Number 184, Scully to McKenna."

Early on I had become aware of a difference about interpretation between Joe and Richard Jordan, the handsome and talented young actor playing Troilus. The issue was whether Troilus, the son of the king of Troy, represented the epitome of valor and honor—in contradistinction to his Trojan ladylove Cressida, representing the nadir of female inconstancy because of her defection to the enemy. That seemed to be Jordan's opinion. I knew that Joe disagreed with this view, but as the director he'd carefully refrained from suggesting his own interpretation to the actor.

"So you don't agree that Cressida betrays Troilus's love for her when she consorts with one of the enemy Greek commanders?" I asked Joe after the show one night, parroting a scholarly footnote I'd read in my paperback copy of the play.

"Quite the contrary," Joe said. "It's Troilus who's the *cad*, and Cressida is his victim." I found that interesting.

One night Joe whispered to me, "Wallow in the lily-beds . . ."

"What?" I whispered back.

"Wallow in the lily-beds," he repeated. "Discuss with Troilus."

When Joe brought this figure of speech in Act III, Scene 2 to the actor's attention in a private note session backstage, Richard Jordan conceded that Troilus' choice of words in anticipation of a rendezvous with Cressida—"Give me swift transportance to those fields where I may wallow in the lily-beds"— suggested the "image of a pig" (wallowing) and reflected some distortion in his makeup and feelings. Although it's a minor note, the lascivious innuendo of the line suggested the inauthenticity of Troilus' declaration of love, and it helped to raise the actor's performance to a more interesting level.

I didn't dare tell Joe that he put me at a serious disadvantage when his verbal notes lacked specificity—for instance, when he whispered something to me like "Tell him not to grab that thing until the other one picks up the other thing."

Tell who? Grab what? Sometimes I had no way of knowing because I hadn't been able to look up from my notetaking to see what was happening on the stage.

After each preview Joe would give his notes to the actors, who had shed their Greek and Trojan armor for jeans and T-shirts and taken seats close to the stage in the emptied-out amphitheater. Standing in front of them, Joe put on his tortoise-shell glasses to consult my handwritten pages as a reminder of what he wanted to say and to whom. I would sit to one side facing him in the first row.

In the middle of his note session one night Joe interrupted himself.

"What's this, Gail?" he asked.

With heart-stopping alarm, I rose unsteadily from my seat and approached him to look at my writing pad over his shoulder.

"Oh, you remember," I replied, "that's when you said the soldier shouldn't grab that thing until the other one had picked up the other thing."

"Oh yes," Joe said, removing his glasses and looking around at the cast. "Ajax—where are you?—Don't swing your battle axe until the soldier draws his sword."

Ajax in this production was played by a young James Earl Jones, probably best known to later generations as the voice of Darth Vader in *Star Wars*. He was on the cusp of theatrical stardom at this time, having appeared in several Shakespeare plays in the Park in the early 1960s before assuming the title roles in *Othello* and *King Lear* at the Delacorte Theater, and in *Macbeth* on a Mobile Theater tour of New York City's five boroughs.

James Earl Jones recalled the value of his early experience in nine of these productions, which besides the four mentioned above had also included *Henry V*, *Richard II*, *Measure for Measure*, *The Merchant of Venice*, and *Hamlet*.

"Being out in the elements, having to fill a different kind of space, was good for American actors learning Shakespeare," he said. "Outdoors, you had the obligation of filling that space with your voice and with your presence. At that time, being a Black actor, I thought 'What role can a Black person play in Shakespeare?' I hadn't discussed with anybody the complications of what they were calling integrated casting in those days." (From an unpublished excerpt in his interview with Kenneth Turan for *Free for All: Joe Papp, The Public, and the Greatest Theater Story Ever Told* by Kenneth Turan and Joseph Papp)

I remained on tenterhooks until Joe had finished his notes to the cast. Only then did I feel free to look up at Belvedere Castle, a gothic fantasy perched on a cliff high above the theater, and listen to the gentle rustling of the poplar trees that Joe had planted on the shore of the lake below it.

Then, strapped into my backpack, I walked along the lamplit pathway in the park to the subway station at 81st Street and Central Park West to take a train home to Greenwich Village.

**

After the previews of *Troilus* were over, Joe and I converged at the coffee machine back at the Great Northern Hotel office.

"The first half was okay," Joe told me with disarming frankness, not adding cream or sugar to his coffee. "My biggest problem was the second half of the play where the scenes pop back and forth between the Greeks and Trojans. It was kind of Shakespeare's 'hook' on Greeks and Trojans."

"What do you mean?" I asked, adding skim milk and fake sweetener to my coffee.

"Well, I compare it to his dealing with British history," Joe said, "where Shakespeare had some wonderful material to draw on in Holinshed's *Chronicles*. Even with Roman history, he had Plutarch. But in this instance, it was kind of a contrivance and Shakespeare had to make up what took place."

I thought about his remark later and concluded that Joe was saying the difficulty he'd had directing *Troilus and Cressida* was partly Shakespeare's fault. Of course I might be wrong about that, but nevertheless I told myself, "Okay, after being tossed into the fray as Joe's unqualified notetaker during this problem play, I did at least manage to stay afloat."

6

On the Way to the Mobile Theater

A strong breeze buffeted the half-open windows of Joe's car as we headed down the FDR Drive along East River on our way to a performance of *Henry V* on the Festival's Mobile Theater in Brooklyn. During the drive Joe briefed me about the audience that would be coming to see the show.

"You'll find that people who don't know what to expect or who have no particular preset notion about Shakespeare respond almost immediately to what is real in the play," he told me. "They'll pick up on lines that you would think are too highfalutin' or poetic."

"Like what?" I asked.

"Like 'I know a bank where the wild thyme blows, Where oxlips and the nodding violet grows . . .'"

"Really?" I said.

"Yes. And you'd say, well that's, you know, poetry. Who's going to listen to *that* in Bedford-Stuyvesant? But they listen."

"That's amazing," I said.

The illuminated Manhattan and Brooklyn Bridges came into view on our left, as Joe reminisced about his first Mobile Theater nine years before. It had been a thirty-five-foot platform truck pulled by a New York City Sanitation Department tractor, a far cry from 1965's state-of-the-art caravans that now rolled into parks and playgrounds throughout the city's five boroughs. His memories of *Romeo and Juliet* on the Mobile Theater's rickety predecessor were still fresh in his mind.

"The actor playing Mercutio was losing the audience's attention during his Queen Mab speech," Joe said. "You can always tell when that happens because people start to cough. Or they walk out. But he was doing it in the usual way. You know, with great *gusto*."

"What was wrong with that?" I asked.

Joe answered by mimicking the actor's overly exuberant approach to Mercutio's speech (which, by the way, is a long flight of darkening fancy about a microscopic fairy queen visiting people's dreams in a chariot made from a hollowed out hazelnut).

"O!!! THEN I SEE QUEEN *MAAAB* HATH BEEN WITH YOU!!!" Joe declaimed to the windshield as he swerved onto the access ramp leading to the Brooklyn Bridge. "But I said to the actor, 'Why don't you play it more secretively, make it magical?'"

Taking his right hand off the steering wheel, Joe studied his index finger with theatrical interest and by way of demonstrating his point, whispered softly, "*Ohhhhhh*, then I see Queen Mab hath been with you. *Sheeeee* is the fairies' midwife, and sheeee comes in shape no bigger than an agate-stone on the *fore-finger* of an alderman . . ."

"And the audience understood that?" I asked in a hushed voice.

"Well here was a noisy street in the park," Joe said, choosing the right-hand lane across the bridge, "and of course you say, well my god, who's going to understand *that?* But the actor did it so magically, it was quiet, and he got the attention."

"That's remarkable for such a complicated speech," I said.

Joe frowned. As I was beginning to learn, he disapproved of any suggestion that Shakespeare was out of reach to the common man or woman. I certainly hadn't meant to suggest any such thing, but apparently that's the way Joe heard it.

"You have to remember that Shakespeare was a *democratic* playwright," he told me, merging now with the bridge traffic exiting at Flatbush Avenue, "and he easily reached the masses of the people because he knew his audience. You had a feeling he was right there in the theater, sitting backstage and writing."

The image that Joe conjured was so vivid to me, it was as if he'd teleported himself to the original Globe Theater on the South Bank of the Thames River in London and had just stumbled into William Shakespeare in the attiring room with his quill pen poised on a page. Momentarily my sneakers sprouted wings and I joined him there.

***

My experience of the Mobile Theater that summer was a revelation. Its *Henry V*, played by the Black actor Robert Hooks with a predominantly Black cast, performed for neighborhood audiences consisting of all ages and ethnicities, including many families with children. They filled the Festival's 1,600-seat portable bleachers every night, reacting to the characters and events on stage with a spontaneity and savvy that was truly exciting to be in the midst of.

Kids wriggled, candy wrappers rustled, babies cried, and bottles of soda rolled under the seats. Unruly boys sometimes threw stones at the stage from nearby trees or fences. When that happened, the show was stopped and a voice over the loudspeaker warned that the performance would be cancelled if it happened again. Peer pressure from the audience would take care of it.

For a while Joe kept a collection of these stones on his desk. He didn't romanticize what he was trying to do. He simply felt that good theater belonged to the people. Just like free library books, which have major institutional support on a national scale, he felt the best access to Shakespeare was free access.

This was my first summer at the New York Shakespeare Festival, during which I had observed Joe and his theater operating at full throttle, riding a crest of unrivaled popularity and public service. I had also learned a great deal from him and acquired a few new skills. Most of all, thanks to Joe, I had developed a keen appreciation of the amazing acting talent that surrounded us. This was due to the fact that in these early days Joe was intensely focused on the challenge actors faced doing Shakespeare in an era dominated by naturalistic plays and speech. At a Theatre Arts Magazine Symposium about directing Shakespeare, Joe had said, "What is it that we look for? We have a name for it, a paradoxical one. We look for a modern-classical actor. George C. Scott and Colleen Dewhurst, two performers who made their mark at the Festival, represent this mixture."

Scott and Dewhurst, who were then unknown, achieved international fame in future years—Scott for his Oscar-winning performance in the film *Patton* and Dewhurst for her powerful performances in the plays of Eugene O'Neill. However, they had both started out playing Shakespeare at the Festival.

During a radio interview with the historian and actor Studs Terkel, Joe recalled Scott's remarkable hold on an audience:

George C. Scott was doing Shylock in *The Merchant of Venice* in Central Park in 1962. I was directing the play. The way you directed George Scott was you leave him alone 90% of the time and just deal with him 10% of the time. It should be true with every good actor. You don't have to bother an actor. You just sort of create a milieu in which he can work.

I remember one moment. Shylock's daughter had just abandoned him. He finds her gone, but she's dropped her handkerchief. George made the most dangerous choice he could make. He goes over and he slowly picks up the handkerchief and—I think it must have taken him three minutes—he wrings that handkerchief. And his back begins to slump. I physically saw him sort of fall apart. His back actually arched to such a degree and his chin almost touched his knees. And he held on to that almost past the point of endurance.

You would say, "Oh no, he can't hold this much longer, I mean it's just impossible. My god he's holding it still." And I thought it would be so melodramatic and so fakey if any other actor did it. But he held that audience. There wasn't a sound. I heard people sobbing. It suddenly becomes an enactment of all human tragedy in that moment.

Joe said that Dewhurst and Scott brought

a spice and other seasoned ingredients which vitalized the productions, along with a particular brand of truthfulness that humanized the language with an understandable, living speech . . . The challenge is to achieve this modernity without sacrificing the form and poetry of Shakespeare. Occasionally there is a fusing of the feeling ignited by the actor with the grandeur of the line. Oh what a glorious blaze is here! The true dramatic poetry of Shakespeare comes to life.

In 1956 Colleen Dewhurst had triumphed as Kate in the Festival's production of *The Taming of the Shrew* at the East River Amphitheater. She met and later married George C. Scott after she saw him play Richard III in the Festival's production at the Heckscher Theater in 1957. Having appeared in seven plays that Joe produced, Dewhurst later reminisced about her long relationship with him:

"Joe really *did* care about the people," she'd said in her husky voice. "That's what he cared about. He really *had* a statement, which was 'Theater should be free.' And it should belong to everyone. And as he went on, his power was in the fact that he believed. Eugene O'Neill said, 'The dream is what keeps man fighting,' and that, really, is the way I think of Joe." (From an unpublished excerpt in her interview with Kenneth Turan for *Free for All*)

The actor Roscoe Lee Browne had a slightly different spin on Joe when he described his first audition at the New York Shakespeare Festival in 1956, which was for Cassius in *Julius Caesar*. He'd never acted before, but the director Stuart Vaughan was impressed. Cassius, however, had already been cast so Vaughan went off to check what other roles might be available.

At that moment, Browne said,

> This rather nifty, ripcord-muscled slim fellow with lots of black hair quite casually came down the aisle and I knew right away, this is the fellow.
>
> "I'm Joe Papp," he said. "How long have you been an actor?"
>
> "Twelve hours," I said. "But I have no intention of bearing any torches."
>
> "No, no, no," he said, laughing. "You'll have words, you're good."
>
> It was just that simple. And it was extraordinary. (From an unpublished excerpt in his interview with Kenneth Turan for *Free for All*)

Roscoe Lee Browne subsequently appeared in nine productions, including two of *Julius Caesar*, in which he played the Soothsayer.

In 1965, as the outdoor season at the Delacorte Theater drew to a close, I knew that my first summer working for the New York Shakespeare Festival was unlike anything else I'd ever experienced, and I was very grateful that Ann had ignored my reluctant feelings about office life and had recommended me for her full-time job with Joe at the Great Northern Hotel.

7

A Radical Change in Mission

I had never been to a board meeting of an organization before, so my first one at the New York Shakespeare Festival in the fall of 1965 was bound to leave an impression, although I had no idea how memorable this meeting would actually prove to be.

I set up three folding tables in Joe's hotel office, covered them with a black cloth that I found in the closet, and put a photocopied agenda at each place. Everything was ready as the Festival's seventeen trustees began to arrive—a diversified group of altruistic socialites, liberal lawyers, wealthy widows, culturally minded businessmen, and heirs of coffee and meatpacking fortunes.

Joe, who was president of the Festival, presided at the board meeting, dispatching the official business in an amiably confident manner. After he adjourned the meeting, however, he asked the trustees to stay a little longer.

"I want to discuss an important matter off the record," he said. "It won't take too much of your time."

Everyone stayed, wondering, as I did, what he had up his sleeve.

"All right, here's the thing," Joe said. "I've always found it difficult to be a summer operation, even a little demeaning, because we have to fight the most fantastic kind of disadvantages. One: we're out of doors which means that weather is an extraordinary factor. And then we have airplanes going over, when all we hear is '. . . *or not to be.*' That forces us to use a sound system, which is always unsatisfactory."

Demeaning? Disadvantageous? Unsatisfactory? These struck me as odd words coming from Joe, whose language about working in the Park was usually so positive.

"It's not only that," he continued. "Shakespeare is a great basis for beginning in the theater as a director or as an actor because the demands are so extraordinary. But you can't base your theater life only on Shakespeare."

I wondered what Joe meant by that. After all, he had been focused on Shakespeare for the past eleven years. What else could he "base his theater life" on now unless he became, say, the dean of a theater department at a university? I knew he'd had an offer recently from one in the Midwest. As I turned that possibility over in my mind, I felt a pang of apprehension. Would Joe want to go there? I didn't think so, but perhaps he needed the stability of an academic job to support his family. He had two young children.

"Throughout the history of the theater," I heard Joe saying now, "every important company has made its most significant contribution by introducing and developing new plays and playwrights. That was the case with Molière, Shakespeare, and the ancient Greeks, for example. In the beginning they were all new playwrights, and any theater in the past that was worth its salt pursued this goal."

Joe then cited the Royal Shakespeare Company and the Berliner Ensemble as contemporary theaters for the New York Shakespeare Festival to emulate by producing, as they did, classics and new work side by side.

To emphasize this point Joe said, "I can't go on doing Shakespeare exclusively because it's not somebody writing today, with their ear, with their mind, with their body—and I feel this lack in my work as a producer."

After a pause, board member George T. Delacorte, the wealthy founder of Dell Publishing Company, spoke up. "So what exactly is it you want to do, Joe?" he asked.

"I want to do new American plays in a permanent year-round theater," Joe replied.

Although he had mentioned this idea to me once or twice, it hadn't dawned me that he would be trying to implement it any time soon. Why? Because I'd witnessed firsthand his tooth-and-claw struggle just to raise the modest sums of money he needed to produce his seasonal Shakespeare plays in the parks, and they ran, as Joe himself put it, "in perpetual crisis mode."

What hope was there of his breaking through that stubborn financial ceiling to fund the ambitious creation of a permanent year-round theater?

This must be something Joe would like to do in the future if the Festival's financial position becomes stronger, I thought to myself. But no, that was not what Joe meant. Nor was it how the trustees around the folding tables responded to his announcement of what was, after all, a radical change in the Festival's mission: an audacious plan to acquire new real estate and to start searching for it immediately.

The trustees hardly blinked.

I observed that the Festival's early trustees were by habit favorably disposed toward Joe's dynamism, relying to a remarkable degree on his inexhaustible energy and resourcefulness to meet the financial challenges of the theater. I guessed that their benign passivity in fiduciary governance was the product of Joe's historic function as the Festival's chief fundraiser—he personally raised 85–90 percent of the money through foundations, individuals, and the new city and state agencies, which, when paired with his unique role as the Festival's founder and producer, gave him unusual power and freedom of action.

Although this money-raising responsibility was always an irksome monkey on his back, on some level I knew that Joe preferred it that way because, as burdensome as it was, it placed the control of the Festival where he wanted it—in *his* hands.

I remembered how he'd once joked to me, "The board didn't engage me. I engaged the board."

Consequently, although he consulted the board members on all major matters, Joe felt free to navigate in unconventional ways.

An unforgettable example of this happened five years later when Joe had to deal with the untimely death in 1970 of board chairperson Joseph "Burt" Martinson. There was no immediately obvious replacement for Burt, nor was the Public Theater yet in the habit of hiring executive head hunting agencies. Instead, Joe asked the actor George C. Scott, the Festival's first Richard III and Shylock, if he would serve as an interim chairman. Scott agreed.

George C. Scott, with his dashing air of malevolent energy and devilish jack-o-lantern grin, was still remembered for his portrayal of the crazed General "Buck" Turgidson in the 1964 movie *Dr. Strangelove*. His only preparation now before chairing his first board meeting at the Public Theater in

1971 was to ask Joe to furnish him with a gavel. Joe understood that he was requesting a prop and bought him one.

It seemed to me then that Scott took charge of board meetings as occasions to *perform* the role of chairman. Calling the first one to order with a rap of his new gavel on its sound block, the actor announced in his commandingly raspy voice: "If there are any ee-mendations, or objections to the previous minutes that the trustees may wish to bring to our attention before we proceed with the business of the meeting, I will gladly entertain them for discussion at this time."

Fantastic! These words could not have been more thrilling to me than if Scott had just said, "Now is the winter of our discontent" or "Hath not a Jew eyes?"

His piercing gaze searched all of our faces for a response. Since no objection to the minutes was expressed, he rapped the gavel again, moving the board's agenda along with a performative air of gravitas and understated authority.

George C. Scott had no involvement with the Festival's business other than these mesmerizing appearances at the board meetings every quarter, which I regarded as a priceless chance to see the great actor adopt a character at close range.

In these early days of the Public Theater, Scott was sometimes available when Joe would call on him for support during difficult periods. They had known each other since 1957 when Joe produced *Richard III* starring Scott in a staging by Stuart Vaughan at the Heckscher Theater. The next year Joe had stage managed a play at the Ambassador Theater on Broadway called *Comes a Day* starring Judith Anderson in which Scott had a secondary role. Joe once told me how a frenzied George C. Scott had slammed his fist into his dressing room mirror there, badly cutting his hands. Joe cleaned and bandaged them, then fitted tight gloves over the bandages so that Scott could go on stage and perform. In the following year, 1958, Joe directed Scott and his future wife Colleen Dewhurst in a concert version of *Antony and Cleopatra*, and in 1962 he directed Scott as Shylock in *The Merchant of Venice* in the first season at the Delacorte Theater.

George C. Scott, a person highly endowed with his own brand of intensity, discussed the effect that Joe had on him:

> Joe is a complex, complex individual. There's a kind of inner tension, like working with a wound-up spring or a gun that's cocked—you have the feeling

that something might happen. You're not sure whether it's going to be good or bad, it could be terrific, but things are not going to stay status quo. Joe was an absolute dynamo. Very few people in my life have had that kind of determination. He was unflappable, unswayable, would not be put off by any goal, would use any tactic, friend, enemy, anybody, to get what he wanted. He's used us all from time to time, and nobody ever objected. (From an unpublished excerpt in his interview with Kenneth Turan for *Free For All*)

During the off-the-record session with trustees at the end of the board meeting in his hotel office in 1965, Joe had stated his strong desire for a permanent, year-round theater dedicated to new American work. When several trustees wished him "good luck" with his proposal and platitudinous "good health" to carry out his intentions—I felt like Alice at the Mad Hatter's tea party because no one seemed to be curious about where the money for this great enterprise was going to come from.

Mrs. Lea Goldwater, a forthright lady in her eighties much given to proclaiming her esteem and admiration for Joe, now praised his courage and vision to the skies.

Mrs. Florence Anspacher, a wealthy octogenarian widow and the theater's principal benefactor who was quietly protective of the special relationship that she enjoyed with Joe, listened to Mrs. Goldwater with elfin attention. When Mrs. Goldwater was finished, Mrs. Anspacher murmured to her tablemate, "My, but aren't we pouring it on thick today!"

Publisher George T. Delacorte, a straight-talking man with a reputation for unconventional philanthropy, spoke up again at this point, saying with avuncular concern, "Joe, I worry that you're trying to do too much."

Joe replied that trying to do too much had never been his problem.

After the trustees left and I had started collapsing the fold-up tables in Joe's office, he said to me, "George has it wrong. I worry about doing too *little!*"

I told Joe that I was excited about his plan for a theater dedicated to new American playwrights, mentioning—because I knew he'd never looked at my résumé and had simply hired me on Ann's recommendation—that I'd been associated with new plays at Lincoln Center Theater.

"That's good!" Joe exclaimed, eyeing me over the tip of a *Romeo y Julieta* cigar as he clipped it with a guillotine cutter and struck a match. "We're going to need writers."

8

The Astor Library

Associate Producer Bernard Gersten's humorous ebullience always struck me as the perfect complement to Joe Papp's irrepressible joking and punning, and the two of them were in giddy high form as they began to look for a real estate property that could be converted into a year-round theater.

"I have no money," Joe told me in 1965 before he and Bernie set out on one of their forays. "I just want to do it."

His headlong risk and derring-do in looking for a year-round space reminded me of a photograph I had seen of a daredevil "Leaping the Chasm at Stand Rock, Wisconsin Dells in 1887," an image symbolic of the fact that, as Joe wrote in one of his notes to himself, "By nature and habit I feel most effective when I am dancing on the edge of a precipice."

When he finally found the building that he wanted, Joe arranged to show it to trustee George Delacorte and asked me to join them. He was hoping that Delacorte might help buy the building in the same way he'd helped to defray the construction costs of the Delacorte and Mobile Theaters a few years earlier.

Because Joe and Bernie had been looking recently at neighborhood churches and small cinemas, I had been imagining something on a similar modest scale, but when we arrived at the Astor Library on Lafayette Street, we found ourselves facing a three-story Italianate Renaissance colossus with a 250-foot-long frontage on the sidewalk.

IN AND ABOUT THE DELLS OF THE WISCONSIN RIVER.
97.   Leaping the Chasm at Stand Rock, Instantaneous.

Henry Hamilton Bennett/The Miriam and Ira D. Wallach Division of Art,
Prints and Photographs: Photography Collection, The New York Public Library

The Astor Library in 1881.
New York Public Library Archives, The New York Public Library

It sat on a wide cobbled trucking avenue in East Greenwich Village, the hippie center of New York City at that time. As Joe, George Delacorte, and I approached the building, we were surrounded by tie-dyed flower children, stoned kids with guitars, and Hari Krishna chanters jostling for space on the pavement.

Joe escorted us into the long-abandoned premises through a side entrance which led to a vast unilluminated interior space. Eager to tell us about the Astor Library's remarkable history, Joe said that it had been built in 1854 as the first free public library in New York City and later became the headquarters of the Hebrew Immigrant Aid Society ("HIAS") which since 1920 had helped Jewish refugees fleeing poverty, pogroms, and the Nazis.

"Here we have a shul," Joe said as he led us into a room on the ground floor (the future Shiva Theater). It seemed frozen in time, looking as it did when it had opened in 1921 as a synagogue for refugees temporarily sheltered within HIAS's walls, as well as for Jewish residents in the neighborhood.

On the second floor he walked us through a few dormitory cubicles that HIAS had improvised between the tall Greek columns of the Astor Library's Main Reading Hall (the future Anspacher Theater). In one of the cubicles, I noticed a dusty photograph of President Calvin Coolidge hanging askew on the wall. In another, a dim shaft of sunlight pierced the dark room as if from an embrasured window in a castle, spotlighting an old mattress and baby rattle that had been left behind on the floor.

I felt a powerful sense of destiny in the building's twin heritage: New York City's first free public library and a Jewish agency in times of persecution and war. What better place for Joe to start a theater! When we reemerged on the sidewalk after the tour, the three of us squinted at the midday sun like people coming out of a cave.

Half-humorously, Joe asked me how would I like to work in such a place. I was enthusiastic. I felt the magnificent ruin had exciting possibilities.

But George Delacorte wasn't so sure.

"I don't know, Joe," the dapper philanthropist said, brushing dust off his expensive suit. "Do you really think anyone will come down to this neighborhood once you've fixed the place up?"

That, however, wasn't the foremost question in Joe's mind at this point. The foremost question was whether the building could be saved from demolition by the real estate developer who had bought it from HIAS with the intention of erecting a condominium tower on the site.

Although the Astor Library had been designated a landmark by New York City's then-new Landmarks Preservation Commission, the law mandated only a few months of grace to allow for the intervention of a preservationist buyer. Without that, the Astor Library would be razed to the ground.

Joe gambled that the grace period would give him enough time to raise the $512,000 he needed to buy the building from the developer. Although he was disappointed that George Delacorte remained dubious about his downtown plans, Joe was able to cobble together the purchase price of the Astor Library with the combination of a bank loan and a generous donation from trustee Florence Anspacher, the self-effacing but astute widow of playwright Louis K. Anspacher. She also donated a youthful portrait of her husband (who bore an uncanny resemblance to Joe) which would be on display in the future Anspacher Theater lobby for many years.

From 1965 to August 1966, however, our offices remained uptown at the Great Northern Hotel because the derelict interior space of the Astor Library was uninhabitable until a part of it could be fixed up for occupancy.

Anticipating our future move downtown, Joe said to me one day, in the manner of an afterthought suddenly infused with urgency, "We need to find new American playwrights. Let's get the word out."

Of course! That was the purpose of acquiring the Astor Library in the first place and Joe's directive galvanized me like a battlefield communiqué. I began calling the play agents I knew from my jobs at the Theatre Guild and Lincoln Center Theater. They were incredulous when I told them about Joe's plan to create a nonprofit complex of five or six theaters in a building dedicated to new plays by American playwrights.

It's strange for me to recall how unusual this concept was in the mid-1960s. Many people were aware of the major performing arts centers for classics and revivals that were proliferating across the country at that time, often with a small experimental black-box theater to which contemporary works were relegated. No one else, however, had conceived such a grand plan to dedicate a large building exclusively to new American work. It bespoke a different purpose on an entirely different scale, and I had to explain it more than once to skeptical agents on the phone.

The idea was worthy of the talent that I had seen emerging at the off-off-Broadway places I was attracted to, such as playwrights Sam Shepard and Mariá Irene Fornés with composer Al Carmines at the Judson Memorial Church, and directors Wilford Leach and Andrei Serban with composer Elizabeth Swados at Ellen Stewart's La MaMa Theater.

One day the first manila envelope containing a playscript arrived in our mail at the Great Northern Hotel. I was so excited that I brushed aside the inconvenient fact that it contained not a new American play, about which we had advertised our single-minded and all-consuming interest, but a new translation of Henrik Ibsen's *The Vikings of Helgeland*. Although I knew that Joe wouldn't launch his future theater with this Norwegian epic about Eric Bloodaxe, a tenth-century sea king in an elk-horn helmet, I was nevertheless thrilled that an agent had heard our appeal for scripts and sent us Ibsen's play.

"We're going to call it the *Public Theater*," Joe said to me at this time. "But if you ask some old cab driver for the Public Theater, he's going to say 'I dunno,' but if you say HIAS, it'll be, 'Oh, Hi-*yahss*! My parents came through there!'"

I was so caught up in the excitement about our move to the future Public Theater that it wasn't until Joe casually mentioned to me one day that he didn't personally know any playwrights that I understood what a vulnerable position we were starting from. Apparently he had few contacts or irons in the fire. What he had instead was a vision that might possibly be as undefined or nebulous as the legendary Astor Library Ghost rumored to have haunted the occult book stacks in the nineteenth century.

This is one of Joe's leap of faith things, I thought to myself. Here he is, unfamiliar with the considerations of starting a theater to present the work of living playwrights, and he's moving into this huge building without having a single play to put in it. It's like opening a movie multiplex without having any films on hand to show or even the faintest idea where you're going to find them.

Nevertheless my heart beat faster and I felt elated. I tried to remember what my predecessor Ann had told me to expect at the Festival after the summer season came to an end. Winter contraction? A slower pace? Off-season tasks?

Well, none of that had happened. Instead here I was, after just a few months in my new job, swept up in the rip-roaring excitement of a new theatrical enterprise!

9

A Blizzard

In the middle of an afternoon at the Great Northern Hotel office in December 1965, Joe pulled on his emerald-green goose-down jacket.

"Christmas shopping," he said.

When he returned a couple of hours later, he was carrying two shopping bags filled with gaily wrapped Christmas presents. These were gifts that he had just bought at B. Altman's Department Store on Fifth Avenue and 34th Street for all twelve of us on the New York Shakespeare Festival's staff.

As he went around the office shaking hands and placing gifts on each of our desks, it wasn't lost on any of us that Joe had personally shopped for them and matched each one to its recipient with tasteful items like silk ties, cufflinks, bracelets, designer scarves, pen sets, and paperweights. When he arrived at my desk, Joe handed me a box that felt heavy, but before I could open it, he'd walked on to the next office.

Guessing that it must be a paperweight, I was startled to find instead a 753-page volume of the selected works of the Marquis de Sade, the notorious eighteenth-century French libertine. It had just been published with scholarly annotations and much fanfare by Grove Press. Its title page announced, "The Marquis de Sade, the complete Justine, Philosophy in the Bedroom, and other writings." On the back cover there were historical endorsements of de Sade by Baudelaire, Swinburne, and Apollinaire, and a contemporary one from Simone de Beauvoir.

I turned to the flyleaf to see if Joe had written an inscription in what was at one time a scandalous book.

He'd done so, and it said: "To Gail on Christmas 1965 with appreciation of your patience, forbearance and kindness. Joe Papp"

It was a gracious note, but it shed no light on the gift. Bemused, I was studying his inscription as one would fortune-telling tea leaves in a cup when Joe returned to my desk after distributing the rest of his presents. I wanted to say something witty and sophisticated to him, but all that came out, with a rather stiff attempt at gaiety, was "Thanks very much for the book, Joe."

"You're welcome," he said. "I knew you were a book person."

The next month a spectacular blizzard transformed New York City into a sugar-crystal wonderland as picturesque as a Currier and Ives engraving. Peeking out at it in the morning from my apartment window in Greenwich Village was like stepping through Alice's looking-glass.

In minutes I was outdoors in my boots and parka, headed for the snow-bound enchantment of Washington Square Park, which was only two blocks from my room above the drugstore. The Park was almost unrecognizable as I trudged past the places I'd known so well when I was a student at NYU's Washington Square College in the 1950s. Just north of NYU's main building, the entrance to Chock Full O'Nuts was blocked by a huge bank of snow. West of the Square on MacDougal Street, the windows of The Peacock Caffe and San Remo Restaurant glistened with frost.

I wanted to find Petit Potpourri, a tiny Russian-Hungarian restaurant whose daily menus I used to type in exchange for dinner during my freshman year at NYU, but I almost walked past it because the basement entrance was buried under a snowdrift. The restaurant's famous hostess had been Romany Marie, a Romanian immigrant known since the 1920s as "The Queen of Greenwich Village." An exotic-looking woman with hoop earrings, she sat at a corner table playing solitaire. Customers came to see her because of her legendary status as a friend to people like Eugene O'Neill, Buckminster Fuller, and Edna St. Vincent Millay.

She'd also been a friend of my Romanian godfather, the art dealer Aurel Lupu, but she was too deaf to hear me when I'd tried to tell her. The bustling owner of the place was Motya Nemiroff. In the *New York Herald-Tribune*'s favorable review of the restaurant in 1953, I appeared by chance in the accompanying photograph sitting with Romany Marie at her table.

Still in my teens at that time, I was living with my mother in a fifth-floor walk-up on East 15th Street. I had received a modest scholarship stipend in music composition to use toward my college tuition, which I was supplementing with an assortment of part-time jobs, such as typing menus for Petit Potpourri, polishing marble floors in townhouses, packing plastic fruits for shipment, transcribing Dictaphone lectures, and sorting index cards of microscopic fossils at the Museum of Natural History for its *Catalog of Foraminfera and Ostracodes*.

I was somewhat aware of the new theater movements in the early 1950s, such as Theodore Mann's Circle in the Square at Sheridan Square, and Julian Beck and Judith Malina's experimental Living Theater at various venues around the city. However, I hadn't yet heard about Joseph Papp's Shakespearean Theater Workshop that was starting up at Emmanuel Presbyterian Church in East Greenwich Village a few blocks from where I was attending classes at NYU.

I couldn't afford to buy tickets to anything then except cheap seats to concerts at the outdoor Lewisohn Stadium at 136th Street and Amsterdam Avenue, or to standing room at the beautiful old Metropolitan Opera House at West 39th Street and Broadway. There I would race long-legged boys up ten flights of stairs to get a standing spot along the dizzying top-tier railing. From that thrilling vantage point, I heard the operas of Verdi, Puccini, Wagner, Strauss, and Mozart for the first time.

Having completed my nostalgic tour around NYU, I paused for a final look at snowbound Washington Square, which seemed to have been transported back in time, before stopping off at the reliably cozy diner. Warming my hands on a coffee mug, I tried to picture the Delacorte Theater and Central Park in this record-breaking blizzard. I imagined eddies of snow swirling across last summer's stage when it had been the Trojans' besieged citadel opposite the enemy Greek encampment in *Troilus and Cressida*. I still remembered the opening lines of the play when an armored Prologue warns the audience of things to come: "Now in expectation, tickling skittish spirits, on one and other side, Trojan and Greek, sets all on hazard."

Bulletins over the diner's radio interrupted my train of thought with news about the cancellation of public transit and school classes. But unlike the furloughed students who were surely rejoicing throughout the city, I wasn't happy about my subway holiday from work because the New York

Shakespeare Festival had become a home away from home for me. It gave structure to my daily life, and I felt unmoored without it.

I thought that Joe, a workaholic unlikely to be deterred by the inconvenience of a blizzard, would undoubtedly make it in to the office. He'd walk the forty-odd blocks from where he lived. It occurred to me that I could do the same—walk to work via the pedestrian pathways that had been shoveled along the avenues. It would be an adventure, certainly better than staying home alone in my room all day, and I could let myself in at the Great Northern Hotel's office suite, even if Joe wasn't there, because I had been entrusted with a master key to it.

Before beginning my hike uptown, I tucked handwarmers inside my mittens. Their heat would protect my always-cold, Raynaud's Syndrome–afflicted fingers against "the icy fang and churlish chiding of the winter's wind," as the banished Duke says in *As You Like It*.

> "Which when it bites and blows upon my body
> Even till I shrink with cold, I smile, and say
> This is no flattery. These are counsellors
> That feelingly persuade me what I am."

I understood that. I was, in fact, finding much in Shakespeare that seemed uncannily relevant to my life.

Booted and hooded like a Klondike prospector, I set out for the Festival's hotel office on traffic-less Sixth Avenue, walking past snowbanks as high as my shoulders and waving to the few hardy pedestrians I passed on the deserted thoroughfare.

When I reached the Great Northern Hotel office after an hour and a half, Joe was the only person there, having trekked through the blizzard's aftermath from his apartment at 98th Street and Broadway. He was very surprised to see me. As I shook the snow from my fur-hooded parka, he joked that I looked like a St. Bernard, the rescue dog trained to carry a keg of brandy around its neck to revive hikers lost in the Swiss Alps.

I eyed the office coffee pot hopefully but it was empty because there was no one around to make coffee. I set about making some. When it was done, Joe fetched a bottle of twelve-year-old Courvoisier from a cupboard in his office and poured a generous amount of it in our paper cups.

"How many blocks did you walk?" he asked.

"Fifty-five," I replied.

"That's amazing," Joe said.

Warmed by the brandy, I settled into my corner at the office, happy to be there and not giving a thought to the slog back to Greenwich Village at the end of the day.

In future years I would interpret my pseudo-heroic trek to work after the blizzard and Joe's provocative Christmas gift of 1965 as idiosyncratic harbingers of the good things to come.

10

The Public Theater

𝕿𝖍𝖊 𝕹𝖊𝖜 𝖄𝖔𝖗𝖐 𝕿𝖎𝖒𝖊𝖘

Papp's Troupe Gets 1850s Landmark for Indoor Home
By RICHARD F. SHEPARD
January 6, 1966

"The large, ornate building at 425 Lafayette Street that opened 112 years ago as the Astor Library will become the first permanent home of the New York Shakespeare Festival."

When the Festival's small staff moved from the Great Northern Hotel on West 57th Street to the dilapidated Astor Library in Greenwich Village in August 1966, we bivouacked in the only reclaimed space, which was on the second floor in the north section of the building. Construction of the first theater, the 299-seat Anspacher, was soon to get underway in the middle section.

Although the second floor of the future Public Theater was at that time a dreary expanse of green linoleum lit by neon tubes hanging from the ceiling, it metamorphosed virtually overnight into a partitioned warren buzzing with the daily transactions of the theater's business. Since it was August, our activity included the end of the current season in Central Park and on the Mobile Theater, along with the annual gearing up for the Festival's tour of a

Shakespeare play in the city's public schools, something that was still possible to do before the Board of Education was decentralized. The administrative offices, which included fundraising, began to expand in accordance with the organization's new purpose in its new building. Joe was excited about establishing in-house technical departments for costumes, scenery, lighting, and sound on a year-round basis, but they were to come at a later stage in the renovation of the premises.

In my office adjoining Joe's, a hole had been gouged through the building's exterior rear wall to accommodate a massive steel girder that temporarily bisected the space. This gaping aperture provided easy access for adventurous birds that flew into the room, winged over my desk, and zigzagged into Joe's office, which had become the creative center of the building where playwrights, actors, and directors now began to gather.

Our startup at the Public Theater took place long before the computer era and of course we had none of the twenty-first-century technology that everyone takes for granted and thinks of as essential today. In other words, we had no computers, no cell phones, printers, scanners, fax machines, email, Internet, CDs, or digital recordings. ATMs and universal credit cards weren't yet on the scene. People still wrote and mailed letters, used carbon paper, and the pinnacle of communication urgency was the Western Union telegram. When one of those arrived, you paid attention.

Our workhorses were bulky IBM Selectric typewriters that bounced around so violently they had to be bolted to tables, and an A.B. Dick Mimeograph Machine whose large rotating drum inked the waxy typed stencils you placed on it to duplicate. This noisy contraption was housed in a glorified closet we called the Supply Room.

When construction of the first theater commenced in the Astor Library's Central Reading Hall, I would often cross the corridor to watch the outlines of the new performance space, the Anspacher Theater designed by Ming Cho Lee, begin to merge with the building's nineteenth-century architecture. Further along, I was delighted to see the Reading Hall's Greek columns, which had previously been obscured by HIAS's dormitory cubicles, come into view again with their capitals newly accented in gold leaf, a detail of the building's architectural restoration created by Giorgio Cavaglieri, a masterful pioneer in the "adaptive reuse" of historic buildings.

From my office I began to see clouds of smoke billowing over Joe's desk as he finger-rolled cigar bands of La Primadora, Romeo y Julieta, Partagás, Cohíba (the Taino word for tobacco), Las Cabrillas De Soto—the names as aromatic as the tobacco from which his connoisseur-grade cigars were made.

"Do you know that it takes one hundred steps to properly produce a single Cuban cigar?" Joe said to me one day. "And they have to be aged like fine wines."

Privately, I estimated that the volume of smoke wafting up to the ceiling from Joe's desk must be related to the mounting deadlines that everyone had begun to feel at the Public Theater: to finish the construction of the first theater, to find the plays to put on in it, to renovate the public space, to raise the extraordinary amount of money to accomplish all of this—with less than a year to go before the scheduled opening of the Public's first season in 1967.

Our new offices in the Astor Library had high ceilings, and unlike the suite we had occupied at the Great Northern Hotel, Joe and I could now see each other and took to speaking in person instead of using the intercom. Despite the practical matters on his mind, Joe got in the habit of talking to me about his larger concerns.

"I formulated my ideas about free Shakespeare in New York City's parks years ago," he told me one day in an urgent tone of voice, "but I've never actually *sold tickets* to plays before. Nevertheless, that's what I'll be doing now here at the Public Theater."

Joe spent a good deal of time thinking out loud about how to reconcile this unfamiliar challenge of selling tickets to audiences with his previous admission-free relationship to audiences in the parks. What did it mean? What was the philosophical consistency of his new role as a producer of contemporary playwrights instead of only Shakespeare?

Joe's musings were never dull stuff. As the *New York Times* book critic and author Michiko Kakutani once wrote, "Listening to Papp talk is like listening to a Renaissance scholar on Benzedrine."

I remember being at a meeting in his office with several other staff members one afternoon when Joe leaned back in his chair and on just a thread of relevance resumed a train of thought he'd apparently had earlier in the day.

"To succeed in any art form, you have to be quite *narrow* in a certain sense," he said to us. "You must have a point of view about what you do and what it means to you and to other people. So what is my point of view? What does all of this mean?"

When he got in this mood, it seemed that the questions Joe asked himself served the same purpose as the human harvester who shakes an olive tree to make the fruit drop.

"I'm planning to create five or six theaters in the building," he continued, "but because space is limited, they can only range from the maximum of the 299-seat Anspacher Theater, to flexible smaller seating in the two skylighted reading halls on the third floor. Then down to just ninety-nine seats in the shul. Of course I'd like it all to be free," Joe added, rolling a cigar band between his fingers, "but that isn't economically possible because it would require massive subsidy for untried new work and nobody is interested in supporting that. Anyway—how can I be sure that anyone will come?"

Just then Bernie Gersten walked into Joe's office. Joe flipped the rolled cigar band into his wastebasket.

"On the other hand, it *should* be free," he said, aiming his next remark conspiratorially at Bernie, "because—first of all—the amount of money that we'll be able to make from the box office at the Public Theater with all its small theaters will be so insignificant, why even charge anything?"

"In fact," Joe went on with a mock jaunty air, "if I *gave* people a dollar to stay away, we'd do much better in our business. We wouldn't have to put on plays at all! We could just say 'Here is enclosed, herewith is one dollar'—or five dollars even, 'cause we'd lose so much money. 'Please don't come to any of our performances!'"

"And it would be only 10 percent of what it will cost us to operate!" Bernie exclaimed.

Despite Joe's easygoing inclusiveness, early on I took note of his edgy sense of ownership of both his successes and failures. It was subtle. I saw that he became difficult to read if anyone identified too effusively with the ups and downs of what he was doing. It was as if he regarded excessive admiration in the same negative context as excessive criticism. It struck me as a territorial reflex. Though he was open and friendly in his working relationships with associates, staff members, trustees, peers, cohorts, citizens, confidantes, boon companions, and punning buddies, Joe never regarded anyone as an equal partner with respect to the artistic control and survival of the theater that he was bringing into existence.

Another interesting aspect of this formative period is that unlike contemporary generations of college-trained arts administrators, there weren't
more than one or two people at the early Public Theater with that precise
kind of background. Certainly not me. And not Joe, who had gone to work
after graduating from Eastern District High School in Brooklyn and then had
joined the navy after Pearl Harbor.

Because Joe was a self-assured person with two decades of theatrical
experience, it took me awhile to appreciate the steep learning curve he was
actually going through in creating the Public Theater. The first sign of stress
that registered with me was when he returned prematurely from lunch with
Bernie and others. He'd collapsed on the floor of the restaurant and thought
he was dying.

That night I wrote in my diary: "Joe's symptoms mimicked a heart attack.
He lay down in his office most of the afternoon, reviving later with some
Formosa Oolong tea and semi-sweet biscuits before leaving for a doctor's
appointment."

Work stress was surely part of it, I thought, but Joe also seemed to be under
some kind of personal strain that I didn't understand.

The next time he returned prematurely from another lunch at the same
restaurant, it was because of a quarrel with his lunchmate, Burt Martinson,
the Public Theater's chairman. During the meal Burt had objected to Joe's
allocation of exhibition space at the Public to the renowned artist Romare
Bearden for his Cinque Gallery. Burt had hoped the space would be reserved
instead for an American folk art museum with which he was affiliated.
Disappointed, he had accused Joe of "opportunistically favoring African-
Americans," and Joe had stormed out of the restaurant.

Joe had every right to be infuriated by what he regarded as racist interfer-
ence in an artistic matter. He also saw this as an infringement of his artistic
autonomy based on democratic access in the arts, something that he would
never tolerate, be it from a board chairman or from the politicized National
Endowment for the Arts in the 1980s. A few minutes later, Burt Martinson
rushed into the office, sat down next to Bernie Gersten's desk, and burst into
tears.

***

Around this time a staffer took a snapshot of me in a 1960s mini dress holding
an overflowing wastebasket in my messy new office.

Also around this time Joe posed for cocky, unsmiling photographs on the sidewalk underneath a large sign announcing the future theaters and resident enterprises that were taking shape inside the building. It said:

PUBLIC
THEATER
UNDER CONSTRUCTION
Facilities will include—
*FLORENCE SUTRO ANSPACHER THEATER
*ESTELLE R. NEWMAN THEATER
*ANTHOLOGY FILM ARCHIVES
*THE OTHER STAGE
*FERNANDEZ PHOTO WORKSHOP
*CINQUE GALLERY

We were off to the races!

11

A Different Sound in Music

We planned to launch the Public Theater in October 1967 with a first season of four plays. Now, only a few months before that date, Joe still hadn't found the play he wanted to open with.

He had, however, settled on the three other plays in the season. One was going to be a hellzapoppin vaudeville called *The "Naked" Hamlet* that Joe had worked on with his directing students at the Yale School of Drama. It would be followed by two new plays by European dramatists: Jakov Lind, an acclaimed forty-year-old Austrian novelist and chronicler of the Holocaust, and Václav Havel, a thirty-one-year-old dissident playwright in Communist Czechoslovakia.

It went without saying that the work chosen to open the Public Theater would have to be a new American play or we would look ridiculous if not downright fraudulent after heralding the Public Theater as a future home for American playwrights. However, the clock was running out on finding an American play, and Joe was not going to open the theater with anything that didn't genuinely excite him.

Up to this point nothing had excited Joe until an agent sent him *Armstrong's Last Goodnight* by John Arden. The fact that Arden was a well-known British playwright and the play had already been produced in England—factors that should have disqualified it as the new American work to open the Public—were outweighed by Joe's immediate enthusiasm for the play's

Elizabethan Scottish vernacular and lusty characters. I was dazzled by it too. However, when we tested *Armstrong* in a rehearsed read-through with a wonderful group of actors in front of a small audience, its rich vernacular proved to be mostly unintelligible to everyone.

Around this time Joe looked unhealthy and not fit. He appeared beleaguered, maybe angry. It showed in his unsmiling photographs. He kibbutzed a lot with Bernie Gersten, but it sometimes seemed to me as if he was winging it on automatic pilot. He smoked constantly, his cigar-band twirlies rolling off the edge of his trestle desk like pine nuts. Was it stress due to the challenge of the launch? Sleepless nights? Frustrations? Vodka gimlet lunches? Depression? Bad diet? He banned cookies from the coffee station, including the Mallomars he'd been keeping around for jolts of energy with his morning coffee.

Since I handled his calendar, I was aware that Joe had appointments with a psychotherapist four times a week, suggesting to me that there was some kind of disturbance in his personal life that he was trying to resolve.

One afternoon after Joe had returned from the directing seminar he taught at Yale, he told me that he'd run into a bushy-haired actor on the New Haven train who had given him a few pages of a handwritten script.

"I read it before the train pulled into Grand Central Station," Joe said. "Some of it actually seems illiterate, but lines here and there sort of caught my fancy."

"What's it about?" I asked.

"There's a fragment of a scene dealing with the war in Vietnam and a few lyrics. I told him to bring me some more stuff when he gets it finished."

A couple of weeks later the bushy-haired actor and his co-writer brought in about fifty pages. They were joined by a composer who sang a few songs for us in a scratchy voice, accompanying himself on the old upright piano in Joe's office.

The music had strong melodies with a jazzy beat, and the lyrics grabbed your attention. *"Ain't got no pot, ain't got no faith,"* one of them began. After a few more songs, including one about the "Age of Aquarius," it became obvious that Joe's chance encounter on the New Haven Railroad had led us to our inaugural production—a counter-cultural hippie rock musical called *Hair*.

The sound of rock and roll now began echoing through the halls of the Public Theater, as our previously Shakespeare-only organization interacted with the living, breathing team of co-writers Gerome Ragni and James Rado, and composer Galt MacDermot.

The story of the musical, which was about the Vietnam War and the loneliness of young people, was authentic. They were all around us in the East Village at that time, sitting on steps and smoking pot. Half the play would be cast from the neighborhood by Gerald Freedman, the director of *Hair*.

However, despite a joyous start, the rehearsals of *Hair* didn't go smoothly and after a couple of weeks I was alarmed to see people treading a path to Joe's office with complaints about artistic differences, usurpations of authority, even threats to quit the production. Such dire problems suggested to me that the Public's first show was lurching toward an ill-advised exposure to audiences with, to borrow the words of poet William Cowper, its "sails ripped, seams opened wide, and compass lost."

But by this point in my job, I had learned that whenever Joe's plans were derailed, as they were most certainly threatening to do now, he got busy dealing with the situation. Setbacks, I found, brought out a fundamental strength of Joe's character—his inclination to counteract adversity with the singlemindedness and application one might expect of someone laying bricks or sawing wood.

Accordingly, Joe addressed the dysfunction in rehearsals by meeting with the aggrieved parties, declining to read the emotionally distraught memos that were left on his desk every day, and trying to mitigate the potentially crippling resignations of both the director and the choreographer of the show.

Somehow *Hair* managed to survive the developmental chaos of its four weeks of rehearsal, and after it opened at the Public Theater, critics hailed it as the first musical that, as Stephen Sondheim remarked years later, "used rock as a way of telling a story." It was a new kind of musical sound in the theater and audiences went crazy for it.

Hair would be the first show to which Joe had ever sold tickets, and it became an immediate success. It was a profoundly different economic model from the New York Shakespeare Festival. For years people had been forming lines at the box office in Central Park to pick up free tickets, but now they were stampeding the box office downtown to pay for them! At showtime, white stretch-limousines pulled up to the curb in front of the Public Theater, a sure sign that the play was a hit among New York City's cognoscenti.

I was accustomed to seeing Joe move decisively when an opportunity was ripe for action, a quality I much admired in him. But with this "hit" rock musical on his hands, he still held on to his antipathy to Broadway's commercialism, a political point of view he had formed during his youth in the Depression, which had become further entrenched during his time at the Actor's Lab in Los Angeles from 1946 to 1950 when he was in his late twenties. It had remained unchanged over the past fifteen years, up to and including *Hair*.

With *Hair* in 1967 Joe now had a critical and box office triumph on his hands along with the general expectation that he would move it to Broadway. For a producer this is the stuff of dreams and the impetus for action. But Joe didn't lean that way. Instead, he developed a rationale for moving *Hair* to a disco club called the Cheetah, which he regarded as a more democratic venue than Broadway.

"I don't believe in putting on shows just to make money," I remember him telling me, "and I believe it would violate the purity of this institution to do anything on Broadway."

I was still young enough to remember my attendance at Marxist Society lectures in New York City at the age of seventeen, and although I had regarded them as boring and ideological, I was inclined to respect Joe's mature radicalism and assume he knew what he was doing. However, *Hair* soon folded at the disco club and lost money. Not a man to compound error in the wake of failure, Joe then decided to license the Public Theater's producer rights in *Hair* to someone else. Having done that, I thought he seemed relieved to be free of any further direct involvement with the false god Mammon.

Years later Joe told me the reason he refused to take *Hair* to Broadway himself was because he didn't feel it belonged on a proscenium stage. (At the Public, it had been on the Anspacher's three-quarter-round thrust stage.) That was true, I'm sure, but I also think he didn't want to risk money on Broadway at that time because he'd just launched the Public Theater whose future growth was predicated on ambitious escalations of debt to make possible the multi-year construction of more theaters and the renovation of the derelict building.

After Joe had licensed the Public's commercial rights to *Hair*, its new independent producer escalated the show to fabulous fame and fortune at the Biltmore Theater on Broadway and at theaters across the United

States—followed by a proliferation of companies in Germany, Denmark, Holland, France, Italy, Japan, Israel, Poland, Lebanon, Czechoslovakia, and South and Central America.

As *Hair* toured and went around the world, Joe had no regrets.

"The Public Theater has made over a million and a quarter dollars on it as its licensor share—without even doing anything!" he exclaimed to me in his office one day. "If I had become involved in running all those productions, I never would have continued on with the Public Theater. It would have taken all my life."

Nevertheless, *Hair*'s independent commercial success had an important effect on the Public Theater's standing, transforming it from an adventurous off-Broadway start-up in 1967 to a national and international player to be reckoned with.

12

The "Naked" Hamlet

Joe planned that each of the four shows in our first season would have a limited run of eight weeks in the Anspacher Theater, which was our only stage at that time. So although *Hair* could surely have played much longer, Joe duly closed it after the prescribed eight weeks to make way for the second show, which was his own hellzapoppin adaptation of *Hamlet*, which he called *The "Naked" Hamlet*. He took the title from Hamlet's letter to King Claudius in Act IV, Scene 7: "You shall know I am set naked on your kingdom."

"I'm absolutely shattering the play," Joe told me during rehearsals. "I'm breaking the entire form of the play in a kind of comedic, mischievous way."

When previews began in December 1967, the audiences were even younger than those who had recently rushed to see *Hair*. Attracted by the low-priced $2.50 tickets, these teens and early twentysomethings responded like kids at a circus to the vaudevillian Denmark that Joe had created around *Hamlet*.

They giggled when Ophelia, sporting black fishnet stockings and a straw hat, sang Shakespeare's lyrics to music by *Hair* composer Galt MacDermot:

"By Gis and by Saint Charity,
Alack, and fie for shame!
Young men will do 't, if they come to 't;
By Cock, they are to blame."

And in this madcap romp of fluid identities, they loved it when Hamlet hawked bags of peanuts in the aisles, or darted around the precarious heights of the theater's gridiron like Lon Chaney, Sr. in the 1925 film of *Phantom of the Opera*.

Hamlet in this production was played by a twenty-seven-year-old, half-Irish, half-Galician actor named Ramón Gerardo Antonio Estévez who was on the brink of stardom as Martin Sheen. He had never read the play before Joe cast him in the title role.

Martin Sheen said

I did "To be or not to be" as a Puerto Rican, with a Puerto Rican accent. At first the audience was in hysterics but by the middle of the speech, they were listening because you began to see *who* was suffering the "whips and scorns." It was the Puerto Rican in the community, the latest immigrants, who did all the dirty work behind the scenes and took all the blame and didn't get any credit. Their words, their emotions, their accent was now coming through the words of Shakespeare. The audience listened like it was the first time. (From an unpublished excerpt in his interview with Kenneth Turan for *Free for All*)

Joe had often said that "Every actor should do Hamlet. It's like being bar mitzvahed. You're never the same again. Women should play it too." Because his understanding of the play was so incisive—almost psychoanalytic, I felt he was talking about himself when he said, "All of Hamlet's energy springs from the hurting place" and that "Hamlet has one precious possession which he holds to himself—his feelings." These were, I had come to believe, defining aspects of Joe's own psyche.

His deconstruction of *Hamlet* as a hallucinatory funhouse was a radical departure for a director who in Central Park had always been a stickler about observing the proper class distinctions in Shakespeare. But with *The "Naked" Hamlet* at the Public, Joe now broke all of his former rules, telling me, "The play is so powerful and has so much richness that you can twist it fourteen ways and you can't kill it."

In his enthusiasm for this experimental production, I don't think Joe gave any thought to his vulnerability as director-and-producer of a play at the just-opened and newly spotlighted Public Theater. Up to this time his directing had taken place in a sort of critic-proof Garden of Eden in Central Park where

Martin Sheen in *The "Naked" Hamlet* at the Public Theater in 1967.
George E. Joseph/Billy Rose Theatre Division, The New York Public Library

free admission and the large outdoor setting offset the usual baneful influence that negative reviews can have on attendance. Now that we were indoors and charging admission for the first time, I feared that negative critics might have a different impact, even though I'd had no personal experience of how aggressive and punishing they could be.

When the reviews of The "Naked" Hamlet came out, it seemed as if a dreadful nightmare had descended on Joe because both the daily and Sunday reviewers at the New York Times—operating as a twin juggernaut of defamation—heaped their supercilious scorn on his production.

"Hamlet Hawks Peanut Shells and Other Nonsense" was the drift of Clive Barnes' weekday review in which he wrote that Joe's production was "for Philistines who wish to be confirmed in their opinion that the Bard is for the birds . . . No no no. I think we need a new approach to Shakespeare but this jejune nonsense is not it."

Walter Kerr, newly hired as a critic by the Times, told his readers that The "Naked" Hamlet was "an enterprise exactly like the shows idiot children used to put on in their basements."

Ye gods, I had never read reviews this terrible before. I felt very bad for Joe who, looking quite grim in their wake, left with his wife and children for a previously planned vacation in Puerto Rico.

After all the excitement we'd been through with the opening of Hair and The "Naked" Hamlet, the office felt very lonely with Joe out of town. I missed him and wished he was there to read the six wonderful reviews that appeared later that week actually praising his "Naked" Hamlet:

CBS-TV: "Explosive and exciting"

Time: "A Hamlet of crystalline intensity"

ABC-TV: "One of the most fascinating departures from the traditional that I have seen"

Newsday: "Sends shafts of intense light on over-familiar passages"

New Republic: "Courageous, bound to have an effect on the theatrical consciousness for some time to come"

Village Voice: "You'd have to be sadly uptight about Shakespeare not to get great fun out of it"

My impulse was to send this new crop of reviews—offsetting the baleful influence of the New York Times theater critics—to Joe, but I hesitated putting them in the mail because he was on a family vacation and I was sensitive to the fact that something related to the theater might be an unwelcome intrusion on the family's time together. I never even considered calling him on the phone. However, the new reviews were at such striking odds to the two dreadful opinions in the *Times* that I finally sent them off to Joe at his vacation address.

He was in high spirits when he returned, thanked me for sending the reviews, and said they had given him the idea of challenging Clive Barnes to a television debate about the show.

Clive Barnes, the powerful, British-born chief drama critic of the *Times*—infamous for sleeping through the Aida trumpet fanfares and cannonades at our Shakespeare history plays in Central Park (I had seen him doze off myself)—readily accepted Joe's challenge. No doubt Barnes felt confident of his mastery of *Hamlet* due to the many productions of it that he had seen in his native Britain as well as in the United States. Those productions, while not surpassing the three hundred performances of *Swan Lake* Barnes was rumored to have attended during his heyday as a dance critic, were nevertheless numerous.

For his part Joe knew *Hamlet* inside out, backward and forward. He knew it by heart. He knew the 350-year-old stage history of *Hamlet* from Burbage to Burton. He was familiar with *Gesta Danorum* by Saxo Grammaticus (1160–1220), a history of Denmark that contains the first mention of the legend of Amleth (Hamlet). He'd plumbed the *Variorum of Hamlet*, containing different versions of the text with scholars' notes and commentaries, which I also read out of curiosity. And needless to say, he knew every nook and cranny of his own action-packed deconstruction of the play.

What prompted Joe to cross swords with Clive Barnes at this early stage in their long and tumultuous relationship was, I think, more than just their differences of opinion about *Hamlet*. It had to do with a hidden aspect of Barnes' attitude toward Joe which the *New Yorker* journalist Phillip Hamburger picked up on when he interviewed Barnes for a profile of Joe that he was working on. Although he never wrote the profile, his interview notes for it can be found in "The Phillip Hamburger Papers" in the Manuscript Section of the New York Public Library on Fifth Avenue. In them Hamburger had jotted that Barnes "Really didn't like Papp . . . didn't find him especially intelligent . . . [Barnes said] 'I don't find him the least bit artistic . . . I don't

Cleavon Little in *The "Naked" Hamlet* at the Public Theater in 1968.
George E. Joseph/Billy Rose Theatre Division, The New York Public Library

find him attractive . . . he isn't inner driven or directed . . . he zips and darts about like a little bug.'"

So this was Barnes' private view of Joe on the eve of their televised debate. Although Barnes' Britannic snobbery had never been expressed in print or to Joe's face, Joe could sense it a mile away. Convinced it had figured in Barnes' reaction to his production, he was itching for a debate with him.

I gathered with the staff around the television set in Joe's office to watch Barnes and Joe square off on Channel 2, the local CBS station. The physical contrast between them on the screen was striking: Joe, lean, trim and handsome; Barnes, in a corpulent phase of his unfortunate weight problem, flashing a rabbit-tooth smile at Joe.

Round One began when Joe, with cheeky nonchalance, produced on camera a bag of unshelled peanuts he'd brought to the TV studio. Throughout the debate he could be seen cracking them open and popping the shelled peanuts into his mouth. This was, of course, a mocking allusion to Barnes' infamous "Hamlet Hawks Peanut Shells and Other Nonsense" review. By the end of the program, the peanut shells piling up at Joe's feet had effectively distracted a viewer's attention from the bloviating points of Barnes' argument against *The "Naked" Hamlet*, making it obvious, at least to all of us watching, who had won the match.

But the TV debate wasn't the end of the attention paid to *The "Naked" Hamlet* in the wake of its baneful reviews in the *Times*, because after its limited eight-week run in the Anspacher Theater, Joe brought it back later in the season for school audiences to see there. This time Hamlet was played by the Black actor Cleavon Little, who would soon win a Tony Award in *Purlie* on Broadway and later become famous for his signature role in the Mel Brooks film *Blazing Saddles*. The school production provoked a public dispute with the Board of Education about its suitability for students, which Joe won.

He then toured it on the Mobile Theater in the summer of 1968, directed by his young Assistant Director Ted Cornell. The next year Macmillan published a handbook of the production, edited by Joe and Cornell, with text, photographs, its rock score, and a full account quoting the "outrage—or delight" that *The "Naked" Hamlet* had stirred up.

13

An Equal Opportunity Employer

It meant a great deal to me that Joe was a nonsexist equal opportunity employer because my young working life had started out in the egregiously sexist era of the 1950s when classified job ads in the *New York Times* were still segregated by gender in its "Help Wanted-Male" and "Help Wanted-Female" columns, exactly as they'd been since the nineteenth century. Professional jobs, even the editorial trainee positions that I sought in my youth, were listed in the Male column, and it was tacitly understood that job seekers of the wrong sex, that is, female, shouldn't bother to apply. It was a hard lesson that I had learned firsthand when a publisher's personnel manager rejected me on sight when I showed up for an interview.

How did I handle this appalling situation? *It's outrageous*, I remember thinking back then as a young girl stuck in a discriminatory social order, *but that's the way things are.* No wonder I was attracted to the egalitarian spirit that I found at the New York Shakespeare Festival when I started there as a summer temp. After we moved into the Public Theater, I was so surprised and pleased when Joe promoted me to "Assistant to the Producer" that I sent my father in Keene, New Hampshire, and my mother in New York City copies of the first program that carried my new title.

It was great to know that Joe valued me in this way. Even though my new title came without a raise in pay, at that point in my personal evolution I couldn't make the synaptic connection in my brain that a promotion should translate into dollars. Nor was it in my wheelhouse to think of, let alone to ask for, a raise.

I later realized that this was probably due to the impact the Great Depression had had on my parents. As a young child I picked up not only on their feeling of helplessness with respect to unemployment but also on their determinedly cheerful enterprise in dealing with it. I think their example shaped the way I dealt with the problem of not earning enough money at the Public Theater, which was to moonlight on weekends as a factotum to people in the arts.

My freelance jobs were quite interesting. They would last anywhere from one day—working for British director Peter Brook, for example, to weeks and months working for scenic designer Boris Aronson and *New Yorker* film critic Pauline Kael. I also worked for the New York Society of Film Critics which included crotchety film critic "stars" of the day like Andrew Sarris and John Simon.

Some of my freelance jobs lasted years—as in the case of the director-critic and Group Theater co-founder Harold Clurman, to whom I became quite attached. I always loved it when Clurman got excited about an idea because he would gesture in a thrillingly dramatic manner while shouting, "THE THEATER MUST SAY SOMETHING! IT MUST RELATE TO SOCIETY! IT MUST RELATE TO THE WORLD WE LIVE IN!"

I shuttled on the subway between my weekend work places—from the elegant Osborne catercorner to Carnegie Hall, to fancy condos on Central Park West, to transient rooms at the artist-friendly Chelsea Hotel—juggling the formidable assortment of egos and professional concerns that I encountered. All of this, of course, was in addition to my demanding job working for Joe. Fortunately, I was young and could handle the weekend commuting and extra hours.

I read Simone de Beauvoir's *The Second Sex* around this time when the Women's Liberation Movement was gaining momentum in 1968. Her brilliant analysis of the oppression of women through the ages opened my eyes as if my long-dead suffragist grandmother had sprinkled fairy dust on my pillow. But the feminist hue and cry of the Sixties wasn't yet in my political bones because I hadn't been able to identify with the angry anti-male rhetoric that characterized some of the early spokeswomen of my generation, many of whom had felt trapped in household drudgery, unrelieved child rearing, and abusive relationships. I'd had to deal with other kinds of difficult conditions, such as illness and unemployment, but not the ones above, which somewhat distanced me from the urgency of the movement and its agitation.

In addition, categorical hostility to men didn't sit well with me because I happened to like a decent percentage of the men with whom I had worked or had an acquaintance, and I couldn't hate them as a class. None had ever abused me. As a result, I was slow to adopt a feminist worldview and was therefore incapable of framing my underpaid salary at the Public Theater as a political issue.

"Gail, come in here for a minute," Joe called out through the open door between our offices one day. He had put on his eyeglasses to study the break-down of an administrative budget.

"I didn't realize you were paid so little," he said, indicating the report on his desk. "It's just come to my attention. I'm going to raise you to $200 a week."

I was amazed. $200 a week was a huge sum in my eyes. I had been making $160 gross, $118 net.

"Thanks very much, Joe," I said. "I certainly appreciate it."

"Well, I better raise you," Joe said, removing his glasses, "or else some guy will come along and you'll get married."

I blinked. Was he being fast, flip, or flirtatious? I shrugged it off with a smile.

But what prompted him to say that? I wrote in my diary that night. *What does it mean? Anything special?*

I decided it was just one of Joe's throwaway lines—the kind of sporting jape he'd toss off to a person and forget about the next minute although, as I had observed, that person might later obsess about the uncertain meaning of it—precisely as I was doing now. I had to admit, however, that it was flattering to be considered a still viable commodity in the marriage market although I had no interest in getting married again.

Feeling good, and anticipating more money in my pocket, I bought a frog-clasp shearling coat I'd had my eye on for a long time. It was by far the best coat I'd ever owned, and I took pictures of myself wearing it in a photomat.

Looking at the strip of mug shots, for which I'd fastened the coat's nifty frog-clasp closures up to the neck, I thought to myself, *Gosh, I don't look so bad!*

14

Birth of the Play Department

In 1967 Joe had only a few people at the fledgling Public Theater who were likely to encounter talented playwrights of potential interest or have plays sent to them. That group included Artistic Director Gerald Freedman, Associate Director Osvaldo Riofrancos, Casting Director Dolores Pigott, Staff Director Ted Cornell (Joe's former student at Yale who was in charge of a projected experimental theater), and me as Assistant to the Producer.

It's therefore strange for me to recall that, for several years, we didn't have a designated department for handling original plays and musicals submitted to the Public Theater. In those early days most everything that would later be sent to a Play Department was addressed to Joe, delivered with the rest of his mail in a U.S. Post Office mailbag left next to my desk each morning. Joe's *name* was the department. At first there was just a trickle of scripts sent to our new address on Lafayette Street, and after I removed them from the bag, it was one of my new duties in Joe's one-person office to read them because I had been a playreader in some of my previous jobs.

A good number of the plays sent to Joe exhibited the free hippie spirit of the mid-Sixties not only in content but also in their format. One was boldly written on a stack of paper napkins. I read it. Another was intricately rendered as an infinity spiral. I read that one too, even though its dramatic ending would remain forever unknown after it disappeared from view in the graphic concept. Other plays were carefully penned on lined paper, and a few reliably arrived in our mailbags addressed to "The Pubic Theater."

I soon became sensitive to Joe's low threshold of tolerance for kitchen-sink drama.

"I don't want to see another coffee cup on the stage, or a refrigerator," he complained to me, "or someone eating an apple. That's the worst."

My pet peeves were plays whose characters, instead of having names, were called "Woman A" or "Man B." The sight of it in a script set my teeth on edge like fingernails scratching a blackboard.

"Have we received Jack Kirby's script yet?" Joe called out to me from his desk one day. "His agent said she was sending it—what's its name?—*Eat Carrots*?"

"Yes," I called back, not correcting the title because I knew Joe had deliberately gotten it wrong. He knew and I knew that the title was not *Eat Carrots*, but *Fuck Carrots*, and he was daring me to say it. The script had arrived on the heels of another play with the similarly very-1960s title of *Eat Shit*, which I also wouldn't say out loud though I had no qualms about reading it.

"Here it is," I said, handing the "Carrots" script to Joe with my report attached.

After the success of *Hair*, the scripts came pouring in and I had to get help. I engaged an experienced freelance script consultant, the poet-playwright Alfred Levinson, whom I had met at Lincoln Center Theater, as well as Rozanne Rich Seelen, the co-owner of New York City's famous Drama Book Shop, and Nancy Golladay, who was then a lighting designer for the Merce Cunningham Dance Studio. I also went to see plays at other theaters almost every night and wrote thumbnail reports on any productions that I thought would be of interest to Joe.

I became in effect the default predecessor of a future Play Department, eventually overseeing a staff of freelance playreaders while keeping Joe's relationships with playwrights, directors, and agents on a priority footing. I still read a few scripts at home. However, at the end of the decade the original people with an ear to the ground for talent (Freedman, Riofrancos, Cornell, and some of their gifted assistants) had left the Public Theater for other jobs.

By the early Seventies we had five theaters operating in the renovated building and Joe had begun to move shows to Broadway. He also began to enlarge the artistic staff at the Public, engaging the wonderful Black actor-director Novella Nelson as consultant to the producer in 1972. As a director, Novella introduced the playwright Edgar Nkosi White and fostered a

Director Stuart Vaughan (center) rehearsing Stephen Joyce and Bryarly
Lee in *Romeo and Juliet* on a temporary stage in Central Park in 1957.
George E. Joseph/Billy Rose Theatre Division, New York Public Library

Colleen Dewhurst and George C. Scott in a concert version of *Antony
and Cleopatra* directed by Joe at the Heckscher Theater in 1959.
Billy Rose Theatre Division, New York Public Library

Aerial view of the Delacorte
Theater on Belvedere
Lake in Central Park.
Courtesy of the Public Theater

The Delacorte
Theater in Central
Park where
New York City's
skyline is always
a backdrop
to the play.
Sam Falk/The New
York Times/Redux

The cast of *King
Lear*, directed by
Joe, in the first
season at the
Delacorte Theater
in 1962 with
Jamaican-American
actor Frank Silvera
as King Lear
(on throne) and
Roscoe Lee Browne
as Lear's Fool
(seated on step).
Friedman-Abeles/Billy
Rose Theatre Division,
New York Public Library

Joe directing *Troilus and Cressida* at the Delacorte Theater in 1965, the year we met. He told me, "It's Troilus who's the cad, and Cressida is his victim." I liked that.

Papp Estate

Scenic designer Ming Cho Lee and Joe studying the model of his set for *Troilus and Cressida* at the Delacorte Theater in 1965.

George E. Joseph/Billy Rose Theatre Division, The New York Public Library

Joe directing the Mobile Theater production of *Henry V* with Robert Hooks, one of the founders of the Negro Ensemble Theater, Ellen Holly, and Lynn Hamilton in 1965.

Paul DeMaria/NY Daily News Archive/ Getty Images

Ellen Holly and James Earl Jones in
Macbeth on the Mobile Theater, 1966.
Friedman-Abeles/Billy Rose Theatre Division,
The New York Public Library

Composer David Amram, shown
in 1960, was involved in many
of Joe's early productions.
Photofest

The Joseph Papp
Public Theater in
Greenwich Village,
home of five
theaters, Joe's Pub,
and the Library
Restaurant. It opened
with *Hair* in 1967.
Afton Merrifield Rodriguez

This is me moving into the Astor Library building in 1966. Construction work on the first of the Public Theater's five theaters had just begun.
Papp Estate

The original cast of *Hair* at the Public Theater in 1967.
Friedman-Abeles/Billy Rose Theatre Division, The New York Public Library

A wary-eyed Joe hosting Mayor John V. Lindsay (L) at the Public Theater's first reception in 1967. Bernard Gersten, the Public's associate producer, is on his right.

Joe and his son Tony at the Public Theater in 1968.

Inaugural reception at artist Romare Bearden's Cinque Gallery on the second floor of the Public Theater in 1969. Bearden (R in light sweater) is shown talking to co-founder Norman Lewis. Their purpose was "To exhibit the work of both new and established African-American artists."

Cinque Gallery records, 1959–2010. Archives of American Art, Smithsonian Institution

Charles Durning as Feste with Barbara Barrie as Viola in *Twelfth Night* at the Delacorte Theater in 1969. I could easily imagine Durning, who was a consummate comedian, as a member of Shakespeare's own company at the Globe Theater.

Friedman-Abeles/Billy Rose Theatre Division, The New York Public Library

(L–R) Gerald Freedman, the first artistic director of the Public Theater, rehearsing *Peer Gynt* at the Delacorte Theater in 1969 with Stacy Keach, Judy Collins, Estelle Parsons (seated), and Olympia Dukakis.

Friedman-Abeles/Billy Rose Theatre Division, The New York Public Library

Playwright Adrienne Kennedy at the beginning of her influential career when her plays *Cities in Bezique: The Owl Answers* and *A Beast's Story* were produced at the Public Theater in 1969.

Friedman-Abeles/Billy Rose Theatre Division, The New York Public Library

Joe multitasking in 1970.

Gail Papp

separate departmental function to handle scripts. Helen Marie Jones, a young woman who had been a casting assistant and playreader at the Public, was put in charge of it. Her program credit was script development, but I thought of her as running a play department even though one hadn't been officially established yet.

Meir Zvi Ribalow, a poet and aspiring director, also started at the Public in 1972, as a result of the following incident.

After receiving weekly piano lessons downtown, Joe's button-bright eleven-year-old son Anthony would spend the rest of the afternoon at the Public Theater, riding home with his father at the end of day. His favorite place to hang out was at the Reception Desk's manual exchange switchboard on the first floor, a still-functioning relic from the Hebrew Immigrant Aid Society. Anthony would sit there next to receptionist Gigi Lilavois as she answered incoming calls in her soft Haitian-accented voice, spellbound by the way she swiftly handled the multicolored trunk lines, jack lamps, and levers of the old console.

One day Meir Zvi Ribalow, the aspiring director, stopped at the busy reception desk to inquire about employment. Anthony, who was sitting there, asked him a few questions in his father's forthright manner and then hurried up to Joe's office on the second floor.

"Dad!" he said. "I just spoke with this person who walked in downstairs. He seems intelligent and I think you should hire him for something."

After Joe met with Ribalow, he hired him as a production associate on a show then in rehearsal called *Winning Hearts and Minds* based on anti–Vietnam War poetry.

Amid the frequent comings and goings that were typical back then (none of them due to anyone being fired, but rather due to people moving on), the script handling function became vacant, and Ribalow was available to fill it. He was joined by Melanie Carvill, the vivacious stepdaughter of Irish actor Jack MacGowran, the great interpreter of playwright Samuel Beckett. Newly enfranchised as a Play Department, Ribalow and Melanie's office soon became a lively precinct in the building.

I recall, however, that Joe appeared to have an agreeable but perfunctory interest in its activities at this time. For someone like him whose eyes and ears were always cocked for talent, the functions of the Play Department seldom commanded his attention. His desire to find new work and new directors, however, increased significantly after 1973 when he took charge of running Lincoln Center Theater with the goal of making it a showcase for diverse American artists, rather than a platform for classics, as before. More than ever the institutional search for new plays required people familiar with the pulse of his current thinking and his sense of urgency about it.

When Ribalow left to pursue his primary career as a director, I sensed an opportunity to ask for the now-vacant job. I hesitated at first because the idea seemed pretty bold to me. But a quick look around at the Public Theater's staff confirmed a fact that I already knew—Joe's strong prejudice in favor of promoting people from within the organization—and this encouraged me.

To my great relief, Joe liked the idea although he said he didn't look forward to losing, that is, replacing me. I was delighted with the title he chose, "Director of Play Development" because it was the first one I'd ever had that didn't have the word "assistant" in it. He announced my promotion at a board meeting in June 1975, saying that I would be joined in the newly renamed Play Development Department by the Black playwright Ed Bullins, who would be in charge of a workshop for playwrights.

In my new job, I felt that the Play Department should be located close to the creative center of the organization, which hadn't been possible recently because free space near Joe's office had become scarce due to the Public Theater's rapid internal expansion. So where was I going to work from? I asked the facilities manager for the small supply room that had once housed the A.B. Dick Mimeograph machine. No one else wanted that glorified closet, but it was ideal from my point of view because of its location next to Joe's office.

Lynn Holst, a future vice president of RHI Hallmark Entertainment, became my space-sensitive and influential associate director in the former supply room and with added staff our department eventually added a modest wing to it. The previous retinue of freelance readers congregated there, expanded now to include theater directors and the involvement of actor-playwright Kathryn Grody, the novelist Deborah Eisenberg, and the author Bonnie Greer. I was also fortunate in being introduced to Arthur Wilson, a charismatic poet-actor-playwright-educator, who became director of the Public's Playwriting in the Schools program.

I was now reading many more plays than before, always a challenging task because you need to fill in many elements that you don't see on the page. In one respect I think I benefitted from having grown up with radio rather than television because it had developed my auditory imagination when reading.

I had also learned a great deal from Joe's intensely personal method of communing with a play.

"I'm using my body as a laboratory," he once said to me. "The play is the nub of my inquiry."

In the course of time, I learned from Joe's astonishing openness to plays of every conceivable kind, running the gamut from a realistic play, directed by Marvin Camillo, about the fate of a white man who is a child molester in a predominantly Black and Hispanic prison (Miguel Piñero's *Short Eyes*, which is slang for pedophile) to music-hall depictions of a little girl's curiosity and spunk in the nineteenth century (Elizabeth Swados/Lewis Carroll's *Alice at the Palace*).

I learned from Joe's receptivity to cultural worlds he had little or no direct knowledge of. They included the early plays of the young Chinese-American playwright David Henry Hwang, such as *F.O.B.* (fresh off the boat), as well as the mature work of the Saint Lucian Caribbean poet Derek Walcott in his play *Ti-Jean and His Brothers*, a folktale about the struggle of a boy and his two brothers against colonialism and the Devil, which Joe produced in Central Park in 1972.

I also learned from Joe's ability to correct his wrongful first impressions of a work, such as Wallace Shawn's *Aunt Dan and Lemon*. His first response had been negative because of an anti-Semitic protagonist in the play, but he re-read the script and ended up producing and defending the play. He said, "I realized that what Wally was saying was that the liberal argument is weak. It's more hypothetical than real."

And I learned from Joe's ability, in the context of an entirely different play, to correct or reconsider his toleration of a horror-show element in John Ford Noonan's *Older People*, which had ended with a highly realistic coronary induced by a maniacally jealous wife. Noonan, a gentle person with a heavily ironic sensibility, thought it was funny. Joe found it hard to take, although he saw the point of it. But when audiences gasped and hid their eyes, it came out.

I believed with all my heart that "a fine play is process caught in flight," as Joe had written in a note to himself. But since I had been close to his creative priorities as the Public's producer for several years, I knew the importance of being aware of what scripts were emerging that might interest directors and

Joe reading a script during a staff party in his office in 1969.
Gail Papp

actors, that were also of a kind that Joe might be interested in producing, and, of course, that were more or less ready to show him. I addressed this matter by encouraging the Play Department staff to function more like assistant producers in relation to some of the work they were developing.

This thinking jarred departmental culture a bit at first. Was I turning my back on the essential process of nurturing talent in favor of end results? No. But since the Play Department's office in the former supply room was next to Joe's, as I had devised, I hoped the possibility of a more active producing role by the staff would take root, and it did.

Somehow the notion of being a dramaturg never got hold of me. Perhaps it was because, like Joe, I was leery of the word's eighteenth-century Germanic origin, or its broad but ill-defined range of activities. Dramaturgs themselves were often hard put to explain what they did and would say things like "I'm a mediator" or "I look for patterns," or even "I don't know the answer." Essentially, however, a dramaturg is a literary advisor in the theater whose role is to help the playwright, director, and actors, if requested. I had excellent dramaturgs on my staff. But for myself, I looked instead to role models for my function in the editorial field that I was familiar with.

My hero was the book editor Maxwell Perkins. I first heard about him and his relationships with many great authors of the early twentieth century from my parents. I had been intrigued by Perkins' process—his own mode of expression intertwined with the author's intentions, and a vulnerable connection to the writing through the filter of his expertise. When I assumed responsibility for the Public Theater's Play Department in 1975, I remembered his rock-solid commitment to writers under the most difficult and flawed of circumstances, which reminded me a lot of Joe's unshakable support of certain playwrights, such as Miguel Piñero, Elizabeth Swados, and others.

The only measure I ever had with regard to a script was a reliance on my imagination and my genuine excitement about someone's talent. Although the process was subjective and always fraught with risk, I knew whether I felt it or not. From that followed my desire and ability to help a playwright with what they needed in the way of commissions, readings, workshops, a place to work, someone to listen and ask questions, and, of course first and foremost, an introduction to Joe.

As to the mystery and responsibility of reading a play, I think the esteemed author-journalist-critic Margo Jefferson has best expressed for me the subjective challenge that's involved, in her article "Revisions: Reading a Play Demands Reading Between the Lines" (*New York Times*, December 11, 2000).

Plays are the missing link between reading and performance, the one kind of solitary reading that makes you as active as you can be posting messages on a Web site. The other participants are the characters, to whom you must give your own vision. And the dialogue is more porous, more open to imaginative entry than fictional narrative.

Whenever you pick up a play, you become designer, conductor, and director. You keep moving between the roles of director, actor and spectator, the observer and observed. When you read then see a play (or see then read one), you must adapt—learn to revel in—contradictory responses and interpretations. You have to go past the boundaries of your own temperament and judgment, at least for a time.

In 1974 I put out word that I was interested in commissioning "Ten-minute musicals." My simple idea was that the short form might encourage young composers and writers to try the longer form. I speculated that six ten-minute musicals could be yoked together for an eclectic evening program, providing, of course, that a talented director could be persuaded to make the concept work. This wasn't as foolhardy on my part as it sounds because the Public Theater's future artistic director Wilford Leach shared my enthusiasm for the idea and wanted to put together a first production.

My call for ten-minute musicals had a gratifying response. As scripts and tapes started arriving, Wilford and I listened to them together, reviewing an assortment of works that ranged from a mini opera buffa titled *I Am the Dog and I Want to Go Out* to a sun-and-surf caper from Barry Manilow called *Away to Pago Pago.*

The growth of the Play Department was rapid. By the mid 1970s—in contrast to that day in 1966 when I had rejoiced over the arrival of a single script in our mail at the Great Northern Hotel—the Play Department was receiving three thousand plays and musicals a year and we had a full schedule of readings and short-run workshops.

The Play Department office in the mid-1970s when we
received 3,000 plays and musicals a year.
Papp Estate

The potential musical talent for the theater was enormously exciting to me. (My co-major in college had been music composition.) Besides the five musicals the Public became known for between 1967 and 1991 *(Hair, Two Gentlemen of Verona, A Chorus Line, Runaways,* and *The Mystery of Edwin Drood)*, we produced forty other original musicals during that time. This group included:

- A musical that Joe commissioned called *Lenny and the Heartbreakers,* a trailblazing work by Kenneth Robins and composers Kim Sherman and Scott Killian that incorporated analog and digital synthesizers, drum machines, vocoders, and a rock-opera orchestra. The fact that *Lenny* was staged by the iconic choreographers Alwin Nikolais and Murray Louis, who enlisted dancers from their companies, pushed the visual and aural boundaries of musical theater at that time.
- *More Than You Deserve,* an ill-fated pairing of the talents of composer Jim Steinman and playwright Michael Weller, which however introduced Steinman to the phenomenal singer Meat Loaf and marked the beginning of their lifelong collaboration. Meat Loaf subsequently appeared in *As You Like It,* singing the role of an exile in the Forest of Arden at the Delacorte Theater, from which his operatic-size voice trumpeted throughout Central Park.
- A memorable series of performances of composer-lyricist Sarah Kernochan's *Sleep Around Town* with Carrie Fisher.
- An early version of Baikida Carroll's musical based on Ntozake Shange's novel *Betsy Brown.* Before that the virtuoso composer-pianist Cecil Taylor had taken a musical stab at the story but it hadn't worked out.
- Meredith Monk's eerie *Specimen Days,* a Civil War opera.
- Composer-lyricist August Darnell's *Fresh Fruit in Foreign Places* featuring himself as Kid Creole with The Coconuts and co-lyricist Andy Hernandez in a mix of disco, Latin American, Caribbean, and Cab Calloway styles inspired by the Big Band era.
- Carson Kievman's *Wake Up, It's Time to Go to Bed!,* three fully designed and plotted acts in which the musicians were the sole actors as they played their instruments in settings that conveyed dramatic suspense. The concept was perhaps ahead of its time when some baffled members of the audience walked out, unable to recognize the virtuoso performers that were right in

front of their eyes and ears simply because they weren't sedately seated and in formal attire.

There were many other new musicals by composers as brilliantly diverse as Nick Bicât, Willie Colón, Doug Dyer, William Finn, Nancy Ford, Rosalie Gerut, Des McAnuff, Nicholas Meyers, Richard Peaslee, Margaret Pine, Todd Rundgren, and David Langston Smyrl, to name just a few. (I have tried, to the best of my ability, to list and remember them all in the appendix.)

In addition there was *New Jazz at The Public*, an outstanding multi-year series of performances by musicians such as the eclectic and influential jazz composer Sun Ra, the saxophonist-composer Anthony Braxton, and Ornette Coleman, a founder of the free jazz genre. There were many others.

These concerts came about after Joe went to hear new jazz saxophonist David Murray at Axis in Soho in 1978. He told a reporter:

> What grabbed me initially was the music's extraordinary velocity. And I don't think I'd ever seen an instrument so totally overwhelmed by a musician. It was a continuous, unrelieved outpouring of really complete expression. After about thirty-five or forty minutes I was aching for some jazz rhythm that was recognizable to me. At some point the musicians did break into that, and I noticed that everyone felt a little relieved. Well, by the second set I began to get more of the whole feel of it. I came away very excited, thinking I should do something with it at the Public Theater.

In addition, Joe introduced musical concerts uptown at the Delacorte featuring world artists such as the Bach pianist Rosalyn Tureck; Cecil Taylor, the virtuosic free jazz composer-pianist; the powerful Chilean singer Mercedes Sosa; and the brilliant Argentinan bandoleonist-composer Astor Piazzolla.

It was a superb moment of historic musical creativity, some of which happily found its way to the welcoming stages of the Public Theater.

15

Dr. Spock's Petition

It was my first business day-trip out of the city with Joe—to Washington, D.C.—and the fact that we were going by train had put me in a holiday mood. I loved trains, hated planes, and was tremendously relieved that Joe had decided not to fly. I brought a script with me to read and, free of flight fright, settled in with it while enjoying the suburban and rural landscapes that flashed past the train's window.

As we neared Baltimore, my mind drifted to the serious purpose of the trip, which was to support the anti–Vietnam War petition to the Senate that Dr. Benjamin Spock, the famous pediatrician and activist, was sponsoring in 1972.

At Dr. Spock's behest, 115 distinguished professionals whose signatures he'd gathered had agreed to convene in Washington on this day to publicize their opposition to the war in Vietnam. When we joined them at a Washington hotel, Joe learned for the first time that the plan was to march to the Senate office building and then lie down in the hallway outside the Senate chamber in order to block anyone trying to go in or out. When asked to leave, they would refuse to do so, an action that would force the Capitol Police to arrest them, which, because of the famous people among the arrestees, would attract the desired media attention to Dr. Spock's antiwar petition.

Joe scowled. No one had told him anything about lying down on floors and getting arrested. How could he do this? At the end of the day he was supposed to be back in Manhattan for a ceremony at which Governor Nelson Rockefeller would present him with the New York State Award, and we were on a tight schedule to catch the Metroliner that would return us to the city in time for it.

Joe moved into his swift and efficient crisis management mode that I had seen on previous occasions. He commandeered a payphone booth in the lobby of the hotel where Spock's group had assembled and, in a rapid series of calls, arranged for his wife Peggy and playwright David Rabe to be his proxies at the ceremony.

Later, as orchestrated by the good doctor, Joe lay stretched out head-to-toe with other supine professionals on the floor of the hallway outside the entrance to the Senate chamber, forcing annoyed senators and congressional staffers to step over and around them. As one man with heavy, black-rimmed glasses was stepping over Joe, he stopped in his tracks. Smiling but incredulous, he said, "What are you doing down there, Joe?" It was Arizona Senator Barry Goldwater, the arch-conservative, half-Jewish Republican candidate for president in 1964, whose ancestors, like Joe's, had come to America from Poland. His recognition of Joe signified to me Joe's ability to make civil connections across the political spectrum.

"With all due respect, Senator," Joe answered from the floor, "I'm against this war in Vietnam."

Soon Joe and the other protestors were hoisted to their feet by a squad of Capitol Police that came marching in. Gripping their arms tightly, the police conducted them one by one down the Capitol building's marble steps, where I had joined a small crowd on the sidewalk cheering the arrestees as they were driven away in paddy wagons.

Hoarse from cheering after the last wagon had departed, I realized that I didn't have any idea where they'd gone, but I asked around and was given the address of the nearest police station. When I arrived there by taxi, Joe was relieved to see me. He was standing in line with other protestors who had been instructed to plead "Nolo contendere" (No contest) at the station to secure their immediate release after paying a fine. But it turned out that unless a person could produce cash to pay the fine, you'd be detained overnight in jail. Joe didn't have enough cash and the annoyance set him off.

"Do you have any money?" he asked me.

"No, I don't have any money," I said.

A police officer appeared to escort him and the other cash-strapped protestors down the station's bleak corridor to its holding pen. As he was led away, Joe turned and called out to me over his shoulder, "Gail! Get the money!"

Then before he disappeared around the corner, he shouted, "I REFUSE TO STAY HERE TONIGHT!"

Minutes later I found myself standing alone on the sidewalk in front of the police station. It was now evening in Washington. Compared to the nighttime high energy of New York City, our nation's capital felt deathly quiet and empty, as if people had deserted it.

How was I going to "get the money"? I knew no one in D.C., had no relatives or friends, the banks were closed, night had fallen, and there were no cell phones or ATMs in 1972.

Then I had a bright idea: theater box offices. I knew that Joe was friendly with Tom and Zelda Fichandler, the founders of Arena Stage in D.C., so I taxied to the Arena's box office and hustled to its still-open ticket window. For twenty frustrating minutes, I tried to convince the Arena's understandably suspicious treasurer that I was a person on a legitimate errand "to get Mr. Papp out of jail." Not having any Public Theater ID to prove who I worked for, I behaved like the industriously seductive bowerbird featured in Sir David Attenborough's BBC documentary, offering up the names of the Public's current plays, its actors, its staff members, our address, our phone number— anything at all I could think of to offset the treasurer's reluctance to hand a wad of box office cash to a perfect stranger. I don't know what convinced him, but my barrage of information did finally succeed, and on the way back to the police station, I settled into my taxi seat with an adventurous sense of my own actions, pleased that I had the Arena Stage cash in my pocket.

Joe was relieved to see me but said he'd actually spent an enjoyable few hours talking with his fellow detainees in the holding pen. After he paid the fine with the cash that I handed him, we caught a Metroliner back to New York City.

Although it was very late by this time, I was wide awake. It felt good being on a train again, listening to its mournful whistle as the dark contours of Maryland and Pennsylvania streamed past the window. I was filled with a sense of adventure and felt the lure of unknown possibilities. Seated next to me, Joe was exhausted and had fallen asleep. Whenever the motion of the train jostled him to one side and his head came to rest on my shoulder, I didn't dare move.

16

Malacology

I was something of a loner during those early days at the Public Theater. Although I enjoyed friendly relations with the small staff when we worked together at the Great Northern Hotel, when we moved into the Astor Library building, and the staff grew, I seldom went out for lunch at neighborhood restaurants like the others did, and never had the inside track on office gossip.

My extreme shyness was the result of a geographically unsettled childhood during which I had attended fifteen different public schools from kindergarten to the twelfth grade in San Francisco, Mill Valley, Berkeley, Richmond, Hollywood, and Colton, California, in New York City, and in Keene and Marlboro, New Hampshire. My sense of being an outlier as the perpetual new kid in class at a new school every year or half-year had been intensified by the fact that I was my parents' only child, tethered to a solitary, adult-centered life at home. As a result, when I was outside of home, I developed the unshakable feeling that nobody ever recognized me.

The years-long repetition of this awkward experience fostered habits of self-reliance and social disguise. Although I'd been lively as a young child, by the time I grew up I had adopted the protective deportment of a quiet person with good manners.

Living in this bubble, I was shocked one day when Joe asked me out to lunch. Had he gone mad? This was unheard of. He only went to lunch with the Parks Commissioner, a philanthropist, a director, and actors like Julie

Harris, Colleen Dewhurst, George C. Scott, or James Earl Jones. Someone like that.

Now he was asking me? I didn't know what to make of it. Actually, I felt like hiding, but, as with Joe's scary request that I take his director's notes at the *Troilus and Cressida* previews during my first summer working for the Public Theater, I couldn't think of a plausible reason to say no. So, as I had done then, I said, "Fine."

From the start of this first lunch together at a restaurant near the theater, our conversation was fun and on an equal footing. We discovered that we both easily read street signs backward (*Rotsa Ecalp*), as well as the food on the restaurant's menu (*slessum*). We also discovered that we were of like mind in preferring W. C. Fields to Charlie Chaplin, Scriabin to Liszt, and Martin Buber's *I and Thou* to Swami Muktananda, a popular cult figure in the Sixties. When I mentioned to Joe that I was surprised a theatrical biography of him hadn't been written yet, because there was a need for something more personal than those columns of information in *Who's Who*, he began to tell me about his boyhood in Brooklyn.

"I grew up in a mixed neighborhood in Williamsburg," he said. "Aside from Jews, there were Italians, and there was an Irish section close by, and then a block away from there was a group we called the Mohammedans. Then not too far from there, a Black neighborhood. This was the community, and it was broken up by turf. No way in the world would I leave my block without four or five people going with me, and then you took your life in your hands."

Somehow I had pictured Joe growing up in the protective embrace of a closely knit family, but evidently that wasn't the way things had been and he'd had to fend for himself from an early age.

The waiter appeared with two glasses of chardonnay that Joe had ordered and set them at our places.

Joe raised his glass. I raised mine.

"There was a lot of violence in my old neighborhood in Brooklyn," he continued. "You stayed within a very narrow confine, and the difference between being Jewish and being anything else was an extraordinary difference." I understood he was saying that it was the Jews in his neighborhood who were most in danger of being attacked.

I took a sip of wine and told Joe that my father had also grown up in Brooklyn.

"Is that so?" Joe said.

"My father's father was a circus banner painter there," I continued. "He used to paint huge banners in a big studio in Coney Island that had platforms and tall ladders. I think he sometimes painted theater sets."

"That's very interesting. So he was in the theatrical profession?" Joe asked.

"Just the circus part of it," I said.

"When I was growing up there, I didn't know anything about the theater," Joe said, "and I spoke like any Brooklyn kid."

"What did you sound like?" I asked.

"I'll give you an example. We had to memorize Marc Antony's funeral oration in school. That's when Caesar is lying there dead in his blood-stained toga. And Marc Antony says, 'If you have tears, prepare to shed them now. You all do know this mantle . . .' We would say it this way: 'If you have teahzz, pree-peah ta shed dem now. You-all do know dis mantull . . . ' That's the way we talked."

Joe said that he'd been able to improve his speech with the encouragement of a wonderful teacher in high school. I later learned that Joe's teacher had been Eulalie Spence, a British West Indian playwright, actress, and director who was a significant member of the Harlem Renaissance.

I asked about his unusual teenage interest in Shakespeare. I wondered if it had been stimulated by memorizing those speeches from the plays in school?

"No, I think it was because I grew up in a home where Yiddish was spoken," Joe said. "That was our first language and English was only a second language. Because of that I became acutely sensitive to the musical sounds of different languages and to the cadences and rhythms of the spoken word."

The rest of the lunch was fun and friendly, and walking back to the theater, we called out some street signs in backward fashion. I was completely surprised, however, when Joe invited me to lunch again the following week at a different restaurant he thought I'd like.

Over this second lunch, he told me that it had taken a war to get him out of New York.

"I joined the Navy after Pearl Harbor and was on a baby aircraft carrier called a Kaiser Coffin."

"I know about those," I said. "My father worked on them as a draftsman at Kaiser Shipyards in Richmond, California during the war. He let me visit him there."

"Is that so?" Joe said. "Well the one I was on had an elevator which used to take the fighter planes up to the main deck. It was a marvelous little stage, so whenever we had time off, I would put some shows together. Bob Fosse was in the navy with me. He was just a kid and I did a show around him. I began to like that. We toured the Aleutian Chain—that's Kodiak and Attu—then we went to Japan and played at the Ernie Pyle Theater in Tokyo. That was really my beginning, but I never thought I'd do it as a means of making a living. That never entered my mind."

Joe also talked about studying at the Actor's Lab in Los Angeles after the war. The G.I. Bill had paid for it.

"I began to read and do things there I'd never done before," he told me. "I sort of fell in love with live actors on the stage."

"But you didn't become an actor," I said.

"If I had permitted myself to be more vulnerable, I would have continued in the acting profession," Joe said, "but the ego of an actor is a very difficult thing to have to cope with because you yourself are the instrument."

I asked how he got involved with the city's park system, and he said that it came about because when he was a kid the only places to get away from the heat in the summer had been the parks and he used to go to them all the time.

"I would go to Prospect Park to listen to the Goldman Band concerts," Joe said. "My father loved bands and we used to sing band songs together. I got to thinking that the parks were the most democratic environment. They were free and people came and so the idea began to form of having performances in the park and not charging admission. There was no deep-rooted philosophy at that time except for my artistic drive to do Shakespeare's plays and to find ways of making them immediate to American audiences."

The waiter arrived just then with our lunches. Joe offered me the bread basket.

"So—what do you do when you're not working?" he asked.

With Joe's question the relaxed and friendly lunch took a different turn for me. Personal questions had always triggered my reflex for secrecy because I'd learned that if you let someone know too much about yourself, you were in a more vulnerable position than if they knew nothing or very little. This wasn't a mature calculation of my adult brain but a reflexive wariness that had developed during my continuously uprooted school years. As a result, I'd never had the occasion, and certainly never the impulse, to tell Joe anything about my personal life. Such as being divorced. Or presently sharing an apartment with the Yale Law School bachelor, who had overcome his former caution about the romantic relationship his parents seemed to favor.

Speechless now over the bread basket that Joe was holding out to me—an image etched in my memory like a moment distilled by Proust—my reflex against revealing personal information stiffened. But needing to answer Joe's question promptly, I decided I could safely tell him about one of my hobbies, malacology.

"Malacology?" Joe said, looking up from his soup.

"Yes, it's the study of mollusks—sea shells," I replied.

"You collect them at the beach?"

"No. I buy them at auctions where only ones that were captured live, with their original colors and patterns intact, are later put up for bids."

"So it's their aesthetic beauty that attracts you, is it, like a work of art?" Joe asked with a cadence he'd picked up from Irish friends, while at the same time displaying his habit of always probing for a better understanding, be it of a person or a play.

"Yes, but I'm also interested in their predatory behavior. Like when the univalves prey on the bivalves."

"Bivalves?"

"Cockle shells, for instance. They have two halves. Univalves don't."

Oh God, I thought. *Why am I going on about this over lunch with Joe?*

"You've seen cockle shells on the beach with holes in them?" I went on in spite of myself.

"Sure."

"That's caused by a univalve secreting a chemical that makes a hole in the bivalve's hinge which disables the muscle so the bivalve opens and the univalve can eat the slug inside."

"Fascinating!" Joe said. "I'm glad I didn't order mussels for lunch!"

17

Buried in the Berkeley Hills

The senior attorney at the Public Theater's prestigious law firm was of the opinion that Joe looked like the great nineteenth-century actor Edwin Booth, who was famous for his portrayal of Hamlet. Privately, I didn't see the resemblance, although in this regard I was undoubtedly prejudiced in favor of my father who in his youth really and truly *did* look like Edwin Booth, an eerie resemblance that was much remarked upon and is evident in early photos of my father. However, the Public's attorney was old enough to have known someone who had actually seen Edwin Booth on stage so his opinion that Joe looked like him carried some weight.

Joe said that he wished he'd been around in 1886 to see Edwin Booth play Iago in English to Tommaso Salvini's Othello in Italian.

"That must really have been something!" he said. "Audiences back in the 1880s accepted dual-language performances on the stage. They also knew the difference between Edwin Booth's Hamlet and Forbes-Robertson's Hamlet. They'd know exactly how each of them would say 'Words, words, words' or 'O what a rogue and peasant slave am I.' Theatergoers then were all experts."

I told Joe that I loved the stories I'd read about Edwin Booth trouping in the 1850s in Alaska's gold mining camps where the miners already knew by heart the speeches in the Shakespeare plays they came to see.

"Well those days are gone forever," Joe said. "We're not doing very much mining in Alaska except for oil right now."

Joe always had a soft spot for "old Broadway"—its stars, colorful producers, traditions, razzmatazz, and the steady march of its nineteenth-century playhouses from the Battery up to Times Square. It was a past that Joe said "conjures up a time when the American theater was alive and flourishing, when great actors strode across the boards of this country's hundreds of stages, when audiences packed the proscenium playhouses to find delight in performances by such players as Booth, Laurette Taylor, Sarah Bernhardt, Edwin Forrest, Mrs. Fiske, and Otis Skinner."

Except for the French Bernhardt, the actors Joe mentioned were all Americans: Edwin Booth, Edwin Forrest, and Otis Skinner were renowned Shakespearean actors; Laurette Taylor had originated the role of Amanda Wingfield, the mother in Tennessee Williams' *The Glass Menagerie*; and Mrs. Minnie Maddern Fiske's portrayal of Nora in *A Doll's House* helped Henrik Ibsen's plays reach a wide audience in the United States.

Ever since we'd moved into the Astor Library, I had observed Joe's impulse-buying of books at the Barnes & Noble on our corner at Astor Place. So in December 1969, with B&N's store windows decorated for Christmas, I thought it quite possible that the attorney's comment about Joe's resemblance to Edwin Booth might send him looking for a biography of Booth at this local bookstore.

If he did, he'd see the store's display of the just-published paperback *The Mad Booths of Maryland* with a picture of Edwin Booth on its cover and probably buy it. The author, Stanley Kimmel, was a friend of my father's, and this edition of his book contained a new "Supplement" called "John Wilkes Booth's Common-Law Family" featuring a previously unpublished letter, written in 1886 by a friend of the Booth family in Bel Air, Maryland, about a purported relationship between my great-great-grandmother and President Lincoln's assassin.

I didn't want Joe to inadvertently stumble across this disturbing and highly questionable information, so rather than brood about it, I decided the best thing was to give him *The Mad Booths of Maryland* for Christmas.

On its flyleaf I wrote "Happy holidays! (See Supplement One for the family skeleton)" and left it on his desk without signing my name.

"So, what's this about the family skeleton?" Joe asked me a few days later over dinner at Japonica Restaurant, tilting the large carafe of hot sake he'd ordered for us as he filled my cup.

Feeling both relieved and unnerved by having outed myself, I told Joe that I'd first heard about my family's purported connection to John Wilkes Booth, a brother of Edwin Booth, as a child when my father gave me an old 4" × 6" photograph of him, saying that he might be my great-great-grandfather and that a long time ago a woman in our family—my great-great-grandmother— had loved him and the photograph had belonged to her.

I explained that my father had learned about the possible relationship to Booth from his mother, a child actress trouping in the 1880s with her mother, who used the stage name Rita Booth. Born in 1859, Rita Booth had been regarded by some people in the theater profession of her time as the daughter of Booth.

"And what's Rita Booth's relationship to you again?" Joe asked.

"She's my great-grandmother," I said.

Finishing my cup of sake, I said that my father's mother remembered being taken as a child in the 1880s to visit John Wilkes Booth's older sister, Rosalie Booth, in a brownstone apartment at 339 West 23rd Street in New York City. She recalled how her mother, the young Rita Booth, and the elderly, white-haired Rosalie Booth had sat at a low tea table talking before an open-grate fire while she played with a good luck sea bean necklace that "Aunt Rosalie" had given her.

"When there were no children's roles for my father's mother in the road companies that hired Rita Booth, she was boarded with Rita Booth's mother, a flamboyant diva whose supposed youthful mésalliance with Wilkes Booth in 1859, six years before he would murder President Lincoln, had allegedly scandalized her New England family. This bizarre story," I told Joe, "has been passed down in my family for five generations."

"What about that photograph of him?" Joe asked. "Do you still have it?"

This was a matter of some chagrin to me because when I moved from Berkeley, California, as a child, I had buried it in a time capsule under a eucalyptus tree in our backyard, placing Booth's photograph in my school pencil box, along with my Brownie Scout pin, a tiny flask of "The Woman I Love" perfume from Woolworth's, and a note to whomever might discover my pencil box in the far-distant future.

"It must still be buried there somewhere in the Berkeley hills," I said.

Joe frowned at his wristwatch.

"Curtain's in forty-five minutes!" he exclaimed, pushing his chair back before heading off to pay the bill. "I hope they've fixed the first part."

We then rushed to a preview of a musical called *Stomp* by a Texas combine led by Doug Dyer that would soon be launching the Public's newest theater, Martinson Hall.

18

An Evening at the Ontological-Hysteric Theater

Since my relationship with the Yale Law School bachelor wasn't going well at home, and I didn't have a best friend at this time, my lunches with Joe and, more frequently, dinners before previews at the Public Theater, had become a welcome substitute for the congeniality and fun that were otherwise in short supply in my life.

I assumed that Joe's desire to associate with me must be due to some similar factor, although I didn't know this for certain because neither of us ever talked about our personal circumstances. Nevertheless, despite the fact that Joe's professional life teemed with people and he had a family, I recognized that he was, if truth be told, *married* to the Public Theater from morning to night, and I guessed that it could be a problem to be in a relationship with someone like Joe unless he also worked with the person.

We ventured beyond our insular world of neighborhood restaurants for the first time when Joe invited me to an off-off-Broadway play in what was then a still run-down Soho, at writer-director Richard Foreman's Ontological-Hysteric Theater.

Foreman's theater was a long narrow space with bleacher seats, and a capacity of about seventy-five, which occupied 25 percent of the total room, the balance being given over to the stage. It resembled the inside of a camera or the narrow hall of a crazy art museum. Since Foreman's style embraced concepts in perspective, the space felt like part of the creative process, like a honeycomb or a web.

Sitting next to Joe in the dark well of this theater which wasn't our Public or Delacorte Theater, I had a heightened consciousness of his presence. For instance, I noticed his shiny black shoes and heard, as if amplified, the rustling of his program and the sound of his breathing next to me.

Good grief, this feels like a date, I thought.

Was it my imagination? I couldn't be sure because it had been a very long time since I'd had such a sensation—a near lifetime away, in the past. But when Joe reached for my hand and held it, I realized with a shock that these feelings weren't all in my imagination, and I was so dizzy with excitement that I could scarcely pay attention to the performance on the stage. Suddenly here was an emotion I no longer thought I was capable of: the overwhelming joy of being alive.

Later, Joe and I agreed that the evening at Foreman's Ontological-Hysteric Theater was our "first date." Our circumstances, however, were hardly conducive to romance. First of all, Joe was married and had two children in grammar school. And—as Joe had accidentally discovered the time he'd brought me a bouquet of roses when I was sick at home on Waverly Place—I was living with someone.

The Yale Law School bachelor was a courteous and formal kind of person and he had invited Joe in, saying that it was an honor to meet him. But Joe didn't move from the doorway. He handed me the roses, said he had to get back to the office, and left.

When the door closed, my partner of several years said in a low voice, "He's after you."

His comment made me sad. Even though our amorous friendship had run its course, I was grateful to him for rescuing me from the fraught aftermath of my first marriage, and I regretted the sudden dismay he had to have been feeling from the unexpected encounter with Joe.

I also worried that it might change Joe's opinion of me. But, as I learned, he was too seasoned in the ways of the world to let that happen. His way was to block it out as if it had never occurred.

Joe's appearance with the roses highlighted a problem in this phase of our courtship. Due to the difficulty of our combined domestic circumstances, there was never an opportunity for Joe and me to be alone. Our time together was always spent with colleagues in the office, with audiences in theaters, with diners at restaurants, or with pedestrians and pigeons in New York City parks.

The situation caused much frustration, mitigated only by an occasional quick taxi ride to yet another public place. But it also set in motion a kind of old-fashioned ardor similar to the yearnings of lovers in the nineteenth century whose restrictive courting rituals mirrored our own.

In this situation I felt obliged to leave my partner, and in doing so I entered a new phase in my life as a single lessee of furnished sublets in Greenwich Village. Joe and I weren't living together, but for the next couple of years these picturesque sublets in the vicinity of the Public Theater would be the home base of our new part-time personal life. There was an unavoidable imbalance in this arrangement because I now lived alone (again), whereas Joe had two ports of call, his home and my sublet, and was never alone. But his overarching concern at this time was his two young children, and he was determined not to lose his connection to them, as he had with three older children from previous marriages.

Whenever I felt out of my depth, as I sometimes did in this entirely new relationship to Joe, my impulse was to reach for the ridiculous. I had noticed Joe occasionally challenge someone by saying, "Okay, what's the first line of *Hamlet*?" Since the person he buttonholed in this merry sport usually didn't know, Joe readily supplied the answer.

"It's '*Who's there?*'" he'd exclaim. "That's a good first line! Shakespeare knew how to start a play. Our contemporary playwrights can learn a lot from him."

Just for the heck of it, I decided to look up all the first lines in Shakespeare's plays that, like *Hamlet*, began with a question. At last I was ready to spring one on Joe when we were alone at my new sublet. I said:

"Okay, what's the first line of *Henry VI, Part 3*?"

"When shall we three meet again?" Joe joked.

"C'mon, I'm serious."

"O for a muse of fire!" he joked again.

"No, I mean it."

"If music be the food of love . . ."

"C'mon. Just say you don't know it."

"Sure: '*You don't know it.*'"

I sighed in frustration. "It's 'I wonder how the King escaped our hands?'"

"That's easy," Joe said. "On his feet."

We talked about the first lines of other plays. Joe mentioned Chekhov's well-known beginning of *The Seagull*, where Medvedenko, a schoolteacher, says to Masha, an unhappy young woman, "Why do you always wear black?" His question gets things moving right off the bat, in the same way that "Who's there?" does at the top of *Hamlet*.

I mentioned Tolstoy's *Anna Karenina*. Although it is a novel, I thought it met the same kind of challenge with its famous opening sentence: "Happy families are all alike; every unhappy family is unhappy in its own way."

For Chekhov and Tolstoy, it was unhappiness that put their characters in motion. And, I thought to myself after Joe had left, that applied to my own life as well. And, apparently, to his.

19

The Rocky Road to Broadway

When the actors took their curtain calls at the end of the musical *Two Gentlemen of Verona* in Central Park, audiences roared their approval as colored balloons were sent sailing into the night sky above the Delacorte Theater.

After observing this spontaneous ovation night after night during previews, Joe told me, "I didn't know whether *Two Gents* would go beyond the Park until the audiences got on their feet and started pounding and cheering. That's the only way I know I have a hit."

It was 1972. Five years earlier Joe had licensed the commercial rights to *Hair* to another producer. Now, these delirious audiences, followed by rave newspaper reviews for *Two Gentlemen of Verona*, had once again thrust the problematical possibility of commercial success upon the Public Theater. By this time, however, Joe's radical animus toward the commercialism of Broadway had ripened into nonprofit entrepreneurship, and he didn't hesitate to move *Two Gents* from the glades of Central Park to the flashing marquee of a playhouse in the heart of New York City's Theater District.

I couldn't imagine there would be very much for Joe to worry about as a first-time producer on Broadway. It would be a challenge, of course, to transfer the magic of an outdoor production to an indoor proscenium stage, but that was a task the talented and experienced team of playwright-lyricist John Guare, composer Galt MacDermot, and director Mel Shapiro was well-equipped to handle.

Sitting with Joe at the first preview of *Two Gents* at the St. James Theater on Broadway, I eagerly anticipated the show's madcap opening that I loved so much—a "cacophony of bird calls" and a white-suited Spirit of Love singing, a capella, "Love is that you, That fills my ears, That fills my nose, That fills my heart . . ." And I could hardly wait for the entrance of the wonderful Raúl Juliá as Proteus and the sinuous Jonelle Allen as Sylvia, both of whom had wowed audiences in Central Park.

But after a few minutes I knew that something wasn't right. There was none of that joy and frolic on the Broadway stage that had been so delightful during the show's summer performances outdoors. Instead *Two Gents* was flat as a flounder.

"What in God's name is she playing?" Joe whispered to me as he watched a new leading actress who had joined the company. "Her character is too broad. It's too vulgar." She was "La Lupe" (Guadalupe Yoli Raymond), an uninhibited Cuban singer known as the Queen of Latin Soul.

Soon, the unimaginable happened. During the first half of the show, theatergoers began to rise from their seats and noisily leave the theater, like flocks of birds startled into flight. During the intermission the ones who had stayed badmouthed the show, sounding a drone of complaints that could be heard on the sidewalk, in the lobby, at the bar, and in the ladies restroom where I eavesdropped on their comments.

"Why do you suppose they brought it to Broadway?" I heard the ladies say in unpleasant voices.

"I dunno. Agnes told me it was good in the park."

And so, instead of a musical hit from the Delacorte Theater in Central Park paving the way for the Public Theater's much-anticipated debut on Broadway, we found ourselves presiding over a disaster.

What had gone wrong? First of all, it was obvious that the unfortunate new leading actress had been miscast, a grotesque miscarriage of judgment not only on the part of the author and director but also of Joe, who had co-equal approval of casting. I wondered how Joe, usually such a canny judge of an actor's talent and appropriateness for a role, ever could have agreed to it.

There was a sober consensus that she needed to be replaced, but to do that the Public Theater would have to buy out her run-of-the-play contract, a large sum of money for a nonprofit theater to write off. But Joe did it, and the director and his colleagues put an ideal replacement in the part on short notice. She was the delicately beautiful Diana Davila, who had played Juliet in our Spanish-language Mobile Theater production of *Romeo y Julieta*.

As another cast replacement and adjustments in choreography and costumes followed, I literally watched the show change from a "flop" to a "hit" in two weeks, just as it happens in Broadway backstage stories in the movies. The theatergoers' noisy walk-outs and bad-mouthing in the lobby mercifully ended like the cessation of a stuck car horn, and the comments in the ladies restrooms about-faced to "It's wonderful! I love it!"—the buzz of success on the Great White Way.

At the same time that this amazing turnaround occurred at *Two Gents*, Joe moved David Rabe's *Sticks and Bones* from the Public Theater to the Golden Theater on Broadway. The move flew in the face of conventional wisdom because Rabe's play about the effect of the Vietnam War on an American family and its soldier son hadn't received the "money reviews" downtown that are usually deemed necessary to drive a commercial transfer, but Joe believed it was an important play that deserved a national platform, and "national" meant Broadway.

Of all the writers that he produced, Joe felt that David Rabe carried the greatest kind of weight. "He's closest to the power of O'Neill," he said. He even wrote to David's parents, Mr. and Mrs. William Rabe, saying, "I see David as a national playwright. What that means to me is that he has an acute perception of the American consciousness. This perception in the theater makes it possible for ideas to transcend the limitations of class, color and economic lines."

Then we had a big surprise. The Public Theater's two shows on Broadway received nominations for Tony Awards. This instantly put the John Guare/Mel Shapiro/Galt MacDermot musical of *Two Gentlemen of Verona* in contention for Best Musical with the super-popular *Grease* and *Follies*, and young David Rabe's *Sticks and Bones* in contention for Best Play with a formidable trio of works by playwrights Neil Simon, Harold Pinter, and Robert Bolt.

***

For the past two years I had been subletting apartments in Greenwich Village and at this time had just moved into one situated in a nineteenth-century courtyard with a wrought-iron gate at 10th Street and Sixth Avenue. I could hardly wait to tell my mother about it because I knew she'd appreciate its historic location.

"It's actually a tiny two-room house at 3 Milligan Place," I told her. "It was built in 1852 and it's like a cozy little home. It even has a fireplace."

"Number Three Milligan?" she asked me.

"Yes, Mother, Number Three," I said. "Why?"

"Well, sweetie pie, did you know that 3 Milligan Place is where I was living when your father was courting me in 1930?" she asked.

"No, I had no idea," I replied.

I couldn't get over that. If you put it in a novel, it would seem like a contrived coincidence. An image of my attractive young parents flashed through my mind. Of my mother dressed like a Nazimova-style flapper and of my Edwin Booth lookalike father turning the handle of the same wrought iron gate at Milligan Place that Joe and I now passed through.

We had never talked about living together, about marriage or divorce, any of those questions that, brought up for discussion, or worse, resolution, have the power to shipwreck even the most loving relationship. I was on guard against them, believing that life would unfold in its own good time and that any speculation about the future posed a threat to my delicate ecosystem in which I never addressed these issues. I was prepared to continue in this way because Joe had young children and they came first, and I really didn't care about getting married again.

However, even though we saw each other every day, I missed Joe terribly when he wasn't with me at Milligan Place. Without him, its picturesque setting only served as a painful reminder to me of his absence. But I never let on that our part-time life together was a cause of sadness.

I tried to offset my emotionally vulnerable condition with what seems, in retrospect, like magical nonsense, but I distinctly remember drawing on my sense of family pride through the mottos that had been passed down to me. "*Nil desperandum*"—"Never despair"—had long been one in my father's family. On my mother's side there had been "*Festina lente*"—"Make haste slowly"—signified by the emblem of a dolphin entwined in an anchor. Even though that image seemed somewhat ambiguous, if not downright alarming, I took hope from it.

And so I found various ways to continue in a complicated situation that had no secure grounding either in the present or in the future—always reminding myself that it was a tremendous blessing, and more than anyone dares hope for in this life: to love, and be loved in return.

20

How I Spent Shakespeare's 408th Birthday

There was, of course, much excitement at the Public Theater when our first two shows on Broadway—*Two Gentlemen of Verona* and *Sticks and Bones*—were nominated for Tony Awards for Best Musical and Best Play, respectively. Now the day of the 1972 awards ceremony had arrived, and the winners would be announced on television.

"It's April 23, Shakespeare's 408th birthday," I thought as I got dressed to attend the ceremony at the cavernous old Broadway Theater at 53rd Street where it would also be broadcast for television viewers.

I wore a midnight-blue velvet A-line dress, not at all anxious in those ultra-skinny days that its hem fell five inches above my kneecap. However, I still wasn't used to the radical change that I had initiated by leaving my Yale Law School partner, with whom I had been living for several years—to start living alone. This reframing of my personal life was recent enough for me to feel strange about getting dressed up to go somewhere without him—but also not being able to go with Joe either, who continued to maintain the outward semblance of a stable family life for the sake of his children.

After exiting the subway at Rockefeller Center, I walked the five blocks to the theater, where a well-known hanger-on around Broadway, a benign fixture on the sidewalk, called out to me, "*Are you anybody?*" The answer that sprang to mind was Emily Dickinson's "I'm nobody! Who are you? Are you nobody, too?" but I just smiled and waved at him.

I took my seat with the Public Theater staff in the balcony of the large play-house, whose décor and furbelowed ceiling reminded one of its earlier use as a vaudeville house and then a movie palace. In the present era many of the best American musicals, from *South Pacific* to *Fiddler on the Roof*, had premiered on its stage. As my view shifted away from the stage to the audience, I spotted Joe sitting there with his wife Peggy. I knew of course that they'd be in the orchestra section, but through some hazy miscalculation on my part, I'd assumed that their Tony Award seats wouldn't be visible from my perch up in the balcony.

For the past two years—until this moment—I had always been sheltered, almost sequestered in the clandestine private life that I led with Joe and I had never been confronted with this kind of visual and emotional dissonance before. Facing it now for the first time, I was seized with a frantic desire to leave the theater but, not being able to do that, I tried to distract myself from my lovesick turmoil by thinking of role models in the lives of famous paramours whose *savoir faire* I might emulate.

Admiral Horatio Nelson's "Hamilton woman" came to mind, but she wasn't a good role model because she'd never labored alongside the admiral in the British navy the way I did alongside Joe in the Public Theater. I thought of Marie Duplessis and Alexander Dumas *fils* and some others, but none of the *inamoratas* who came to mind had been working colleagues of the men with whom they were involved.

My silent musings on unsatisfactory role models were interrupted by the sudden appearance of Joe sprinting into the balcony of the theater, looking very handsome in his tuxedo and bow tie as he greeted the staff there and discreetly signaled a happy glance in my direction.

At the end of the telecast—when the Public Theater's two maverick shows unexpectedly won the Tony Awards for Best Musical *and* Best Play—we, the minions in the balcony, went BANANAS NUTS CRAZY, while down below in the orchestra I saw Joe, elated by the Best Play award to David Rabe—who was his favorite playwright—scramble out of his seat and leap on stage to congratulate him.

Having won these double Tonys for a play and a musical, Joe and the Public Theater now pole-vaulted into national prominence in the 1970s. This was a decade that took all of us on a rollercoaster ride toward more Broadway shows and Tony Awards, Pulitzer Prizes, touring and foreign productions, television deals, and the proprietorship of Lincoln Center Theater.

For the first time I was startled by Joe's picture on the covers of national magazines and at phone booths on the sidewalk, which displayed large illuminated photographs of Joe-in-a-phone-booth promoting Public Theater plays. His smiling face also looked out at me from Public Theater posters on subway platforms and from a giant wraparound radio ad banner on the sides of buses that had him saying, in quotes, "When I can't read all about it, I hear all about it on WCBS News Radio 88AM."

I laughed at his photograph on the July 3, 1972, cover of *Newsweek* because it made him look like Richard III, apparently as a way of illustrating Associate Editor Charles Michener's story "on the brilliant and stormy producer."

"A short time ago Joseph Papp was fighting to keep alive his free New York Shakespeare Festival as well as his Public Theater," Michener wrote. "Now he has emerged as the single most creative and controversial figure in American theater. At a time of esthetic and financial crisis, Papp is finding brilliant new writers, building audiences, winning prizes and telling off the critics."

During the hoopla surrounding the Tony Awards, Joe signed an agreement with the William Morris Agency to represent the Public Theater for film and television, and a group of us went to Los Angeles with him to meet the mega-agency's legendary president, Abe Lastfogel. When Mr. Lastfogel's chauffeured white stretch limousine picked Joe, Bernie Gersten, and me up at our Hollywood hotel, the opulence of its soft leather interior and chrome bar inspired a merry ride to the agency with Joe and Bernie matching wits the whole way about what might have happened to the First Fogel.

Back in New York Joe was somewhat ambivalent about the agency connection. When a magazine interviewer asked him if he was going to capitalize on his amazing Broadway success by branching into film and television, I saw him bristle with impatience.

"My job is building theater and my job is my life," Joe replied. "*Theater* is the most forceful expression for me. This is the only form in which I can articulate my own feelings about life and do something about society."

Robert Brustein, drama critic for *The New Republic*, cast a wary eye on Joe's new celebrity status, warning him from his Theater Department eyrie at Yale University, "What the media would destroy, they first make famous."

But Joe was Joe, and, as I had learned when I began working at the Festival, cultural stardom wasn't new to him. He found it useful, but he didn't seek it for personal ends. People couldn't figure him out because although his mind was always teeming with creative ideas inextricably intertwined with justice and human rights, he took umbrage if he was referred to as "idealistic." And he was downright scathing about the word "liberal."

"Liberals are the most confusing," he said. "They have two feet firmly planted in midair. They lose self-identity. Who the hell are they? And what are they operating from—some kind of mystic ideal?"

"If you never met him," the British playwright David Hare wrote, "you can't imagine how completely Joe Papp dominated a room. One of the most striking things about him was his fabulous handsomeness. Short, lean, with thick dark eyebrows, Byronic brow and an intense air of windswept concentration, he was everyone's idea of a man of action—never lost either for an analysis or an unlikely way forward. You could never quite rely on being your normal self in his presence."

With the new media celebrity of Joe and the Public Theater that arrived after the Tony Awards in 1972, I was reminded of what I had once read in a book review about Winston Churchill: "All people of great achievement are ambitious, but the key question is whether they are ambitious to be, or ambitious to do."

Joe had always been in the second category—"ambitous to do." Personal fame affected him only to the extent that he felt it advanced his goals for the work of the Public Theater and Free Shakespeare, to which he was, as everyone knew, joined at the hip.

21

Traveling with Joe

In 1973 the plan was for me to fly to London with Joe for the opening of the Public Theater's musical *Two Gentlemen of Verona* at the Phoenix Theater. This would be my first trip abroad and I was so excited that I pretended my mortal fear of flying, which I had never told Joe about, didn't exist. I don't know what I expected to happen, but by the time our departure was in just two days, my excitement had evaporated and the flight to London loomed before me like a rendezvous with a firing squad.

"I'm afraid of flying," I finally told Joe, who tried to reassure me with the oft-cited fact about the superior safety of airplanes compared to traveling by car.

"Anyway, I'll be there to hold your hand," he said.

Not wanting to defeat such loving encouragement with the importunity of my phobia, I resolved to deal with it. Someone suggested that I bring a flask of spirits with me. I could administer it in flight as needed, taking nips as efficiently as if I had an IV drip and it not costing me the exorbitant in-flight price for a drink. I thought that made sense, so I bought an eight-ounce hip flask for the flight and filled it with tequila.

During the take-off, I clutched the hand that Joe offered, my heart pounding so furiously I could scarcely breathe. I couldn't even cry. If I were facing the firing squad that I had hypothesized, what would my thoughts be at that last moment? I knew I would gladly die for Joe if it would save his life. This was serious, not a feeling to be dismissed.

Meanwhile the plane was rising off the ground with its four fired-up jet engines shrieking over the aircraft's wings. In a state of abject terror in my aisle seat, I wondered how any sane person could pretend that this grossly unsafe mode of travel was *acceptable*?

Joe loosened his grip on my hand a little. "Do you have your flask?" he asked in a kind voice.

I fished it out of my purse. I had never tilted a flask to my lips before, as they must have done in the Yukon in days of old, and I choked on the first sip. Still, the healing power of the tequila even in that small measure managed to make its way to my heart, lungs, stomach and, eventually, head.

I got the hang of the flask and offered it to Joe. He declined. He'd already ordered a vodka gimlet.

We began reading the newspapers we'd brought with us. The Watergate investigation had begun.

"Gosh, it says here that three of Nixon's main people at the White House may have to resign," I said.

"Yes," Joe said. "There's a good analysis of it on page thirteen."

Our national politics diverted me more and more as I took nips from my flask. By the time the aircraft's great wings began to tilt in the direction of Heathrow Airport, I was no longer feeling anxious and had become enthralled instead by the lights of London which shone like glow worms outside our window.

My God, I thought as I looked at that twinkling horizon from our airborne elevation. *Here Joe and I are, arriving in the land of Shakespeare, the land of the Brontës, of Chaucer, John Donne, Virginia Woolf . . .*

Tears welled in my eyes as a powerful emotion swept over me: the thought of my literature-loving but poor parents who had given me so much yet could never afford to travel themselves. And here I was about to land in the enchanted isle of their literary imagination with the incomprehensibly loving support of Joe for which I was so grateful.

Our landing at Heathrow Airport oddly left no lasting impression on me. In fact, I only remember Joe and me standing at a curb as he hailed a taxi and one of London's big square black hackneys that seem to have been fabricated in King Edward VII's reign glided smoothly to our side. We got in.

"Dorchester Hotel," Joe told the driver.

"Very good sir," the driver said and began steering his cab through an intricate course of narrow streets and traffic circles—which are called "circuses"—looping dizzily around Piccadilly Circus, before streaming onto the straight boulevard of Park Lane which took us to the Dorchester Hotel, a tall modern building on a park corner. Joe had booked it because when he'd stayed there before, the Dorchester's Concierge had always welcomed him as a special guest with full VIP courtesies.

It was late at night when we entered the huge lobby of the hotel. Joe said that I should wait with our bags while he checked us in at the Registration Desk. With feelings intensified by the tequila I'd sipped during our flight, I watched Joe stride toward the Dorchester desk in his energetic manner, a sight that instantly reminded me of Shakespeare's description of Antony— "His delights were dolphin-like: they showed his back above the element they lived in . . ."

Then, biding my time until he returned, I tried to remember Shakespeare's famous lines about England.

"*This scepter'd isle . . .*" I murmured to myself, feeling a little dizzy and wishing I could sit down somewhere. "Then it's something-something, *This happy breed of men . . .*"

Suddenly Joe was by my side again.

"Let's go!" he said, grabbing our bags and walking briskly toward the exit. I trotted after him. The next thing I knew we were standing on the sidewalk outside of the Dorchester Hotel.

"What happened?" I asked, flabbergasted.

Joe demurred. He was in one of his subjective and action-driven unruly states. Something was storming through his brain but I had no idea at first what it was. The only thing I could think of was that he had stayed at this hotel before with his family, and just now he had been checking us into a room. *Of course that's it,* I thought to myself. *He should have chosen a different hotel where the staff wouldn't know him from previous visits.*

Joe hailed a taxi.

"Take us to the best hotel you recommend," he told the driver.

"Very good, sir."

I don't remember where we stayed that night, but the next morning the sun was shining and neither of us was in a mood to rehash the previous day's upsetting moments.

In future years I flew to London with Joe for the openings of other Public Theater productions on the West End, such as Jason Miller's *That Championship Season* and *A Chorus Line,* as well as the filming at Shepperton Studios of *The Pirates of Penzance* and the film of David Hare's *Plenty,* which he coproduced with Edward R. Pressman.

Our theater-related travels increased dramatically in the 1980s when we visited more than twenty countries and forty cities in Europe, the eastern Communist bloc, and South America. Joe also visited Vietnam with a delegation of veterans. I never got used to all the flying that involved, but I managed to do it, even on eleven-hour-long flights to Moscow and Rio de Janeiro, with the help of the handy flask.

Trips to London assumed a new importance in 1982 when an exchange got underway between Joe and the Public Theater and the Royal Court Theater's Artistic Director Max Stafford-Clark, who shared a similar commitment to cutting-edge work. The two theaters' relationship came at a time when Joe had become intensely dissatisfied with the superficiality of domestic playwriting. The trans-Atlantic sharing of plays, directors, and actors created an exhilarating atmosphere at the Public with a new focus on the provocative work of British playwrights such as Caryl Churchill, David Hare, Ron Hutchinson, and Michael Hastings, and at the Royal Court on the challenging work of American playwrights such as Wallace Shawn, George C. Wolfe, Larry Kramer, and Thomas Babe. Far more than an exchange program, it was an augmentation of perspective that had a deep and lasting effect on the Public Theater.

22

A Bastion of Bourgeois Patronage

After the departure in 1972 of Lincoln Center Theater's producing director, Jules Irving, no one was waiting in the wings to replace him. The building's dark shuttered presence stood in woeful comparison to its glittering neighbors on the main plaza of the sixteen-acre Lincoln Center complex: the Metropolitan Opera, the New York Philharmonic Orchestra, and the New York City Ballet.

It was now the responsibility of Lincoln Center's umbrella corporation, known as "Link Ink," to get its theater component up and running again under new leadership. It was headed then by two arts-loving executives: Amyas Ames, a New England investment banker who was the chairman of Lincoln Center for the Performing Arts, and John Mazzola, a New Jersey lawyer who had been the president of Lincoln Center since its incorporation under John D. Rockefeller III. These two had already begun the search for someone to run the theater when they invited Joe in January 1973 to discuss his views about Lincoln Center Theater's future stewardship. This was going to be an informational meeting, and Joe asked me to go with him.

As I knew, Joe had given a lot of thought to the "edifice complex" that had spread across the country, and he had spoken about it in public a couple of times. Essentially he was against the idea of bunching cultural organizations all in one place.

When we met with Ames and Mazzola in their uptown corporate head-quarters, Joe at first analyzed several factors that in his view had historically plagued Lincoln Center's moribund theater, such as its flawed stage design, inadequate sight lines, and poor acoustics. He then suggested the names of a few experienced theatrical directors and producers who, he ventured to guess, would be able to run a theatrical organization, if they were so inclined.

Then Joe paused, saying, "But, you know, what you really need is an *institution* to come in, because you have nothing here and you can't just call in a guy and say, 'Okay, start something up.'"

"Like who?" Amyas Ames asked.

"Like me," Joe said.

Ames and Mazzola had immediately declared their interest, but explained that before they could pursue the idea they would have to consult with the Link Ink board, which would ultimately decide the matter.

I was startled. Although I understood the allure of the uptown establishment, I didn't think that Joe might actually want to be in charge of this theatrical bastion of official art and bourgeois patronage, as I then regarded it, let alone put the resources of the Public Theater at the service of Lincoln Center Theater. In the past year he had already been producing at maximum capacity, I thought, with twenty-four shows spread between the Public and Delacorte Theaters, Broadway, Washington, D.C., and ABC Television. The prospect of adding full seasons at Lincoln Center's Beaumont and Forum Theaters gave pause for further thought.

However, later that day when Joe related what had happened at the meeting, Bernie was enthusiastic about the idea of operating from Lincoln Center. Unlike Joe, his theatrical background had been mostly in commercial theater and he was strongly attracted by the fact that Lincoln Center Theater's 1,200-seat main stage was an accredited Broadway house which made it eligible for Tony Awards, from which our shows at the Public and Delacorte Theaters were excluded.

Joe now began to view Lincoln Center Theater as a strategic opportunity to give American playwrights a national platform, in the way that Broadway does, by producing their plays on its main stage instead of the customary classics and revivals. With this new emphasis he would be able to build a more diverse audience. In the meantime, he waited to hear from Amyas Ames.

When I went with Joe to that meeting with Ames and Mazzola, I had felt a kind of capricious fate in possibly being linked again to the theater that had fired me as a playreader nine years earlier. I was inevitably reminded of my last-ditch effort in 1964 to save a talented play from being lost in the transition to the new Blau and Irving regime, when I had asked to meet with the new team so I could hand them the play with my verbal and written recommendation. To my surprise they had agreed.

The play was *In Three Zones* by Wilford Leach, whom I didn't know at the time but who would later become the artistic director of the Public Theater. Leach's play, inspired by the Brothers Grimm and Brecht, was about a soldier's progress through a war zone, an occupied zone, and the frontier. Later Mr. Blau announced that he was going to direct *In Three Zones* to open Lincoln Center's experimental Forum Theater. But the next news was the cancellation of the play after he'd squandered the entire year's budget on it.

***

In February 1973 the scent of burning marijuana was pungent in Radio City Music Hall as Joe and I hurried down an aisle seconds before a David Bowie concert would begin. We scrambled into our seats next to Associate Producer Bernard Gersten and his wife Cora Cahan just as the rail-thin Bowie, wearing a silver lamé suit in his androgynous persona of Ziggy Stardust, floated down a skyway and onto the Radio City stage.

As Bowie set foot on Planet Earth in an explosion of glam rock music, galactic mist, strobe lights, and a seismic roar from the mostly stoned audience, Joe, unable to contain his excitement about the news he'd just received, leaned forward in his seat and said under his breath, "Get ready, Bernie. We're going to Lincoln Center!"

The official story announcing Joe's whispered news appeared "above the fold" on the front page of the *New York Times* on March 7, 1973, with a large photograph of Joe and Amyas Ames headlined "Papp Troupe to Replace Lincoln Repertory: Producer Will Stress New U.S. Plays in Major Policy Shift"— as if it was breaking news from the Oval Office.

The *Times* story noted that in addition to becoming the new head of Lincoln Center Theater, Joe would continue producing plays and musicals on the six stages of the Public Theater, at the Delacorte Theater in Central Park, on the Mobile Theater touring the boroughs, "as well as his work on Broadway and television. Such a concentration of power is unprecedented in modern theatrical history."

The *New York Post* picked up on Joe's jaunty mood at a press conference in its story "Papp Moving to Lincoln Center." Reporters there had asked him why he was going to Lincoln Center, of all places—a question that reflected the widespread perception of him as a maverick expected to challenge Lincoln Center's establishment culture rather than join it.

Joe answered in mock seriousness, as if dictating an official response for attribution, saying that the reason he was taking on Lincoln Center Theater was "For personal aggrandizement and to establish a cultural power base here in New York and to take over the rest of the repertory theaters in the country and to create a liaison with China and Russia. Another reason is it's here, like Mount Everest. Another reason is it's closer to where I live." It was quoted with evident relish in the story. With a crazy answer like that, it seemed obvious that he hadn't sold out.

At this time the journalist Stuart W. Little was at work on a book called *Enter Joseph Papp: In Search of a New American Theater*. For it he had interviewed former New York City Parks Czar Robert Moses, then in semi-retirement at age eighty-four.

The news about Joe's takeover of Lincoln Center Theater prompted Moses to relive parts of his old dispute with Joe about free Shakespeare in Central Park. But, as Stuart Little wrote, he also wanted "to pay some final tribute to an adversary who had achieved a kind of fame and public importance Moses well understood."

"Now don't think I feel Papp is a bad fellow," Moses had said. "When he gets up to the pearly gates, he may find he has made a mark. Maybe he's made even more of a mark than I have."

When Joe heard about the interview, he told Stuart Little, "You know, we never met. Our paths almost crossed a couple of times, but we never met."

When Joe announced our first season on the main stage at Lincoln Center in 1973—featuring not the usual classics and revivals but new plays by Black playwrights Bill Gunn and Ron Milner, Puerto Rican playwright Miguel Piñero, and Vietnam veteran David Rabe—it was met with a perfect storm of rebellion from Lincoln Center Theater's 25,000 culture-loving subscribers inherited from the previous regime. They made their dislike of the season of new plays unmistakable by canceling their subscriptions in droves, many with letters to Joe lambasting his policy of showcasing new work.

I saved a few samples:

"My dear Mr. Papp: This is to inform you that your inclusion of a play concerning all black performers should not be made a must as part of a subscriber's bill of fare. The overwhelming majority of the audience is white and doesn't want anything thrust down their throats."

"Dear Mr. Papp: I do not wish the theater to play a role in urban society and to add minority theatergoers."

"Dear Mr. Papp: I find your choice of plays quite abominable . . . I wish you the worst of luck."

Besides these retrograde subscribers, we also faced the distempered audiences who continued to attend Lincoln Center Theater. I saw their ill-suppressed ire come to a head when Joe directed one of the new plays himself, Anne Burr's *Mert and Phil*, a self-styled bizarre comedy about the effects of a mastectomy on a working-class married woman played by Estelle Parsons. No doubt the subject matter was ahead of its time by twenty or thirty years, and from the very first preview I could sense the audiences' squeamish hostility to the play's content and style.

One night, seated next to Joe during the intermission, I saw a man heading in my direction like an oncoming locomotive.

"Are *you* the playwright?" he asked me through clenched teeth.

Every night theatergoers noisily left their seats before the first act was over while others lay in wait for Joe in the lobby to tell him how much they hated *Mert and Phil*.

"Mr. Papp, *why* are you doing this play?" an outraged woman asked him there. Another said, "We don't want to see this kind of garbage!"

The critics found the play as hard to take as the audiences did. The *Times* critic Clive Barnes warned his readers that *Mert and Phil* would send them "running out of the theater in search of water, air or even brandy." The *Daily News* critic suggested that the playwright, being a woman, should have "stayed home."

A pall hung over the postmortem staff meeting that I joined in Joe's office downtown at the Public Theater. He didn't try to lighten the mood.

"I don't want to feel depressed every time I do a play and get fifty or sixty people writing me the most horrendous letters," Joe said. "I want to feel we have support. I want to create an audience base that supports us. A political base. I can't submit myself to this kind of savage attack constantly over and over again."

It didn't surprise me that Lincoln Center failed to shape up as a political base for the antihero characters and harsh, irreconcilable themes that Joe chose to present on its main stage. Unlike Shakespeare in the Park and the Public Theater, which he had established from the ground up, he had attempted, I thought, to impose his idea of theater from the top down at Lincoln Center, where an entrenched base of 25,000 subscribers already existed before he arrived. When you serve that kind of audience, you have to stay somewhere in the "center," a position that was anathema to him.

I had seen how Joe's tactics, out of necessity, could change, but never his commitment to new plays and diverse audiences. Nevertheless, after being pummeled by criticism from audiences at the Lincoln Center Theater and in the press for two years, he finally reversed his unpopular new-play policy and produced classics again on its main stage.

These were met with universal acclaim, the result of Joe inviting nontraditional directors such as Andrei Serban to do *The Cherry Orchard* with Irene Worth, and Richard Foreman to do *The Threepenny Opera* with Raúl Juliá. These were both superb productions that drew popular audiences and are still remembered as artistic benchmarks in the history of American theater.

However, Joe's frustration about his failure to establish Lincoln Center as a platform for new American playwrights never subsided, and I think it's still a credit to him that he felt so deeply about this. After his first all-classics season in 1975, he wrote: "I'm trying a little bit of the center and my God, it makes me dizzy. I'm thrashing around trying to find a reason not to leave, although my whole being is saying OUT! OUT!"

Joe finally quit Lincoln Center in 1977. Once again the story about his association with Lincoln Center featured a large photograph above the fold on the front page of the *Times* headed "Papp Quits Lincoln Center, Citing Artistic-Fiscal 'Trap'."

Later Joe wrote in a note to himself: "The essential reason I took Lincoln Center on was economic. The Public Theater was over a million dollars in debt. I couldn't raise the million, but I felt if I tried to raise five million for Lincoln Center, I could raise the million for the Public. Which I did. I was able to do it. I kept the Public Theater afloat because of that."

23

When James Earl Jones Played King Lear

Joe threw a big party to celebrate the fifth anniversary of the Public Theater to which he invited all of the writers, composers, directors, choreographers, and designers who had been associated with the Public Theater during its formative period from 1966 to 1971.

I found the party in full swing when I arrived, with a lively crowd dancing on the Anspacher stage to Stevie Wonder's "Superstition." I spotted Joe—looking, I thought, like Ophelia's description of Hamlet as the very "glass of fashion and the mould of form"—as he touched base with guests in a whirligig of laughter that followed him from group to group.

I felt at a remove from the party's carefree atmosphere, since Joe and I were scrupulous about never acting demonstratively toward each other in public. I compared my external self in this respect to Nicklausse in the opera *The Tales of Hoffmann*. This Nicklausse, whom we first meet as a female "Muse of Poetry," transforms herself into a male confidante of the poet Hoffmann, who has stories to tell him about his past loves. Nicklausse takes on the role of a concerned friend who listens and comments on these events of Hoffmann's colorful life but is never actually a part of it.

Besides Nicklausse, I had another image for my complicated relationship with Joe: that of a Balinese dancer in Auguste Rodin's famous watercolors. I have two of them on my wall at home in which the Balinese dancer strikes a pose that looks both fluid *and* taut, as if tentatively staging herself for an unknown next move. That's exactly how I felt.

During the anniversary party I went over to a table for a glass of wine. The woman next to me commented on how "dark and alert" Joe looked, saying that he must be very happy about the theatrical institution he'd created and the vibrant artistic community it had spawned in such a short time.

"Yes, it's quite remarkable," I said.

But this anniversary for the Public Theater happened at the time of Joe's fiftieth birthday and his mind was not at rest. He wrote: "What is fifty, What means fifty? It is no different than zero. Without a few essential ties to the human race, a ring-tailed baboon has a greater claim to life."

A few pages later Joe added: "One lesson must be learned before you cross the threshold from forty-nine to fifty:

> to receive you must give
> to be loved you must love
> to grow you must learn
> to learn you must receive, must give,
> *must love, must be loved.*"

***

There had been a certain pleasure in the vagabond charm of my serial sublets, but after two years I became tired of their periodic expirations and yearned for more stability in my life. Accordingly, I signed a lease in 1973 for an unfurnished two-room apartment on East 9th Street near Broadway. The rent was *half* my monthly salary, a scary expense, but the place had large sunny windows overlooking a tree-lined street, and it was just four blocks from the Public Theater.

Since the only possessions I owned were my clothes, a few books, and a typewriter, I bought, on credit at Bloomingdale's, the living room and bedroom furniture, lamps, linen, and dishes that I would need to set up my apartment. It felt like spendthrift madness and I was unnerved by it. What if I defaulted and lost everything? I vividly remembered that happening in my childhood when creditors had repossessed a houseful of furniture because my parents weren't able to keep up the installment payments. Everything had been carried out through the front door—beds, sofa, tables, even an apple-green child's chair—and driven away in a large van. Haunted by that memory, I had always been vigilant about never saddling myself with debt.

Now, however, I had stepped into a potential quagmire of monthly department store bills and interest charges.

Nevertheless I was relieved to have my own place instead of a stranger's apartment, and as the trees bloomed outside my window that summer, I enjoyed the feeling of being a legitimate stakeholder on East 9th Street.

In retrospect I have always thought of this time as "The Summer that James Earl Jones played King Lear in Central Park."

King Lear had opened at the Delacorte Theater on Tuesday, July 31, 1973, but for some reason I didn't go to the press performance and party after the show as I usually did, so I was home in my new apartment when the doorbell rang at 2 a.m. I was reluctant to answer it because I couldn't think of anyone who'd be coming to see me at such a late hour.

But when the bell rang insistently several more times, I cautiously opened the door a crack, careful to keep the chain lock in place, and was astonished to see Joe standing in the hallway holding a large suitcase.

Without a single conversation between us about it, he had evidently come to stay.

24

Living Together

Joe's arrival at my door with a suitcase in the middle of the night may have startled me, but, as I realized later, he and his wife Peggy Bennion Papp, who had become a full-time family therapist after she left acting, had been preparing their children for a future separation.

The first hint of this had actually been in 1971 when Joe arranged for him, me, and his two youngest children—Miranda age thirteen and Tony age ten—to have lunch together. "So you can get better acquainted," he said to me before making a reservation at a tea room restaurant near the Public Theater. I would have preferred keeping a low profile, but he was intent on getting us together. Although he didn't say what he'd told them about me, I knew the lunch was going to be awkward and that I would be under review for some kind of acceptability by his children, who might be rooting for me to fail and sending smoke signals to each other to that effect.

Miranda looked very striking at the restaurant table with her strong facial resemblance to Joe and straight raven-black hair falling to her waist. Her little brother was restive. When I asked about Miranda's plans for the summer, she told me about the camp she'd been going to for several years. This summer she'd be a counselor to the younger children there for the first time.

Rolling his eyes, Tony suddenly catcalled from his chair, "Yeah, Miranda gets to torture the little kids now!"

"And what are you up to this summer?" I asked him. The restive child made a face.

Joe volunteered that Tony would be starting day camp the following week.

When the menus arrived, food was discussed in detail. Tony was fussy about what he would eat and I saw that every time Joe suggested something to him from the menu, he clutched his throat and made gagging sounds.

Halfway through lunch, Tony suddenly said to me in what I recognized as a mischievously "pitiful" little-boy voice, *"Are you going to be our new mother?"*

Speechless, I looked to Joe for help.

"Isn't that the reason for this lunch?" Tony asked, turning to his father.

I can't for the life of me remember what Joe said, but Tony's question plucked a sympathetic string in my heart because I had been an unhappy child of divorce and in some recess of my limbic brain, I was on Miranda and Tony's side of this uncomfortable issue. What surprised me most about the lunch was that Joe had evidently discussed with his children the possibility of separating from their mother, although he had never uttered a word about it to me. Nor did he in the months and the year following the lunch. We just continued as before.

In the fall of 1973, after Joe's arrival at my door with a suitcase, we rented a larger apartment directly across the street from the one I had just moved into only two months before.

On our first night there, my Bloomingdale's furniture hadn't crossed the street yet, but we placed a turntable on the floor, hooked it up to my pair of two-foot-tall KLH speakers, and sat beside them listening to an LP recording of Taneyev's "Prometheus" by the U.S.S.R. Chorus that Joe had bought for the occasion. As the thrilling music boomed in our empty living room, we clinked wine glasses to mark this miraculous milestone of our new life together.

Less than a minute into the "Prometheus" recording, however, an odd percussive beat began to assert itself in the choral performance. Was it something on the LP? A defect in the turntable? But no. It was the tenants in the apartment below us hitting their ceiling with a broomstick. They rang our doorbell to complain about the noise. Then they wrote to the owner of the building, who brought the matter to our attention in a remonstrative letter.

Joe wrote him back:

I have no idea of what morning "noise" you refer to in your letter of October 10th. There was, I recall, an evening "noise" last week—the playing of eighteenth century choral music on my record player, which evoked from your complaining tenant a pounding on his ceiling, a continual chiming of my door bell, and an incessant buzzing of my intercom. Since the time of evening was 9:15, I must assume that my disturbed neighbor is not only a late riser, but an early bedder. I have no intention of tiptoeing around my apartment to accommodate an ill-mannered, hysterical complainant. I happen to live a rather conservative home-life existence, and I believe in peace and quiet. But I am still ambulatory, and a breather. If people want to retire, they should not take up residence in an apartment building where life goes on.

A most important aspect of our new life in the apartment building was the decision by Joe's two youngest children about who they wanted to live with in the wake of their parents' agreed-upon separation. Miranda, by then fifteen, chose to live with her mother. I'd gotten to know her a little bit after our lunch when she was about to begin work as a camp counselor. In 1973 she had attended the dedication of Milton Hebald's large bronze sculpture of *Prospero and Miranda*, a gift of George Delacorte, on the lawn in front of the Delacorte Theater. During the past year I'd been impressed by her no-nonsense, matter-of-fact manner, which seemed mature beyond her years—except, as I soon learned, when she connived in horseplay with her mischievous younger brother.

By then, Tony—the former Anthony who liked to greet people at the Public Theater's reception desk after his piano lessons—chose to live with his father. I'd gotten to know Tony quite well during the past year, an unanticipated benefit of my occupancy of the old supply room as the new site of the Play Department when I became in charge of it. Whenever Tony left his spot at the switchboard reception desk downstairs, he'd bustle around our offices on the second floor, his irrepressible restlessness a mirror image of Joe's.

"I'm bored," he'd complain to his father.

"Tell Gail," Joe would say.

I kept poster paints and large sheets of drawing paper for these occasions, spreading them on the floor of my office so that Tony could busy himself with making paintings of the black Molly Fish that he had in a tank at home. His interest in them was fervent. After they all died, his interest switched to painting his new parakeet. One afternoon, as I stepped over one of his paintings to attend a meeting in another office, I looked down and saw that he was painting not the new parakeet but me as a smiling Addams Family witch-mother at my typewriter.

Tony's choice to live with his father had come with an unnegotiable condition, which was that he'd live with Joe (and me) providing that his father bought him twelve birds on his twelfth birthday. At this time Joe was completely vulnerable to his son's childish manipulations, and so on Tony's twelfth birthday that fall the twelve birds that he wanted were delivered to the new apartment in a scene that reminded me of the comical march in Prokoviev's opera *The Love for Three Oranges*: Six pet shop handlers paraded single file into the living room, four of them carrying tall stands attached to swinging cages that housed different kinds of birds hopping around in them, each one furnished with trapezes, ladders, mirrors, troughs, seed blocks, and perches. Two more men followed them carrying a 3-by-3-foot wood-and-wire pen that housed a "peace dove." Tony was beside himself with joy.

* * *

Besides the twelve birds in Tony's bedroom, our new apartment quickly acquired a lived-in appearance with scripts, books, pens, and notepads scattered about. Joe mounted a four-foot-long Aida trumpet from a Central Park production on a wall, and I set out my auction-bought seashells on a shelf next to the copy of *The Complete Works of the Marquis de Sade* that Joe had given me the first Christmas I worked at the Festival.

"By the way," I said to Joe, as I placed a bookend next to the de Sade, "I've always meant to ask what on earth possessed you back in 1965 to give such a licentious book to a new female employee?"

"Oh, I don't know," Joe said. "You looked so prim and proper and I just wanted to shake that up a bit and get the blood stirring."

"You're lucky I had a sense of humor," I said.

My robust sense of humor was a childhood gift from my divorced parents, and around this time Joe met them.

My mother, Gladys Merrifield, who was an editor at *Family Circle Magazine*, put her most vivacious self on display when we took her to dinner at her neighborhood Indian restaurant in Greenwich Village. She surprised Joe by matching his punning prowess with her own. My mother's truly amazing skill in this (she was also a prize-winning poet) was the reason I didn't groan, as others did, about Joe's irrepressible love of puns. I had been raised on them and appreciated the nimbleness of mind and love of absurdity they required.

On the summit of Mount Monadnock in New Hampshire in 1972 with (L) my nieces Afton and Sienna Merrifield, me, Joe, and my cousin Charlotte Stanley.
John Stanley

Meanwhile my father, Richard Merrifield, who was the editor of *Yankee Magazine* in New Hampshire, had proudly spread the news to his relatives there that Joe and I were together. It therefore seemed an appropriate time to introduce him to Joe, along with my stepmother Janet, two aunts, uncles-in-law, thirteen cousins, stepgrandfather, and my half-brother Richard Jr. and his wife and their three children.

We drove to Keene, New Hampshire. I harbored no illusion that Joe would bond with my family there—he had after all been through three sets of in-laws when he was younger. However, since my father and Joe had both grown up poor in Brooklyn, I encouraged that as their most likely point of connection.

***

From the table in our dining nook, Joe and I could watch the full moon rise over Wanamaker Place, the site of the still-standing emporium of that name that had once flourished at our corner of Broadway and 9th Street. I remembered Wanamaker's from my early childhood in New York City when I had been taken to visit Santa Claus there and had asked him for a doll with eyes that opened and shut. Afterward I'd hammed it up in the store's photomat that took rapid-fire snapshots of me, a gleeful four-year-old on holiday from Lad and Lassie Nursery School in Greenwich Village.

That same year, 1938, seventeen-year-old Yussel Papirofsky, recently graduated from Eastern District High School in Brooklyn, got a job in Manhattan at Dinhofer Brothers, a jewelry wholesaler on Lafayette Street just a few blocks south of Wanamaker's. On his way to work, teenage Joe would walk past an imposing building that was the headquarters of the Hebrew Immigrant Aid Society (HIAS), where, twenty-seven years later, he would create the Public Theater.

Joe and I were conscious not only of our personal roots along this Lafayette/ Broadway boundary but also of the neighborhood's glittering theatrical history dating back to the nineteenth century when most theaters and the opera had been located downtown. Edwin Booth's then-record-breaking one hundred performances of *Hamlet* in 1864–1865 had taken place just three blocks south of the future site of the Public Theater at the beautiful triple-balconied Winter Garden Theater that used to be at West 3rd and Bleecker Streets.

When Joe and I started living together, I already enjoyed a frisky relationship with Tony, an adorably sensitive boy who looked like a diminutive Persian prince. Although I had little notion of how to raise a child (having no prior experience other than having once been one myself), I found it easy to be playful and affectionate with him. I was keenly sensitive to the limits of step-parenting, especially since his father and I weren't then married, and I left matters of discipline and rules of the house entirely up to Joe.

One evening when Tony had asked Joe for something to which Joe had said "No," Tony started whining, then threw a tantrum. When the high-pitched childish racket had continued unabated for a half-hour, I thought I would go crazy and wondered why Joe didn't put a stop to it. But he was reading a script and seemed oblivious. However, he wasn't the only adult in the room trying to read a script. I also had one in hand to read, but not having Joe's ability to zone out, I finally whispered softly to Tony, "Please quiet down now or go to your room," falling back on a now-disapproved-of parental admonition that my parents had once employed with me.

The adorable little boy was shocked. These were the first disciplinary words he'd ever heard from me, the person he'd come to regard as his friend and advocate, his "Other Mother" as he'd written on a card. Erupting in tears, he screamed, "I HATE GAIL!" and ran into his bedroom, slamming the door. The twelve birds behind it squawked in unison.

Unnerved and on the verge of tears myself, I wondered if this is what it meant to be a *"parent."*

Joe looked up from his script.

"You did the right thing," he said. He seemed grateful.

Sometimes, Miranda would spend a weekend with us, so we fixed up the walk-in closet off our entry hall for her with a bunk bed and a built-in desk underneath it. In an excess of zeal to render this cramped space more appealing, I put red satin sheets on the bed and pasted glow-in-the-dark moons and stars on the ceiling. Sometimes in the morning I would see Miranda's still-sleepy face blinking above a red satin sheet on the edge of the bunk bed, her eyeglasses askew, looking like a fledgling owl contemplating its first flight from the nest.

Miranda's visits were always an occasion for her and her little brother to whoop it up. I would hear shrieks and cackles coming from behind Tony's bedroom door which set his twelve birds screeching in their cages and his new pet hamsters racing frantically on their hamster wheel. A few times Tony and Miranda hogged our single landline phone in the living room calling tobacco stores and asking, "Do you have Prince Albert in a can?" When the store answered "Yes," they would scream *"Well let him out!"* and run back into Tony's bedroom.

Arriving home from the Public Theater at the end of one day, Joe and I were confounded by dozens of magic-marker signs that Tony had taped on the living room walls, windows, and furniture, saying, "IF YOU REALLY LOVED ME, YOU'D LET ME HAVE A DOG!"

All of this juvenile mayhem was new to me since I had grown up as an only child and didn't have children of my own. But there was an untapped part of me that was crazy enough to enjoy it, so long as Joe and I still had our own time together.

25

A Three-Way Oath of Integrity

Joe had just finished listening to audio tapes of dancers talking about their lives that choreographer Michael Bennett had left with him.

"I cried through the whole thing," he told me. "The hurt of the young people and their families was so painful, but they said it with such brightness. There was no *sadness*. They sort of said it lightly and that made it even more moving."

Joe said that Michael Bennett wanted to create a musical based on the dancers' conversations and had proposed doing so in a developmental workshop at the Public Theater. His proposal was startling because at this point Michael's dance musical had no story, no script, no music, no lyrics, and no choreography.

Further, contrary to Joe's fundamental orientation in the nonprofit theater world, Michael's destination for this work was unabashedly Broadway. The workshop he proposed at the Public Theater would serve merely as a subsidized stepping stone to its intended commercial transfer.

Nevertheless, Joe decided to proceed. Not only had he earlier been impressed by Michael's extraordinary talent as a choreographer and as a director of other productions, but Joe also connected very strongly with Michael's genuine identification with the personal stories on the tapes that had also moved Joe.

Bernard Gersten, the key person who had introduced Joe to Michael's work, was enthusiastic and supportive, and so the Public's workshop was launched with a company of dancers gathered around Michael Bennett, along with an A-list creative team that he'd assembled consisting of lyricist Edward Kleban, composer Marvin Hamlisch, and book writers Nicholas Dante and James Kirkwood Jr.—all collaborating in a multi-month, multi-hundred-thousand-dollar developmental workshop subsidized by the Public's Chairperson, LuEsther T. Mertz.

Several months into the workshop, Joe invited Michael over to our apartment for a chat. Before he arrived, Joe told me that he was concerned about a plotline in the story about two characters who are ex-lovers.

"It's too long and it's gotten sentimental," he said.

But Joe didn't say a word about that to Michael after he arrived. Instead, he simply asked Michael if he thought he'd be able to "bring the show in," a very uncharacteristic phrase for Joe to use. I remember Michael listening to him, seated on the edge of our sofa, and then saying with passion, "Joe, I know what's wrong and I *promise* you I can do it."

"Good," Joe said. And that was it.

Now, just a few weeks later, Joe and I were at the first preview of *A Chorus Line* at the Public Theater. Thirty-two-year-old Michael Bennett, looking very boyish in a striped T-shirt, appeared on stage before the show began.

"I'm afraid the mirrors haven't arrived yet," he told the audience with a sheepish smile, "but I hope you'll enjoy it anyway."

Twenty-one dancers in memorably individualistic rehearsal clothes designed by the incomparable Theoni V. Aldredge then took their places along a white line that ran the width of the bare stage of the Newman Theater.

The absence of the mirrors—a stunning and essential feature designed by Robin Wagner—was forgiven at that first preview because by the end of the show when the cast had told, sung, and danced their individual and collective stories, the 299 theatergoers in the Newman Theater simultaneously leaped to their feet and began clapping their hands in ecstatic appreciation. They cheered joyously, tearfully, and endlessly. When they realized that *A Chorus Line,* by design, would have no more curtain calls after Lighting Designer Tharon Musser's heart-stopping fade-to-black on the dancers' synchronized kick steps in the finale, this only increased their delirium. Joe and I watched in amazement as the audience kept cheering the dark and empty stage, refusing to leave the theater.

"I guess they like it," Joe finally said.

The reviews of *A Chorus Line* were sensational. Despite the fact that *New York Times* critic Clive Barnes seldom saw eye to eye with Joe, he bubbled with unqualified enthusiasm in his rave review: "The conservative word for *A Chorus Line* might be tremendous, or perhaps terrific . . . The reception was so shattering that it is surprising if, by the time you read this, the New York Shakespeare Festival has got a Newman Theater still standing in the Public Theater complex on Lafayette Street."

I remember thirty-one-year-old composer Marvin Hamlisch, having just read the reviews, dashing around Joe's office shouting, "We did it! We did it!"

However, in the midst of this euphoria about the show's downtown premiere, Joe worried that when he moved *A Chorus Line* to Broadway, it might precipitate a fault line in his relationship with Michael. He didn't explain why he felt this way, but I guessed that it sprang from his knowledge of the frailty of human nature when subjected to the potentially corrosive influence of over-the-top success and sudden wealth.

My hunch proved correct when, twenty-one days after *A Chorus Line* opened at the Public Theater, Joe arranged for us to have lunch with Michael at Orsini's, a fashionable restaurant on West 56th Street in our old work neighborhood near the Great Northern Hotel. Joe ordered a bottle of Perrier Jouët Champagne brought to the table in an ice bucket stand. Then he produced from his inside jacket pocket an "Oath of Integrity" he'd composed in Dickensian legalese and read it to Michael and me. (This is the typed copy of the Oath that we signed two days later.)

After Joe had finished reading it, the three of us hugged each other and made a champagne toast to the imperishable "power" of our "blood knot."

Writing twelve years later, after Bennett's death at the age of forty-four in 1987, Joe recalled his reaction to that three-way oath of integrity sworn at Orsini's Restaurant.

"His face was sweet and boyish and he smiled that engaging Italian-Jewish smile. Then, with characteristic impetuosity, he grabbed my hand and Gail's, and swore mightily to keep the proposed pledge."

*Being sound in mind and body and pure in heart, we do solemnly vow, promise, swear, pledge and affirm to perform all the duties, obligations, expectations, as they are construed and understood to apply to the term "friendship" such as loyalty, fealty, mutual assistance, honesty, truthfulness and trust in all dealings, arrangements, both verbal and written, both spoken and unspoken, both at home and abroad, in all companies, at all hours, for all times, to set a shining example of integrity in human affairs, in contradistinction and toward the obliteration of backbiting, undermining, innuendo, opportunism, greed, the devil's larder of subtle seductions preying on man's weakness for aggrandizement at the expense and over the corpus of his fellow.

Be it understood and acknowledged that this signature, though set down in ink, shall be as binding as the power in a blood knot, and whosoever shall attempt to sever or untie it shall suffer the penalty of the damned and remain forever in a dark and empty theater.

SWORN UNTO EACH OTHER THIS ___13th___ DAY OF ___June___, 1975 IN FAITH AND HOPE:

_____
Joseph Papp

_____
Michael Bennett

WITNESSED BY:

_____
Gail Merrifield

*As originally sworn at Orsini's Restaurant, June 11, 1975.

Courtesy of the Public Theater

26

Family Affairs

"There's something I should tell you," Joe had said to me quietly over lunch in 1975 at a hillside hotel in Port-au-Prince, Haiti, where he was waiting for a finalized decree of divorce. "I have a daughter I've never met. Her name is Barbara."

I was intrigued and surprised. I knew that Joe had four children by three wives, but now he was going to tell me about a fifth child. Of the four children I knew, the two younger ones were Tony, who lived with us, and his sister Miranda, who lived with their mother. There were also two older half-siblings, a daughter and a son.

I'd already met Susan Lippman (neé Papirofsky), Joe's daughter by his first marriage to a girl who came from a welcoming Jewish family in his Brooklyn neighborhood. It hadn't worked out and Joe had only seen Susan as an infant shortly before his discharge from the Navy. During Susan's childhood in Brooklyn after World War II, Joe had been working in Los Angeles as the Manager of the Actor's Lab and had remarried. In the 1960s, when Susan was in her teens, she had called the Public Theater office for an appointment to meet her father. She was a very pretty and lively girl with a positive connection to his career in the theater, which I learned while chatting with her before Joe came out to greet her. Susan became a professional librarian and later, the mother of Joe's first grandchildren, Jodi and Jonathan.

A few years later Joe's oldest son Michael Faulkner (né Papirofsky; changed later to his stepfather's surname) also called the Public Theater office for an appointment to meet his father, having just moved to New York State to start college. He was the son of Joe's second marriage to a woman with a richly documented Jewish heritage whom he'd met at the Actors' Lab. The marriage had ended, however, when their son was three years old. When Michael arrived at Joe's office, I picked up on his quiet sense of humor and learned that he was a practitioner of transcendental meditation. He later became an IT manager for a Midwestern university.

Joe deeply regretted that he'd been an absent father to these two older children, saying that it was proper grounds for them to harbor murder in their hearts toward him. He was grateful that they themselves initiated these later reunions with him.

Now, at the hillside hotel in Haiti, Joe had just told me about Barbara, an older daughter he had never met. Visibly tense, Joe said that she was the child of a relationship during World War II with a WAVE, an acronym for Women Accepted for Voluntary Emergency Service, the Navy's corps of female members. Having met when they were both stationed at the U.S. Naval Training Center in Bainbridge, Maryland, their off-base liaison had lasted for the better part of a year until Joe shipped out on an aircraft carrier for duty in the Pacific. At the end of the war she had returned to her husband, and had informed Joe about the existence of their daughter for the first time when the child was sixteen years old due to the need to learn Joe's blood type.

All of a sudden Joe became uncharacteristically silent. I understood why he'd told me this story and the difficulty he had experienced in doing so. The reason had to be that he didn't want any shadow of deception lurking in our life together. I was perfectly aware that he'd been through twenty years of psychoanalytic therapy to reach this point. It's okay, I'd said to him. It wasn't an issue. It had been wartime. There were similar circumstances in my own theatrical family and I embraced them. Most importantly, I looked forward to meeting Barbara someday.

When he saw that I took his confession in stride, Joe looked very relieved.

However, I felt honor bound now to reciprocate his candor by telling Joe about *my* closely guarded secret, which was that I had once been hospitalized for almost a year with an eating disorder called *anorexia nervosa*. As I began to speak, I was afraid that bringing up this grievous chapter from long ago in my life might pathologize me in Joe's mind. After all, I hadn't been someone suffering from a sympathetically familiar illness like depression, but from a delusional self-image and obsessive-compulsive behavior so severe that it had become life-threatening and required medical intervention. It was my turn to feel relieved when Joe replied as calmly to my confession as I had to his, saying it was a blessing in disguise because it had made me a stronger and more empathetic person.

Reflecting on our past lives, Joe and I agreed that if we had been much younger when we met, we might have fallen in love but probably would have had an unhappy marriage. Looking back, I reproached my younger self for having been dysfunctional and difficult, and Joe reproached his younger self for having been unfaithful and untruthful. During the confessional intensity of this lunch, Joe quoted Othello's words about Desdemona because he said they were the way he felt about us: "She loved me for the dangers I had passed, and I loved her that she did pity them." I felt the same way, but with the personal pronouns reversed.

***

In 1979, Joe finally met Barbara Mosser, the daughter he'd told me about while awaiting confirmation of his divorce in Haiti. Accompanied by her ailing mother, Barbara, a thirty-four-year-old nurse married to an army lieutenant, arrived from out of town for an emotional meeting in Joe's office. She had seen the road company production of *A Chorus Line* in Washington, D.C., and was astonished to learn that her biological father was its famous producer. Why her mother had kept Joe's identity a secret from her, and then had changed her mind, remained a mystery. For years, however, Barbara's mother had saved clippings about Joe's theatrical career and had just recently showed them to Barbara.

After Joe introduced me to his newfound daughter and her mother in his office, he went over to the telephone on his desk and called Barbara's little daughter and son, Stephanie and Michael—two new grandchildren he had just learned about.

"Hello, this is your Grandfather!" Joe exclaimed to the excited children at the other end, promising them that we would all get together for a wonderful first-time visit the following Christmas.

27

Our Haimish Wedding

Joe and I chose January 18 for our wedding in 1976 because "chai" in Hebrew means both the number "18" and "life" and because it was his day off from directing a musical at the Public Theater.

We had decided to be married at home with only a couple dozen guests, no printed invitations, and just wine and cheese afterward. After all, this wasn't a first marriage for either of us, and even those previous ceremonies had been extremely modest. Joe's first one at the age of nineteen had taken place at the home of a rabbi near where he lived in Brownsville, Brooklyn, and mine, also at the age of nineteen, had been held at the Ethical Culture Society in the office of its leader, for which I had worn a navy blue suit.

On the morning of our wedding day, the apartment bell rang. I thought it must be a wedding guest arriving too early, but instead it was a photographer in a heavy winter coat who said he was on assignment from United Press International (UPI). Reluctant to come back later because of January's bitter cold weather, he sat down on our sofa and prepared to wait it out. I made him some coffee and for the next three hours he was the only person around besides me, Joe, and Tony until I lost track of him as our twenty-seven guests began to arrive at the apartment.

After everyone was settled on the sofa, chairs, and floor pillows, Joe and I took our places on either side of Judge Samuel Silverman for the ceremony in the middle of our book-lined living room. It had been Joe's happy inspiration to ask Silverman—the lawyer who, seventeen years ago, had successfully defended the Festival's free admission policy in Central Park against Parks czar Robert Moses—to marry us.

Samuel Silverman, born in Odesa, had risen to prominence representing Anne Frank's father in a suit instigated against him over the stage adaptation of his daughter's famous book. Dignified, but with a twinkle in his eye, Silverman was now a justice on the Supreme Court of the State of New York. He hadn't performed a civil marriage in forty-five years.

When he asked Joe to place the wedding ring—a beautiful band of enameled flowers—on my finger, Joe didn't find it in his pocket because he'd left it on the bureau in our bedroom.

"Excuse me a moment," Joe said and went to fetch it.

"I don't know," Judge Silverman said to the guests when Joe was out of the room. "I think maybe we should make them rehearse their lines."

Returning with the ring, Joe joked to the guests, "We have a lousy Prop Department."

After the ceremony we danced to an LP recording of George Schwartz's *Jewish Dances*, the wild drumming of its *freilach* tunes competing with the sound of our guests' clinking wine glasses as they chatted about the theater and the bitter cold January weather.

Joe was pleased that for the first time all of his siblings (though not his parents, who were no longer living) were present at a wedding of his: his brother, his two sisters, their spouses, and his brother's young daughter Diane.

My parents in New York and New Hampshire were ecstatic. My mother wrote me the next day from her Greenwich Village apartment, "I couldn't take my eyes off you last night—except to look at Joe who was so handsome in his blue velvet suit. The wedding was one of the happiest experiences of my entire life."

My father, too ill to attend, wrote from New Hampshire, "The happy vibrations up here haven't simmered down even yet. You're certainly the most glowing romantic story since Petrarch and Laura."

As the wine continued to flow, Joe left the living room for a few minutes, reappearing in the full-length ecclesiastical red costume that Edwin Booth had worn when he played Cardinal Richelieu, the powerful chief minister to Louis XIII in Bulwer-Lytton's nineteenth-century melodrama *Richelieu*. Joe had purchased it at an auction to raise money for the Lincoln Center Library of the Performing Arts. Ever since then it had been hanging among his suits in our closet.

Seeing Joe in Booth's Cardinal Richelieu costume for the first time at our wedding party, I noted with surprise how the scarlet cassock with its long train, caplet, and button-down sleeves, fit him so perfectly; it was as if they had been tailored for Joe instead of Edwin Booth.

When Booth was photographed in his Richelieu costume in the nineteenth century, he used to strike a finger-pointing pose associated with the Cardinal's famous line: "Set but a foot within that holy bound, and on thy head—yea, though it wore a crown—I'll launch the Curse of Rome!"

Joe had some fun improvising on this heaven-rattling malediction, caricaturizing Richelieu as a stumbling drunk with myself cast as the beneficiary of the Cardinal's intoxicated blessings.

I can't explain why the United Press photographer stayed on assignment during this horseplay. Perhaps when he saw Joe appear in a Cardinal's cassock—holding a lighted candle and mumbling benedictions and curses in fake Latin—he mistook it for a delayed religious component of the wedding, I don't know.

In any event, when the wedding photographer sent us his photographs the following week, there were just twelve of the wedding—and forty-two of Joe hamming it up as Cardinal Richelieu.

That same week the Public Theater's clipping service sent us a sackful of syndicated stories about our marriage. The most startling one was from a small local newspaper in the Midwest. It ran the United Press photograph of Joe and me cutting our wedding cake with the caption, "Producer Weds Assassin's Kin."

28

The Public's First Cabaret

The day after our wedding in 1976 Joe and I gave a buffet and wine party at our apartment for everyone on the staff of the Public Theater. For many of them it was the first time they'd been with us in a personal setting, but for others our living room was a familiar place because Joe had occasionally held meetings there.

In the glow of our first year as a public couple, we decided to make a joint down payment on a cottage in the country. After I had carefully read the proposed real estate contract at home, I wrote Joe a memo about a couple of its provisions, which I ended with a rhetorical question:

"Why is the name of the Female partner (myself) in this real estate contract followed by the expression *'His wife'*? While I'm <u>proud</u> of it, I object to being labeled in this way when the Man is not labeled *'Her husband.'* And why is my name the <u>only</u> one missing on the Title Page listing all of the other Financial Parties, e.g. owners, lawyers etc., involved in this transaction?"

I rolled the memo up like a scroll, secured it with a rubber band, and left it for Joe on our dining table. When I got it back from him, he'd scrawled in large capital letters across the top: "I'LL KILL THE MAN WHO LEAVES YOU OFF TITLE PAGE!"

This was the same year that we announced the opening of the Public Theater's first cabaret. It received a great deal of media attention in 1977, reflecting, I guess, the excitement that Joe and I felt about its possibilities.

Variety reported, "Papp has entertained this concept for some time as having 'a liberating effect on composers, playwrights and performers that would not confine them to a finished product.' . . . Merrifield said that the casting news item, which has been appearing in *Variety* for some weeks, as well as other trades has produced an overwhelming response."

The *New York Post* said, "Papp wants to go considerably beyond the pleasant blend of music and 'light satire.' He's talking about a thick theatrical brew which is 'musical, topical, satirical, political, both serious and funny.'"

The *New York Times* announced "Gail Merrifield and Craig Zadan, who will run the cabaret theater, are talking about staging musicals, new plays, political satire, monologues, works in progress and virtually everything else. The idea is to keep things flexible."

The stories then shifted to Joe and me as a new theatrical couple who had been married the previous year. *Playbill* ran a photo of us captioned "Life Is Just a Cabaret, Old Chum," followed later by an article about "Broadway couples," which said, "The reasons Broadway couples give for getting together, for staying together or coming apart are personal, complex and diverse. Papp, for example, had previously been married three times when a little over a year ago he married Gail Merrifield, Director of Play Development . . . The day for Gail and Joe begins at 6:30 or 7:00 a.m. and ends in the wee hours of the morning. And their apartment, says Papp, is an extension of the office—'We try not to talk business but there are four telephones and piles of scripts and we spend weekends reading endlessly.'"

A *Daily News* story at this time explained, "Their marriage is the ultimate in togetherness. Gail and Joe Papp work together, eat together, live together. Twenty-four hours a day, seven days a week. 'And it's not too much,' insists Papp . . . Generally they arrive at their adjoining offices at the Public Theater a few blocks away by 9:30 a.m. and rarely return home before 6:30 p.m. 'Then we bolt in, bolt down our dinner and race off to one of our productions,' jokes Papp. 'We see them all many times. There is a thin line between our personal and professional lives.'"

Our first cabaret was situated in the Public's existing Martinson Hall on the third floor. Performances took place on its large end stage—the same as always—with food and drink originating in a makeshift kitchen on the first floor. Waiters bringing trays from there up to the third floor had to navigate a tricky obstacle course of stairs, bleachers, railings, platforms, chair legs, and

Raúl Juliá as Proteus in the rock musical *Two Gentlemen of Verona* at the Delacorte Theater in 1971. It became the Public Theater's first move to Broadway, where it won the Tony award for Best Musical.

Friedman-Abeles/Billy Rose Theatre Division, The New York Public Library

Morgan Freeman and Novella Nelson in *One: The 2 of Us* by Ilunga Adell, a play in *Four for One* at the Public Theater in 1972.

Friedman-Abeles/Billy Rose Theatre Division, The New York Public Library

A. J. Antoon's delightful *Much Ado About Nothing* at the Delacorte Theater in 1972, with (L–R front row) April Shawhan as Hero and Kathleen Widdoes as Beatrice, and (L–R second row) Glenn Walken as Claudio and Sam Waterston as Benedick. *Much Ado* was also seen in an acclaimed adaptation for CBS Television in 1973.

Friedman-Abeles/Billy Rose Theatre Division, The New York Public Library

Ruby Dee in *Wedding Band*, a searing drama by Alice Childress about an interracial couple in South Carolina in 1918. Public Theater on ABC-Television 1974.
Walt Disney Television Photo Archives/Getty Images

Playwright Alice Childress, whose *Wedding Band* was produced by the Public Theater in 1972.
Schomburg Center for Research in Black Culture, Photographs and Prints Division, The New York Public Library

(L–R) Associate producer Bernard Gersten, chairperson LuEsther T. Mertz, and Joe on the sidewalk near the Public Theater in 1972.
Frederic Ohringer

Joe and me
walking home
from the Public
Theater in 1973.
Papp Estate

Joe and me at a dinner
with friends in 1975.
Papp Estate

The original cast of *A Chorus Line* singing "Who am I anyway?
Am I my resumé?" at the Public Theater in 1975.
Martha Swope/Billy Rose Theatre Division, The New York Public Library

Choreographer-director Michael Bennett in front of a poster announcing the move of *A Chorus Line* from the Public Theater to Broadway in 1975.
Martha Swope/Billy Rose Theatre Division, The New York Public Library

Theoni V. Aldredge, resident costume designer of more than eighty productions at the Public and Delacorte Theaters.
Sal Traina/WWD/Penske Media/Getty Images

Scenic designer Robin Wagner is the recipient of many major awards for his design of theatrical productions, including *A Chorus Line*, as well as for ballet and opera.
Martha Swope/Billy Rose Theatre Division, The New York Public Library

Lighting designer Tharon Musser created the illuminating ambience of *A Chorus Line* with its haunting fade-to-black finale.
Paul Hosefros/The New York Times/Redux

Cutting the cake at our home wedding in 1976.
UPI/Bettmann Archive/ Getty Images

Joe with his daughter Susan Lippman, her husband Richard, and their son Jonathan.
Gail Papp

Joe and me in 1980 with his daughter Barbara Mosser, her husband David, their
children Stephanie and Michael, and philanthropist George T. Delacorte.
Papp Estate

Joe's son Michael Faulkner and his wife Randy.
Courtesy of Michael Faulkner

Miranda and Tony Papp, Joe's youngest children, dancing in our living room.
Gail Papp

Meryl Streep as Princess
Katherine in *Henry V* at the
Delacorte Theater in 1976.

Celebrating an opening of Ntozake Shange's *for
colored girls who have considered suicide/when
the rainbow is enuf* at the National Theater in
Washington, D.C., in 1977. (Center) Ntozake Shange
and jazz musician David Murray, (L) her parents
Eloise and Dr. Paul T. Williams, (R) Joe and me.

Frances Conroy as Desdemona and Raúl Juliá as Othello with (L)
Mark Linn-Baker as an Orderly and Richard Dreyfuss as Iago and (R)
Bruce McGill as Lodovico at the Delacorte Theater in 1979.

people's legs before delivering them safely to the tables that had been set up in Martinson Hall.

Joe said, "I'm beginning to realize that you have to worry as much about what's being served as what's going on up there on the stage."

The Public's inaugural cabaret earned high marks for excellence and originality. Most important was the premiere of Elizabeth Swados's groundbreaking musical *Runaways*, performed by twenty-two children who tell through songs, monologues, and poems about the lives of the young runaways they portray. It moved to Broadway, as did David Mamet's haunting *The Water Engine*, presented as a 1930s radio play about an inventor who's found a way to run an engine on distilled water.

Despite the cabaret's success, however, it ran out of steam after its first year. In retrospect, my private view was that it really hadn't been a cabaret but a theatrical season of four off-Broadway shows unnecessarily complicated by food service. I also felt that it had been fitted into an uncongenial space and had lacked an experienced programmer to conceptualize and run it on a full-time basis.

Twenty-one years later, director-playwright George C. Wolfe, who was then in charge of the Public Theater as its new producer, would name and launch the hugely popular "Joe's Pub" in a professionally designed space adjoining the first floor lobby.

This time the Public Theater got everything right, and "Joe's Pub" has flourished ever since its opening in 1998.

29

Handling Controversial Issues

In 1976, the musical that Joe took a day off from directing so that we could get married was *Apple Pie* by playwright Myrna Lamb and composer Nicholas Meyers. Myrna was a leader in the Women's Liberation Movement (WLM), whom the renowned critic and memoirist Vivian Gornick called "the first true artist of the feminist consciousness."

Apple Pie told a challenging story about a girl who had escaped from Nazi Germany to the United States only to find herself persecuted here by anti-feminists. The role of her Black lover was sung by the young Robert Guillaume whose operatic aria of rage and breakdown remains a riveting moment in my theatrical memory. Later he became famous as the star of the ABC sitcom "Benson."

Male critics indulged in fatuous jokes about the title of Myrna and Nick's musical: *Apple Pie* was "fairly flakey" . . . "difficult to digest" . . . "indigestible no matter how you slice it" . . . "Did the pastry have to be so dry?" and so forth.

Six years earlier Joe had directed another musical by Myrna Lamb with composer Susan Bingham called *Mod Donna*. It had inspired noisy picket lines of feminists in front of the Public Theater protesting the fact that it was directed by a man—Joe.

Although Joe never went looking for problems, they seemed to find him by virtue of what he did and what he believed in. It was clear to me that his work would seldom be free of controversy and that much of it would be of a political nature. The bicentennial year of 1976 wasn't a tranquil time any more than it is as I write this memoir decades later in the politically riled up twenty-first century.

Joe's brand of social activism was a revelation to me. I had been in nursery school in New York City during the movements of the late 1930s that were so important in his life, and my sense of those tumultuous times during the Depression had mostly come from my parents. I also had a vivid memory at age four of my fastidious schoolteacher grandmother in Southern California allowing hobos into her kitchen to give them a meal. Seeing my wide-eyed stare, she reassured me, "Don't be scared, sweetie. They're good men who are just down on their luck." I had no idea that the reason I was living with my grandmother in California was because my parents had lost their jobs back in New York City. My mother had brought me to California to begin kindergarten, saying that my father would join us later.

I told Joe that when I was eight, my father had been the editor of the magazine of the International Longshore and Warehouse Union (ILWU) in San Francisco. This was during the ascendancy of its famous leader Harry Bridges in the 1940s. I remembered my excitement when my father brought home several 78-rpm records of Artie Shaw playing the clarinet that a friend in the International Longshore and Warehouse Union had given him.

I especially remembered when my parents were active members of the Joint Anti-Fascist Spanish Refugee Committee in Berkeley, a group that helped veterans who had fought against the dictator Francisco Franco during the Spanish Civil War of 1936–1939.

When I was nine years old, my parents agreed to let me appear in a benefit performance for the Spanish Refugee Appeal. It was to be the melodrama *East Lynne* with my father playing the villain, Sir Francis Leveson, and myself cast as "Little Willie." All I had to do as the dying child in the play was cry, "Mother!" and expire in a bed tilted toward the audience at a forty-five degree angle.

When I began to work at the Festival in the mid-sixties, the United States was in the last throes of the infamous McCarthy era during which Joe had been tailed by FBI agents and called before the House Un-American Activities Subcommittee investigating supposed Communist infiltration in the entertainment industry.

How Joe handled these early controversial issues, as well as later ones, such as the right-wing politicization of the National Endowment for the Arts in the 1980s, were instructive lessons for me about political protest. His responses were principled and shrewd, usually proportionate, sometimes aggressive, and they resonate with me even now, in an era of political upheavals in the twenty-first century.

In 1971, for example, Richard Nixon's vice president, Spiro Agnew, launched a hard-swinging attack against the CBS documentary *The Selling of the Pentagon*. On March 19 Joe fired off a letter to Frank Stanton, the respected president of CBS, criticizing his tepid response to Agnew's attack.

Dear Mr. Stanton:

I heard some of your remarks over CBS answering the Vice-President's attack on the network, and I am really amazed. When do liberals ever learn that the only way to handle a bully is to give him a dose of his own medicine? Not to use his tactics, which are based on the big-lie technique, standing truth on its head, but taking the initiative forcefully and without pussyfooting, expose the demagoguery. A bully must be hit and hit hard.

This man is a real threat to democracy—a protégé of Joe McCarthy. Say out loud what he is attempting to do. Everybody knows it . . . The bully tries to censor the news media. He wants to control the press. He wants to be the arbiter of opinion. He is Mr. Thought Control in person. He is a walking violation of the free speech and free press amendment. He uses his position to undermine the only independent means this country has to find out what is going on in it . . . He aims for the jugular of democracy . . .

Of course, be reasonable, but God, man, shout a little.

Joseph Papp

Good for him, I thought to myself, feeling the same positive surge I'd experienced six years earlier when I read Joe's manifesto answering Walter Kerr's rant against free Shakespeare.

In the footsteps of Agnew, a new TV controversy erupted in 1973, but this time it was one that directly involved the Public Theater.

It began with the celebratory announcement of Joe's agreement with CBS Television to produce thirteen plays for the network. The story was major media news in 1972.

The New York Times

August 1, 1972

"Papp Will Produce 13 Plays for C.B.S. in 4 Years"

"Robert D. Wood, president of C.B.S. Television, called the alliance with Mr. Papp a venture in prestige . . . In response to a question, Mr. Wood said, 'I wouldn't characterize our role here as veto power. This is really a partnership.'"

Joe's first production for CBS Television was director A. J. Antoon's captivating rendition of Shakespeare's *Much Ado About Nothing* in 1973 with Sam Waterston and Kathleen Widdoes as Benedick and Beatrice, the sparring pair of uncommitted lovers from the Central Park production in 1972. It received wonderful reviews.

Kathleen Widdoes, an enchanting actress, had appeared in Joe's early productions, playing Titania in *A Midsummer Night's Dream*, Miranda in *The Tempest*, and Juliet, beating Sam Waterston by a couple of years to his first part in 1963 as Silvius in *As You Like It*, after which he appeared in a succession of major roles including Hamlet and Prospero in *The Tempest*.

Joe's second production for CBS Television, also in 1973, was an adaptation of *Sticks and Bones*, David Rabe's powerful Tony Award–winning play about a blind Vietnam veteran returning home, brilliantly directed by Robert Downey Sr. Downey was famous for his satirical film *Putney Swope* (1969) about a Black advertising executive in a corrupt world of white power. After Joe and I saw his *Greaser's Palace* (1972), an absurdist Western, Joe gambled that Downey Sr. could render for television the nightmarish distortions of Rabe's family-based story.

It received rave reviews. Over lunch at a restaurant with Associate Producer Bernard Gersten and myself, Joe was reading aloud the rave television reviews of *Sticks and Bones* in *Time* and *Newsweek* that had just been published in advance of its prime-time broadcast in two days. As we were celebrating them, a waiter came over and told Joe there was an urgent call for him on the public telephone mounted on the wall near our table.

It was the president of CBS, who had been frantically trying to reach Joe to let him know that despite the wonderful reviews, the broadcast of *Sticks and Bones* had just been cancelled. He didn't want him to find out about it in the afternoon newspapers.

On his end I heard Joe say, "Well, I don't have any respect for *you!*" before slamming the earpiece back on the wall.

Not finishing lunch, Joe, Bernie, and I hurried back to the Public Theater where Joe got the story from a reporter about what had just happened.

In an action described as "virtually unprecedented," the network president, Robert Wood, who only minutes ago had called Joe at the restaurant, had given a press conference that morning at CBS headquarters in Manhattan announcing his cancellation of the broadcast of *Sticks and Bones*. The reason he gave was that it "might be unnecessarily abrasive to the feelings of millions of Americans whose lives . . . are emotionally dominated by the P.O.W.s returning from Vietnam." So much for the network president's assertions to Joe about "partnership" and his corporate disinclination to exercise veto power.

The real story became much more complicated, however, when Joe learned that the director of Nixon's Office of Telecommunications Policy had pressured CBS to "delay" the broadcast, and that William Paley, the founder of CBS (who had disliked both the cinematic creativity and the point of view of *Sticks and Bones*) had then "asked" his CBS affiliates to tell network headquarters in New York City that they wouldn't air it.

Seventy-one affiliates out of 154 complied, and although that number wasn't a majority of the affiliates, it ostensibly made the cancellation "necessary." It was a front page story in the *Washington Post* on March 7: "CBS Cancels Controversial TV Show."

Joe was beyond furious, and his response was to launch a two-week-long media blitz against CBS in which he blasted the network's behavior as "a cowardly act, a dastardly thing. It is frightening that this monster corporation has decided to put its tail between its legs and back away from this program because some affiliates find it too strong stuff."

Joe booked himself solid for two weeks of newspaper, radio, and television interviews, hammering away at CBS's action as "a cop out, a rotten affront to freedom of speech and a whittling away at the First Amendment."

This was a vigorous demonstration of Joe's refusal to be discreet or go along quietly with the suppression of an artistic work. However, he was under no illusion that he could undo the cancellation of the *Sticks and Bones* broadcast. Instead, his idea was to let the world know that it was happening, and why, in such a forceful manner that people would be forced to notice, and no one would forget. I don't know how David Rabe felt about this fracas, during which Joe led the attack defending Rabe's work as well as his own free speech rights as its producer. Later that year CBS did finally broadcast *Sticks and Bones*, airing it in the middle of the night during the off-season month of August.

In subsequent years a number of our productions that were adapted for television and film became available on DVD, the notable exception being *Sticks and Bones*. I've been able to watch my old VHS cassette of it several times since the controversy of 1973 and can testify that it registers as a powerful and uniquely artistic film in any era. It's an important addition to Downey Sr.'s body of work as a director. Unfortunately, however, it isn't currently available, although it certainly should be.

In 1978, Joe told me that he was depressed about the Bakke Case which had reached the Supreme Court challenging affirmative action on the grounds that it supposedly constituted "reverse racism." He felt the case reflected a conservative countermovement in the country where whites and legislators were tired of the progressivism of the 1960s and early 1970s and didn't want to be bothered with the problems of minorities. Few people understood that Joe's indirect response to the Bakke case was to raise more than $750,000 to establish a Black-Hispanic-Asian Shakespeare Repertory Company in residence for six months at the Public Theater. He persuaded Michael Langham, the renowned Shakespeare director who had headed the Guthrie Theater, the Stratford Festival in Canada, and the Juilliard School, to be in charge of it, along with many fine actors to join the company.

"It's never happened before," Joe said. "I don't see it in political terms. I just felt it was time that we did something like this. To keep a theater alive is to reflect what's happening."

If you were around the Public Theater during our 1978–1979 season, you had a chance to see a powerful young Morgan Freeman and Gloria Foster in *Coriolanus*, as well as *Julius Caesar* with a hair-raisingly regicidal cast of actors who made you believe that Caesar *could* be assassinated.

What was the point?

"Perhaps if we had decided to create such a company in the Sixties, we would have been welcomed," Joe said. "But it's an entirely different situation now in the late Seventies when there's a kind of frustration, powerlessness, and an ignoring of minorities in New York. I know I'm going against the grain, and it isn't too popular a move, but I feel it's necessary."

A decade after the Bakke Case, we were drawn into the culture wars of the 1980s triggered by the rise of the Religious Right.

Washington Post

July 27, 1989
"Senate Votes to Expand NEA Grant Ban.
Helms Amendment Targets 'Obscene Art'"

The campaign against the National Endowment for the Arts (NEA) was led by North Carolina's Republican Senator Jesse Helms on the spurious issue that the Endowment was sponsoring the exhibition of allegedly obscene art in museums. By 1990 the spurious issue had spread from museums to the performing arts, arriving on our doorstep in the following manner.

The National Endowment had just awarded a $50,000 grant to the Public Theater for its International Latino Festival. But when Joe received the grant documents, he found that they required him to sign a form agreeing to obscenity restrictions set forth in legislation that Senator Helms had gotten passed in Congress that barred NEA funds being used to *"promote, disseminate or produce obscene or indecent materials, including but not limited to depictions of sadomasochism, homoeroticism, the exploitation of children, or individuals engaged in sex acts . . . ."* The list went on.

Joe said, "Just to have that language in any kind of agreement makes my skin crawl."

He sent a long letter to the newly appointed Chairman of the National Endowment for the Arts, John E. Frohnmayer, in which he argued that "A work of art is extremely complex and to judge it on a political basis is impossible and wrong . . . I can't accept the grant as long as the Helms inspired amendment on obscenity is part of the agreement."

But Joe was tormented by his decision to turn down the $50,000 grant because funds for the International Latino Festival were hard to come by and he had to struggle every year to raise the money for it. He did so because he believed in the program and was committed to its directors, Oscar Ciccone and Cecilia Vega, whom he regarded as a vital part of the Public's artistic leadership. In his office one day, as he was telling a trustee about his decision to refuse the grant, Joe broke down and cried, something I had never seen him do before.

After he fired off his letter to the NEA Chairman, Joe began a personal campaign to get the obscenity restriction withdrawn from the new legislation by calling key senators on the phone—a new group every day—to explain his opposition to its impact as a prior restraint on the artistic freedom of seekers of NEA grants. He recruited supporters to write and call their legislators. He did print, radio, and TV interviews. He wrote op-ed pieces for West and East Coast newspapers. On television he debated Representative Dana Rohrabacher, a pugnacious right-wing congressman from California. In our current age of Facebook and Twitter, I have no doubt that Joe would have also explored the positive uses of social media in his campaign.

The overall lesson I learned from Joe's different modes of protest is that although technologies may change, the underlying strategy of civil resistance remains the same: organize, recruit, be visible, be heard, and don't stop.

30

Country Matters

Joe still remembered the faux lyrics he'd been taught in grammar school to a wordless and possibly worthless composition called "Narcissus" by Ethelbert Nevin:

> "Narcissus was a little boy so bright
> A fairy changed him into a flower white.
> And so to help this boy along
> Narcissus by Nevin wrote this lovely song."

Joe said, "I remember being hard put to fit that last hurried phrase into the music bar."

I remembered the faux lyrics that I'd been taught to the first four bars of Haydn's Symphony No. 94:

> "Papa Haydn wrote this tune,
> And a chord is coming soon.
> It will be a big surprise.
> Open sleepy eyes! BANG!"

Occasionally such nonsense relieved the tedium of a drive to our cottage in upstate New York. One time Joe surprised me by reciting Robert Browning's very long narrative poem about a battle in 1809 that the French army, led by

Napoleon, had fought against the army of the Austrian Empire at Ratisbon, a city in Bavaria.

I was astonished when Joe began to intone it at the wheel, "You know we French stormed Ratisbon a mile or so away . . ." because my father had recited the same poem for me when I was a child, having learned it in his school days in the 1910s. The words stirred a rush of memory in me that Joe was unaware of. The best part had always been the poem's dramatic final stanza where a Boy Soldier comes running up to Napoleon, who is standing on a hill waiting to hear who has won the battle of Ratisbon.

At the wheel of our car, Joe (as the Boy Soldier) exclaimed, "Emperor, by God's grace we've got you Ratisbon!" Then (as Napoleon) Joe said:

> "The chief's eye flashed, but presently
> Softened itself, as sheathes
> A film the mother-eagle's eye
> When her bruised eaglet breathes.
> 'You're wounded!'
> 'Nay,' the soldier's pride
> Touched to the quick, he said:
> 'I'm killed, Sire!' And his chief beside,
> Smiling the boy fell dead."

On one of our car trips to the country I asked Joe if he'd ever heard the first line of a poem I'd learned from my mother that went "Hork! Pidwar foifee tray? And the dawn came creeping in."

"No I haven't," Joe said, "but it reminds me of poems in the thirties when Vachel Lindsay was all the vogue and he was making a thing of chanting like—'BLOOD! screamed the skull-faced, lean witch-doctors . . . THEN I had religion. THEN I had a vision . . . Boomlay, Boomlay, Boomlay, BOOM!'"

"Yes, my mother used to do that one too," I said.

For me these snatches of poetry and song linked the distant pre–World War I childhoods of my parents to Joe's boyhood in the Depression, braiding together the primary people in my life.

***

"I can't believe this is ours!" I often exclaimed when Joe and I walked around our field of goldenrod, sumac, and Queen Anne's lace in the country.

"Well it may be God's acres, but right now it belongs to us," Joe replied, marking the field's perimeter to make sure our property stakes were still in place.

What little time we were able to spend at the cottage was precious. Joe built sheds. I sowed clover. We had to draw straws for turns to mow the grassy hill next to the cottage because we loved our big gas-powered, fire-engine-red Gravely lawn mower so much that we were both inclined to hog it.

We learned to identify common birds and watched with surprise whenever a wild creature came into view—such as a testy mother hedgehog swatting her train of rambunctious babies, or an immense snapping turtle waddling across a sandy mound pockmarked by large ant holes. At night we followed the moon's trajectory above our hill and listened to crickets.

During a hurricane one autumn, our huge walnut tree came crashing down, pelting its green walnuts outside the cottage. That evening I went out after the storm to gather broken twigs for firewood. As I flung them up the hill towards our woodpile, my wedding ring suddenly flew off my finger. Horrified, I stared at the dark hill before scrambling up the slope, slipping and sliding on muddy walnuts, to get a flashlight from the house. Hovering over its narrow beam, I searched for the ring in the rain-soaked grass.

Then, as if in a dream, the soulful voice of mezzo-soprano Janet Baker singing Bach's "Wachet Auf Cantata" drifted across the drenched landscape from our brightly lit cottage. It was Joe's latest purchase from Tower Records. He appeared on the deck.

"Come back in," he called. "It's too dark. It's too wet and chilly out here."

"But I have to find the ring," I said.

"No you don't," Joe said. "I'll get you another one. Come back in. I've lit a fire."

I didn't want to give up.

"If you come back in, I'll make you a margarita."

When I dragged myself indoors, tear-stained, cold and muddy, he put the margarita in one hand, on which my fingers had turned white down to the knuckles, and led me by the other to the chair he'd set in front of a glowing log in our fireplace.

In the aftermath of a heavy snowfall one winter, Joe suggested that we take a walk along a picturesque back road near our cottage. To protect my

Raynaud's Syndrome–sensitive extremities from the cold—especially the finger that had a new duplicate wedding ring on it—I activated my pocket handwarmers before setting out on a hike with Joe through the magical landscape of snow-etched trees and glistening white fields.

Captivated by the quiet beauty of the countryside, we stayed out longer than we intended, and as we headed home I began to experience difficulty pushing my boots forward in the snow. Finally I had to stop.

"I'm afraid I can't walk any further," I said to Joe. "My hands are okay, but my feet have frozen up. I can't push them forward anymore."

There weren't any houses in sight that Joe could go to for help, nor could he call a friend because this was before cell phones. Worse, the chances of hitching a car ride on this untraveled back road were nonexistent. I had been through too many incidents in which my frozen hands and feet had turned purplish-black to risk that happening again. This condition had first appeared in my early teens when my parents moved from California to New Hampshire and I had experienced my first New England winter there.

"You should leave me here, walk home, and drive back in the car," I said to Joe with, I thought, irrefutable commonsense.

By this time, however, early evening shadows had tinted the snowbanks purple, and he wouldn't hear of it.

"Now listen," Joe said, placing his hands on my shoulders and turning me to face him in the middle of the road. "I'm going to hypnotize you."

I dismissed the idea. "Oh no," I said. "People have tried to do that in the past but I'm resistant to hypnosis. I'm not a good subject."

"I know how to do it," Joe insisted. "I used to hypnotize guys in the navy and it always worked."

I told him that I hated the idea of gazing into his eyes knowing that I was bound to disappoint him.

Joe brushed my objection aside.

"You don't have to gaze into my eyes," he said, gently tightening his hold on my shoulders. "When I count to three, the blood will start to circulate in your feet again, they'll feel warm, and you'll be able to walk."

"But—"

"One, two, three," Joe said quietly, but firmly.

He did it so fast that I had no time to resist and then, *mirabile dictu*, I began to feel the blood pulsing from my ankles down to my frozen toes.

"I can't believe this!" I exclaimed, throwing my arms around him in a grateful hug.

"Okay, now we can walk home," Joe said, gripping my arm as he steered us along the darkening backroad.

***

With the advent of spring, a bird-watching neighbor in the country mourned the absence of an avian population that she said used to be native to the area.

"It's a shame you'll not be seeing the bluebirds here any more," she called out from her doorway when she saw us filling a bird feeder near the road. "They used to be everywhere, but when people started moving into the countryside twenty years ago, they cleared the woods and planted lawns. That drove the bluebirds away."

This seemed like an injustice in need of redress, the kind of challenge that Joe was constitutionally disposed to answer. Accordingly, he set about restoring the bluebirds' habitat by hammering together eighteen pre-fabricated bluebird houses according to instructions that came with them.

"They have to be at least five feet off the ground," Joe said.

"How far apart?" I asked.

"Twenty feet," he said.

We installed them on eighteen posts in a small clearing in the woods on the far side of our brook, near enough so that we'd have a view of the bluebirds, if they came back. We hoped to be able to see them from the sun deck or through the sliding glass doors of the living room.

The bluebirds did return, delighting us with the flash of their blue wings and rusty breasts as they swooped among the trees and the bird houses we'd built for them.

Observing them, Joe scribbled a note that now seems eerily prescient: "I compare myself to a bird. A bird's life is so fragile. It can die in a minute, but its buoyant energy is so fantastic as it goes."

31

Irreconcilable Differences

When *A Chorus Line* shot into the stratosphere of success in 1975, it won every prize there was to win, including a Pulitzer, and spawned an enormous industry of road, national, and international companies.

We had *Chorus Line* merchandise galore in those days, an aspect of Broadway shows I hadn't paid much attention to before, but I now started collecting *Chorus Line* towels, T-shirts, tote bags, mugs, and umbrellas because they were popular gifts.

Images from the show were everywhere. The cover of *Newsweek* had a wonderful photograph of dancer Donna McKechnie as "Cassie" posed for her "Music and Mirror" number in an iconic red leotard and matching wraparound skirt. I was crazy about the look of that outfit and bought it at my neighborhood dance shop in maroon, red, black, even in turquoise. Joe tucked a snapshot of me wearing the turquoise one in his wallet.

The profits rolling in now to the Public Theater from *A Chorus Line* were extraordinary. This was thanks to the charitable contribution of Chairperson LuEsther T. Mertz which had enabled the Public Theater to be the sole producer of the show. Presciently from the beginning, however, Joe worried about the Public's future financial viability when it would no longer have a mega-hit show supporting its operation.

Three years later, in 1978, with *A Chorus Line* still flourishing, Michael Bennett had a new musical in preparation called *Ballroom* which he was developing at his own studio for a Broadway opening. In an atmosphere of excited anticipation about Bennett's next work, Associate Producer Bernard Gersten proposed to Joe that the Public Theater invest $1 million in *Ballroom* as a way of acknowledging the debt of gratitude he felt the Public Theater owed to Michael. After all, it was thanks to *A Chorus Line* that the Public Theater no longer had a yearly deficit and was even in a position to start an endowment fund. In Bernie's considered judgment, investing in Michael Bennett's new show would be more than a gesture of gratitude. For him it also represented, as he termed it, a "moral obligation."

Joe felt gratitude, but he pointed out to Bernie that Michael was in terrific shape these days. He'd become a millionaire. He now had his own very fine producing organization and had just purchased the building at 890 Broadway to use as rehearsal studios for theater and dance. For the first time in his life he didn't need anyone's financial help. Most important, however, Joe felt it was unacceptable to invest and put at risk the Public Theater's nonprofit funds in a commercial show that wasn't related to the work of the Public Theater. Bernie respectfully disagreed and their unreconciled points of view hung in the air.

On Thursday, June 22, 1978, Joe suggested that we drive to our country cottage. It was his fifty-seventh birthday.

"Let's go!" he said. "The weather's perfect and I can rehearse my songs there in peace and quiet."

He'd been invited to sing for a week at a small nightclub in Soho whose owner, Greg Dawson, had liked Joe's singing at a charity gala. Although Joe had a fine natural voice, he'd never been professionally trained and hesitated to accept at first. He finally decided to do it only when our friend, composer Stanley Silverman, agreed to help him. The young director Craig Zadan, who was affiliated with the nightclub, later joined them.

After choosing fifteen songs of the 1930s and 1940s, Joe had set about learning them over the course of the summer. Initially that had seemed like ample time. However by the end of June, with his nightclub debut only six weeks away, he was feeling under pressure and now saw his birthday as a golden opportunity to practice his nightclub songs undisturbed in the country.

We drove up from the city and settled ourselves on the sun deck. I was in the hammock as Joe began his first song.

The weather's getting fine.
The coffee tastes like wine.
You happy hobo sing,
"Hallelujah I'm a bum again!"

Just then the phone rang inside the cottage.

"I'll get it," I said.

It was Bernie Gersten with an urgent problem. In a quiet voice as if not to be overheard, he told me that he'd organized a huge surprise fifty-seventh birthday party honoring Joe at the Delacorte Theater *for that very evening*. I was amazed. This was the first I'd heard of it. Apparently the event had been prepared in secret for months, and Joe's absence from the city on this critical day was completely unanticipated. Bernie needed my help to get him back there that afternoon.

Glancing furtively at Joe still singing on the sun deck, I held the receiver close as Bernie outlined a last-minute strategy to save the surprise party, which required me to initiate a benign hoax to persuade Joe to return to Manhattan that afternoon.

I felt a twinge of discomfort because I'd never lied to Joe about anything before, but of course I had to go along with the ruse due to the astonishing scope of the party that Bernie described to me on the phone—with a famous host and actors, singers, composers, and playwrights participating in on-stage entertainments, as well as a multimedia show. There would also be phoned-in greetings from stars, and a VIP audience of two thousand in which four Mayors of New York City would be present—Robert F. Wagner Jr., John V. Lindsay, Abraham Beame, and Edward Koch.

Bernie said that the first part of the hoax I was to initiate consisted in my telling Joe that a surprise birthday party for him had been planned by our board chairperson and dear friend LuEsther T. Mertz. I was to say that it was going to be held at a restaurant and we would, of course, have to go back to the city for it.

Theoretically this would work, but in reality there was an unfortunate consequence to the plan because it obliged Joe to drive back to the city that afternoon, and this put him in an extremely bad mood. Why, he angrily asked me, had we even bothered to come up to the country? Since he assumed that I'd known all along about LuEsther Mertz's dinner plan, Joe's implied criticism was that I had shown incredibly poor judgment in this matter by letting us drive up to the cottage knowing that we'd have to head back to the city that same afternoon. He must have also wondered how I could shamelessly lie to him about these truncated hours in the country being a "good time" to rehearse his songs. His irritation grew and had become so intense that when we left the cottage and got in the car, he'd stopped talking to me.

After we were home, another part of Bernie's strategy fell into place: an actor in rehearsal at the Delacorte Theater for the next Shakespeare play phoned and told Joe he was urgently needed there to resolve a dispute between actors. Joe therefore agreed to drop by the theater on our way, supposedly, to the Mertz party at a restaurant. He was still not talking to me.

Accordingly, early that evening we drove up the path to the Delacorte Theater and parked the Jeep Wagoneer at Gate #1.

Joe got out of the car and entered the right wing of the darkened stage. As he did so, the house lights suddenly shone on two thousand guests in the audience, now singing "Happy Birthday."

Joe was staggered. He laughed and shook his head in amazement.

On stage, Master of Ceremonies Mike Nichols joked, "If it's really true, Joe, that you had no idea that all of this was going on right under your nose, I'd be *worried*."

After Joe recovered from his initial shock, he was hugely impressed by Bernie's miraculous coup as the producer of the surprise event and thanked everyone who participated in it.

Bernie made a happy comment about the good feeling his spectacular effort had generated: "Why wait until a person is dead to celebrate them?" It wasn't until we were home after the event that Joe realized I had never been told about the party beforehand and had been impressed at the last minute into Bernie's well-intentioned hoax.

A few days after the surprise birthday party, Joe told me that he thought Bernie should become an independent producer on his own.

"God knows he has the talent, skill and experience required in abundance, although it would probably be in conflict with his loyalty to the Public Theater."

During that summer Joe tried to reconcile his recent differences with Bernie concerning a Public Theater financial investment in Michael Bennett's new show. In deference to the entreaties of his old friend and colleague, as well as the warm feelings he'd always had toward Michael Bennett, Joe finally agreed to become a nominal producer of *Ballroom*, although such a role was contrary to Joe's way of working in the theater.

It came as no surprise to me that he soon found the contradiction of that role insupportable and couldn't go on with it. At the end of July he wrote a long, heartfelt letter to Michael Bennett explaining his reasons for withdrawing from the nominal relationship. This "Dear Michael" letter is worth quoting almost in its entirety because it reveals for the first time, in his own words, Joe's process as a producer:

> Pressured by matchmaking tactics and well-intentioned friends and colleagues, I tried as hard as I could to rationalize the Festival's involvement in a Broadway-bound production. But in deciding to go ahead and produce *Ballroom*, I was going against a 25-year way of working in the theater, a process which is second, if not first nature to me. It has been not only a way of work but a way of life, a way of looking at life. Therefore of necessity the role of a nominal producer was not a concern for status, but a resistance to surrender the very life process that dictated my way in the theater.
>
> I did not select the work to be produced—the most significant and meaningful act of any producer, and for me the entire basis of the growth and meaning of the New York Shakespeare Festival . . . Then, all the casting and all the hiring had already been completed, a *fait accompli*.
>
> Here again it is not a matter of vanity or pride—any number of commercial producers would not give a damn how and when and under what conditions they can lay their hands on a property with such potential for audiences as *Ballroom*. But to me (and you can certainly understand this) that process of decision-making is integral to the running and operating of a theater. The choices involving personnel, scenery, costumes, etc. are of no less significance than the choice of the play.
>
> So what was left for the Festival was the chance of investing over a million dollars in a show directed and produced by the most bankable creator on Broadway today—you—and the opportunity of cashing in on the destined success of the Broadway musical. Ultimately I could find this no basis for proceeding.
>
> At no time in the history of the Festival have we moved into the commercial arena without the Public Theater process—readings, workshops, full productions and then, if warranted, a move uptown. This is not a formula, or a pattern of steppingstones to success. It is a way of work and it is the work of a theater. To bypass a Public Theater production is not a violation of form, but a

reorientation of our goals, which have nothing whatsoever to do with a move to Broadway. Broadway is a by-product of our theater—not the product.

I was in the process of setting up my own work and signing my own contracts for an exciting season of new plays, new musical works, a Black theater company doing Shakespeare, a Puerto Rican musical, and 15 workshops, cabaret, etc. etc. I was in the dead center of all of this activity which I had initiated and been deeply involved in with artists, writers, actors, directors, designers, etc. The ferment was rich and fulfilling and full of great expectation. What in hell was I doing signing a contract for an actor I hadn't met let alone cast, for a show which I was not really producing, at a time when my own work at the Public Theater demanded my full-time attention?

Anyway all this is not your problem . . . *Ballroom* will be a hit . . . You will mount it with your unmatched brilliance and it will have a great director's flair.

Mainly I want you to respect my decision. It would have become intolerable, feeling the way I do, to have continued to pretend and play games. I do not have any desire to let our good feeling about one another lapse. I stand ready to be of any assistance I can to you for the time you desired it. In short, let us continue to remain friends. I assure you I wish you nothing but happiness. Joe

But Joe never sent the letter. Nor did he share it with anyone, choosing instead to handle his withdrawal from *Ballroom* in person.

Joe had assumed that this marked the end of his and the Public Theater's confused involvement with *Ballroom*. But then he received a request from Bernie for a leave of absence from the Public Theater in order for him to work on *Ballroom*.

Joe was taken aback. All summer long he'd been dealing with the issue of *Ballroom*, first with Bernie's insistence on a Public Theater financial investment in the show, which Joe said was unacceptable, and then on Joe being a nominal producer of it from which Joe, in good conscience, finally had to withdraw. Now came Bernie's request for a leave of absence in order to offer his expertise to *Ballroom* at a most inopportune time for him to be absent from his important job at the Public Theater. At this point I myself was confounded by Bernie's position and distinctly remember feeling that he was provoking an explosive situation, though he truly seemed to be unconscious of it.

I knew that Joe's intense focus at that moment was on the musical work of three talented, and very different, women. He had been in close consultation with writer-composer Elizabeth Swados, whose groundbreaking musical

Runaways, which she was also directing, had gone through a developmental process in partnership with a cast of twenty-two children and teenagers before it premiered in our new Martinson Cabaret to rave reviews. In previous productions Liz Swados had always relied on Joe as a sounding board and conscience for her work, and when he moved *Runaways* to Broadway his support had become all the more essential because Liz had no prior experience directing on Broadway.

Joe was also involved with writer-singer Gretchen Cryer and composer Nancy Ford, whose moving and timely musical, *I'm Getting My Act Together and Taking It on the Road*, had opened at the Public. There it had developed a tremendous word-of-mouth following, and Joe was now planning to move it to an off-Broadway theater in December.

Meanwhile, he had opened a new stage at the Public called The Old Prop Shop Theater featuring the work of the Mabou Mines company with director-writer Lee Breuer's unforgettable *The Shaggy Dog Animation*.

He had also asked future Artistic Director Wilford Leach to direct two plays at the Delacorte for the first time that summer, and great moments from Wil's *The Taming of the Shrew* with Meryl Streep and Raúl Juliá had just been captured in a wonderful PBS documentary called *Kiss Me, Petruchio*.

Besides the two Shakespeare plays at the Delacorte, Joe had produced sixteen shows at the Public that season, and presented a music series, a dance company, and a film program. He also had five shows running on Broadway (*A Chorus Line*, *for colored girls who have considered suicide/when the rainbow is enuf*, *Paul Robeson*, *The Water Engine*, and *Runaways*).

It takes tremendous organizational resources to mount and oversee producing on this scale, yet the permanent staff of the Public Theater at that time was only eighty-seven people.

It was just at this moment, when Joe most felt the need for a strong second-in-command, that he became understandably concerned about adequate administrative oversight of the theater's resources in production, personnel, and financial management if Bernie, the associate producer, went on an extended leave of absence to work on an unrelated commercial show.

From Joe's perspective, the associate producer's priorities no longer seemed to be in proper alignment with those of the Public Theater, having become attached instead to a sense of moral obligation to Michael Bennett and the assumed future commercial promise of *Ballroom*. But the most important point that Joe finally made clear to Bernie was that he needed him and therefore couldn't agree to the leave of absence. Bernie, apparently not regarding this as an executive decision, continued to insist on it, which I guess was sort of understandable in light of their close eighteen-year-long relationship in the theater.

However, from the time that I started working at the Festival thirteen years earlier, I recognized that Joe had established one-person leadership in creating his theater. As he told me then, the hard lesson he'd learned in the late 1940s, when he was the managing director of the failed Actor's Lab in Los Angeles, was that divided leadership didn't work and was likely to foster institutional chaos. He said that he'd never forgotten it, and it seemed to me that the current debate about *Ballroom* had probably triggered his recollection of that experience.

By the beginning of August Joe had arrived at institutional clarity about his disagreement with Bernie's desire to involve the Public Theater with Michael Bennett's *Ballroom*. Joe now felt that what divided them had become more than just a difference of opinion or Bernie's opposition to his judgment in the matter. It had evolved into an unwelcome challenge to Joe's contractual responsibility to the Board of Trustees to handle the financial interests of the Public Theater in a reasonable manner, a situation that did not yet apply to the position of associate producer, although it would in the future.

There are other strands at play in the story, but this was its basic outline. Unfortunately, Bernie's intransigent passion about *Ballroom*, inflamed and unresolved over the course of the summer, finally precipitated a rupture between Joe and his long-time colleague, whose employment he terminated at the end of the month after they were unable to agree on a mutually acceptable way forward. Bernie hadn't foreseen this outcome and the shock of it to him was traumatic and painful.

Joe, it seemed to me, became stoic and went into "survival mode."

First reactions to the announcement of Bernard Gersten's departure from the Public Theater were highly critical of Joe. Bernie had always been popular with the Public's trustees, some of whom asked why Joe couldn't have worked out a compromise about the leave of absence. But the situation was much more complicated than that. It was beyond compromise and no one had been able to help.

When the news broke in the press, I received a call from Michael Bennett in my Play Department office. This was a first.

Michael told me that he "understood" the "real" situation. He knew that Joe wasn't the "villain in the case" and that he was in no way to blame. He even said that he had done the "right thing." Michael warned me that Joe would be "unfairly cast as the heavy." He said he just wanted to let me know that despite the criticism of Joe in the press, he knew the "true story"—although he didn't explain exactly what he meant by that.

Did I hear an echo in Michael's voice of the Oath of Integrity that he, Joe, and myself had sworn three years ago pledging "loyalty . . . honesty . . . to set a shining example of integrity in human affairs"? Yes, I heard the echo. But Michael had a strategic mind and no doubt expected I would tell Joe about the call, which I did. Whatever was going on behind the scenes, it was obvious to me that he wanted to keep Joe's friendship, and in the end, the only sympathetic support that Joe got was from Michael.

These events occurred in a different era than the present where the top executives of a nonprofit theater would be hired by its board of trustees. Oddly, in retrospect Joe, the supposed maverick, was more strictly aligned on the side of institutional accountability back then than his long-time colleague.

In his subsequent career Bernard Gersten held important jobs in the entertainment industry, eventually as executive producer of the highly successful Lincoln Center Theater which he headed from 1985 to his retirement in 2013. Despite their differences, Joe always unreservedly credited Bernie with a major role in the creation of the Public Theater.

After his departure in the fall of 1978, Bernard Gersten became an independent co-producer of Michael Bennett's *Ballroom* on Broadway.

This was about the same time that Joe began his week-long singing engagement at the nightclub in Soho, the name of which was, coincidentally, "The Ballroom."

32

When Joe Sang at The Ballroom

Joe had rehearsed all summer long in 1978 for his singing debut at a Soho nightclub. Now the moment had arrived. For the next week he would be doing two shows a night of diverse songs by Irving Berlin, Harry Warren, Hoagy Carmichael, Richard Rodgers, Joe Bushkin, Jay Gorney, Gilbert and Sullivan, and one in Yiddish by Nellie Casman and Samuel Steinberg.

He'd never done anything like it before. The last time he'd sung in public was long ago, in the Gilbert and Sullivan operettas that his Eastern District High School put on in Brooklyn. As a boy he'd also sung at a synagogue. Later his natural stage presence had been polished by training at the Actor's Lab after World War II, but singing hadn't been part of it. As an adult he occasionally sang a song for a benefit. But *that was it.*

Before his first performance in Soho, Joe waited outside his dressing room in the club's basement as the string instruments above him on the first floor played Fritz Kreisler's rambunctious overture "Liebesfreud" ("Love's Joy"). Then he listened for the five musicians to begin a slow vamp, which was his cue to climb the basement stairs and saunter onto the club's tiny stage in his tux and Fred Astaire top hat singing:

> The weather's getting fine.
> The coffee tastes like wine.
> You happy hobo sing,
> *"Hallelujah I'm a bum again!"*

Between the songs Joe talked to the audience. He never mentioned his career in the theater. Instead he reminisced about his childhood. He told them about being trained as a boy soloist for the High Holy Days at a Portuguese synagogue in Brooklyn whose elegant architecture was a far cry from the poor storefront shul that he'd attended with his father. At the end of this story Joe sang, in a cappella cantorial style, one of the chants he'd sung there as a boy:

> Tsadik, Tsadik!
> Tsadik Bekhoi Darkhov.
> Eylohim Barukh Khasdekho.
> Eynini b'emes Yeshekho
> Asher lo hayam,
> Vehu oso Hu—
> Veyebeshes yodov
> Yatsaru . . .

The soulful sonority of Joe's unaccompanied tenor voice always deeply moved me. I knew it affected others too because the nightclub audiences grew quiet when Joe paused afterward to tell them, "I still love those beautiful chants. I believed everything I sang, too, and on the holidays I sang with my father sitting in the front row. He felt very much out of place in that fancy shul. He was wearing his old tallis, you know, the one he brought with him from Poland. Everyone else had this gleaming silky kind of tallis. I think he liked his old shul and the old tailor with a wheezy little voice. I think my father loved that wheezy voice because it seemed to have the idea that a man sang directly to God without any intermediary."

Although I was used to seeing Joe in a public role, I felt a new excitement now watching him as a performer. One night as Joe was climbing the stairs from his dressing room in the basement to make his entrance on the stage, his knees suddenly buckled under him and he collapsed on a step. Clutching the banister, he shouted, "Gail! My legs are paralyzed. I can't walk!"

Due to my inexperience as a backstage wife, my first impulse was to call 911 on the club's phone, but just then the musical vamp for Joe's entrance began above us, and I heard myself saying lines that seemed to be lifted from an old movie.

"Of course you can walk," I said to Joe. "I know you can walk. Just take a deep breath. Try the next step. You'll be fine once you're singing *I'm a bum again.*"

And he was.

Another night, as I watched Joe's performance from my perch by the front door, I saw his top-hat nonchalance falter for a moment when he recognized a face staring at him from a candlelit table at the edge of the stage. It was the great Broadway composer Richard Rodgers, who had come to hear Joe sing "Hallelujah, I'm a Bum Again," a little-known song that he and Lorenz Hart had written for a film starring Al Jolson in 1933. Rodgers hadn't heard it sung in forty-five years.

It never occurred to me that Joe's Ballroom gig would be reviewed, but it was a pleasant shock when reviews did appear, because they were all excellent. One of them had an interesting take on the evening: "Part of the fascination of Joe Papp's nightclub act at The Ballroom is watching the feisty, abrasive, arrogant public figure reminisce quietly about his childhood, telling stories about being 'discovered' at the age of eleven and enjoying short-lived stardom in cantorial circles in Brooklyn. The contrast between the mature Joe and this poignant youth is like reading one of those nineteenth century novels about an indigent young man's determined rise to fame and fortune."

Toward the end of his show, Joe would turn up the collar of his tuxedo jacket to portray a down-on-his-luck vagrant as he launched his eleven o'clock number with a heldentenor rendition of "Once I Built a Railroad," the thrilling anthem of the Great Depression. At its conclusion Joe sang:

> Say, don't you remember, they called me Al—
> it was Al all the time.
> Say, don't you remember, I'm your pal!
> *Buddy, can you spare a dime?*

The cheering and applause after this brought down the house every night. When we got home after the show, we were both so wound up, neither of us was able to fall asleep in the bedroom. Instead, I made up the sofa bed in our living room each night, and Joe and I slept on that for the rest of the week. Half-awake in the morning, it sometimes seemed as if I was in a hotel room and we were on the road with Joe's Ballroom show. Then I'd remember that we were home, and it was time to get up and start our day at the Public Theater.

Later Joe said, "I thought of my father when I was singing at The Ballroom. I got a real sense of what he'd given me, and I'd never thanked him. You never know. I'd taken it for granted. In some way I felt that this was an expression of that. It was a tribute to my father, my mother—people who gave me something without making a point of it. They left me no money. They were poor and broke at the end. I'd never expected that. But what I was given was very, very important. They gave me a heritage."

33

An Affinity for Comedy and Tragedy

One of the benefits of working at the Public Theater was that I went to all of the shows many times with Joe and over the years got to see several generations of marvelous actors in Shakespeare, often in multiple roles. And, being around for a long time, I've also had the special pleasure of seeing an actor play King Lear whom I could remember as a young Laertes in *Hamlet* (John Lithgow). Or a mature Prospero in *The Tempest* whom I could remember playing Orlando, the young swain in *As You Like It* (Raúl Juliá). Or a young actor who convincingly portrayed the old and corpulent Falstaff in *Henry IV, Part 1* who only four years later played *Hamlet* (Stacy Keach). The versatility of actors has never ceased to amaze me, and I've loved so many of their portrayals in both leading and secondary roles that I could fill this book with my memories of them.

Although the actor Kevin Kline has been acclaimed for his numerous major Shakespearean roles at the Delacorte and Public Theaters, he began in Central Park as a humble soldier in 1970's *The Wars of the Roses*, a four-part conflation of *King Henry VI* and *Richard III*. Ten years later Kevin returned to the Park in a starring role, not yet in Shakespeare as it happened, but as the Pirate King in Wilfred Leach's innovative staging of Gilbert and Sullivan's nineteenth-century operetta *The Pirates of Penzance*, in which the young lovers were played by the singer Linda Ronstadt and the teen rock 'n' roll idol, Rex Smith.

"I didn't know Gilbert and Sullivan at all," Kevin later recalled. "I went through *Pirates* and I thought, 'This is really silly, funny, wonderful stuff. It's like the Marx Brothers.' I was hooked. I decided the Pirate King is like an Errol Flynn who misses—someone who's carried away with the romantic image of being a pirate and kind of overdoes it a bit." (From an unpublished excerpt in his interview with Kenneth Turan for *Free for All*)

After *Pirates* became an unexpected hit at the Delacorte in 1980, it moved to Broadway, where Kevin won the Tony Award for Best Actor. In 1983 it was adapted as a feature film with most of the original cast. It's still a delight to watch.

This high-flying success preceded the major Shakespearean roles that Kevin played under Joe's auspices, which included Richard III, Henry V, Benedick in *Much Ado About Nothing*, the Duke of Vienna in *Measure for Measure*, King Lear, and Hamlet (on PBS Television and twice on stage)—not to mention Chekhov and Brecht. Throughout the many outdoor and indoor seasons that he appeared in this demanding repertoire, audiences were treated to his superb performances as an actor with a unique affinity for both comedy and tragedy—a quality which strongly reminded me of Joe's own similar inclinations.

In the course of a dozen years Kevin and Joe had many serious conversations about Shakespeare. Kevin acknowledged that Joe was "one of the most serious and dedicated people I know"—before talking about a different side of him.

I always think of Joe as one of the silliest people I know. Silly in the best way. In the last couple of years I've spent a lot of time with Joe, just as a friend. We were asked to do a benefit for The Acting Company. Was there something we could do together? I called Joe and he said "Well, come on over and have lunch at the house and we'll talk about it." And he had this idea—you know he loves to sing—so he said "Let's sing Stout-hearted Men." He had a couple of kazoos and he said "We'll do a kazoo solo in the middle!" We just started goofing around. We had an accompanist and we started singing it, and we were both rolling on the floor, laughing.

Give me some men who are stout-hearted men
Who will fight for the right they adore

We've always had this ability to crack each other up. He's a terrible punster, you know, and he loves a really good/bad joke. My father's the same way, and I think I have a streak of it running through me. So we just love being silly, and whenever we get together to have a serious conversation, there's always at least a major segment of the time spent in making dumb jokes or making each other laugh. (From an unpublished excerpt in his interview with Kenneth Turan for *Free for All*)

In the first rush of the success of *Pirates of Penzance*, WOR radio host Ruth Franklin discussed the production at length with Joe on her radio program, during which one can discern Joe's nimble handling of a slightly loopy interviewer:

Ruth Franklin: Well the actors I saw in your "Pirates of Penzance" were terribly good because they had pulled all the stops out.

Joe Papp: What do you mean by "pulling all the stops out"? I've heard you say that four times.

Ruth Franklin: Me? Have I said it before?

Joe Papp: You just said it—by "pulling all the stops out." Don't you think we could use a little more *reserve* on the stage from time to time?

Ruth Franklin: Well the wonderfulness of your "Pirates of Penzance" occurred because there *wasn't* any reserve—

Joe Papp: Oh yes there was.

Ruth Franklin: —because *you* pulled all the stops out.

Joe Papp: Oh no we did not pull all the stops out.

Ruth Franklin: It was an honest production—

Joe Papp: It was honest but we didn't pull all the stops out. We had reserve where it was necessary and no reserve where we didn't want it. Every performance on the stage has to have some reserve. There's no such thing as "pulling all the stops out." Otherwise you spill your guts on the stage. We don't do that.

34

Exploring Parameters

One day as I was passing the open door to Joe's office, I heard him whistling a tune from Elizabeth Swados' musical *Alice*.

This was a song that had delighted me when I first heard it a few years prior in the work's infancy, when I introduced him to Elizabeth Swados. Joe had been equally enthusiastic about her unusual talent, and now in 1980 he had just directed her musical at the Public Theater with Meryl Streep as Alice.

Joe stopped whistling when he saw me.

"What's happening with the TV adaptation of *Alice*?" he called through the doorway. "Who's working on it? I haven't seen anything thing yet."

Joe was referring to the fact that Liz Swados still needed to adapt her stage musical for a prime-time special on NBC-TV which he was going to produce after the show closed at the Public Theater. For television, *Alice* was to be a cinematically reconceived version, not a film of the stage production.

Feeling a little like the bumpkin who plays "Wall" in Shakespeare's "Pyramis and Thisbe"—because the question seemed to be addressed *through* me rather than to me—I said, "Well, probably you should have a meeting about it."

So later that week the television team that the Public Theater had engaged arrived for a meeting in Joe's office. Everyone gathered around his coffee table. The key person there was composer-lyricist Elizabeth Swados, impeccably dressed in baggy designer pants, funky sneakers, and orange and green socks.

Sitting to one side of her was the suave TV Director Emile Ardolino and on the other side the vivacious Argentinian choreographer Graciela Daniele.

Stage managers, designers, and technical staff filled the rest of the room. I was there because Joe had asked me to do a transcript of the meeting for future reference.

"O-*kay!*" Joe announced in his enthusiastic manner as everyone scrambled to settle down. I pressed the record button on the tape recorder.

There was no hint of his recent vexation—that he had learned the TV studio where *Alice* was to be filmed had to be shared at the end of each day with a news hour whose huge set occupied a quarter of the studio and couldn't be struck.

Talking rapidly, Joe started the meeting by throwing down a conceptual gauntlet.

"All right," he said. "Now the idea of the television show of *Alice* is that it's being done in a television studio. The *entire studio* will be the set, UNABASHEDLY acknowledged, but it will hold aspects of a Victorian theater with an olio curtain and there will be representations of boxes and a gallery. Sometimes this gallery will be filled with fifteen little girls in Victorian nightgowns."

Fifteen little girls in Victorian nightgowns? That was a new and outlandish idea, but there was no response to it from the staff around the coffee table except for a young costume assistant who wrote something in her notebook. Continuing with excited conviction, Joe turned to Emile Ardolino, the TV director.

"We can have a free shooting style," he said to him. "For instance, when the White Rabbit jumps over the hedge, we could stop and replay it. Or when Alice sings 'Jabberwocky'—'His vorpal sword went snicker snack'—she could be fighting a mic on a boom pole."

Throwing his arms out in the manner of an orchestra conductor about to give the downbeat for Beethoven's Fifth, Joe said, "Here's the way I see the sequence of events happening."

Because he'd directed the stage production of *Alice*, Joe knew every bell and whistle in the show, and he went through it, portraying all of the characters (Rabbit, Queen, Caterpillar, Cheshire Cat, Mad Hatter, Duchess, Mouse, etc.) with agile mimicry to make various points.

"MMMMMGRAGHHMMMMM!" Joe groaned ominously, imitating a time-warp sound effect . . . And D-O-O-W-W-N the hole Alice goes. Then *there* she is. *AAAGGHH!* She's *alone.* Then suddenly there is a little rabbit standing there. 'Have you been invited to play croquet today?'" Joe mimicked a tiny rabbit voice. Then turning to me, he asked in his normal voice, "What's the next song?"

"The Caterpillar's Raga," I said after checking the list of Liz Swados' quirky song titles that I had in hand.

Looking deferentially at Liz, Joe asked her, "Do we want to call it The Caterpillar Raga or The Caterpillar's Raga?"

"The Pillarcater's Raga!" Liz said merrily.

Finger-snapping the rhythm, Joe scatted, "The-Pillarcater's-Raga-the-Raga-caterpillar-one-is-reggae-the-other's-raga-put-that-under-the-ruggah. Yeah. Alice goes through a small door and sees a big Caterpillar."

Then, referring to the old-fashioned signs that were going to announce the scenes in the future TV production, Joe said, "Gail, what's the next olio card?"

"We seem to be at the Mushroom Sequence," I answered.

"Okay, I want to see the *effect* of the mushroom on Alice here. What it does to her, because right now we have no effect."

Rising to his feet, Joe sang, "One side will make you grow taller, the other side will make you grow smaller . . ." before pantomiming "Ooh-aah-ooh! She gets BIGGER-and-smaller. BIGGER-and-smaller. She goes through this whole thing, see? Then suddenly there she is. Aaah! And Alice says 'The other side . . . of *what?*' And that's when we hear a spooky voice saying THE *M-U-S-H . . . R-O-O-O-M . . .*"

The television team took advantage of the spooky moment to take swigs from their coffee cups before Joe continued.

"THEN SUDDDENLY Alice-finds-a-Little-House! And BANG!-CRASH! *Whizzzzz!* A-dish-comes-out-of-it-goes-past-her-face.There's-all-this-*noise*-inside-and-smoke-coming-out. She opens the door. '*WAAAH! WAAAAH!*" Joe hollered, mimicking an unruly baby in the story. "And the next thing, see, is, Alice looks, and ten messengers are there rushing in during all this tumult."

Ten messengers? Had Joe just dreamed them up? Ten messengers plus those fifteen little girls in Victorian nightgowns would have added twenty-five people to the cast! That was patently absurd, but you wouldn't have guessed it looking at the disconcerted faces around the coffee table. Everyone had been transfixed by Joe's energetic mimicry and the way he called out the action of the scenes with such assurance. No one seemed to understand that his free-wheeling ideas weren't literal instructions to them but were simply meant to get the television adaptation of *Alice* unstuck and moving forward.

After two more antic hours, the meeting adjourned with Liz Swados and me the only ones left in Joe's office. Sunk deep in the sofa cushions with her long hair falling below her waist, twenty-nine-year-old Liz looked like an older, careworn version of Alice—although the expression on her face, as she looked at Joe at this moment, was more like that of a cross-eyed bird in front of a snake charmer.

Taking this in, Joe felt the need to set her mind at ease.

"You know me, Liz," he said to her reassuringly. "I have to work through a process all the time on everything. I have to go to an extreme idea before I come in to something that's workable, right? I have to fulfill the feeling. I have to take it to its optimum or to its depth. I have to go to *death* to come back again, to really understand it. I have to explore the parameters before I make a decision about the detail."

"Yes, I'm aware of that," Liz said in a small, matter-of-fact tone of voice.

"So I go *way* out and come back in," Joe continued. "I always do that, and, as you saw, people here get very nervous. They think *that's* my decision, and *that's* the end, and *that's* what it's going to be, and suddenly there's no appeal. But it isn't. It's just something I have to go through. Sometimes in the middle of talking, we can be gathered together, like we are right now and talking, and I get the idea—and change my mind."

In the long process of creating the TV version of *Alice*, one of my very favorite things in the stage version got cut. This was Meryl Streep's instantaneous and convincing transformation, without the help of costume or lighting changes, from the child Alice into Lewis Carroll's Humpty Dumpty, who is a large talking egg. When I saw her do that, it confirmed my belief that she could act *anything* brilliantly, as indeed she has throughout her remarkably diverse stage and film career. Lucky audiences at the Delacorte and Public Theaters have seen her unforgettable portrayals as Kate in *The Taming of the Shrew*, Isabella in *Measure for Measure*, Princess Katherine in *Henry V*, as well as in plays by Anton Chekhov, Sir Arthur Wing Pinero, Bertolt Brecht, Thomas Babe, and a film by David Hare.

Several months after the production meeting in Joe's office, when the filming of *Alice* was about to begin in the television studio, the stage manager appeared before us.

"Fifteen nightgowns for little girls have been delivered backstage," he announced. "Who are they for and what should I do with them?"

Ho-ho, I thought to myself. Joe had only himself to blame for these costumes for children who never existed in the show. You couldn't fault the note-taking costume assistant at that early meeting in his office. How was she supposed to know that Joe was merely "exploring parameters" when he talked about fifteen little girls in Victorian nightdresses?

The stage manager waited for an answer. After a pause Joe said, with sphinxlike authority, "Okay. Hold on to them in case they're needed."

Long before this, I had finished the transcript of that early production meeting that Joe had asked me to do, but neither Joe nor anyone else ever had the slightest interest in looking at it.

Forty years later, the first and only use of that transcript has been to reproduce for the purpose of this chapter some of the sounds that Joe felt compelled to make to get the television adaptation of *Alice* moving forward.

35

Feuding with Critics

I look back in amazement at Joe's feuds with the drama critics of the *New York Times*, which attained in my opinion a magnitude worthy of Sherlock Holmes pitted against Professor Moriarty, or Batman against the Joker.

It would be hard to imagine any theater producer or artistic director today wading into such fierce journalistic battles with critics as Joe did back then, but in his way of thinking the Public Theater's very survival and everything it stood for, including the future of playwrights, was at stake.

Among the performing arts in New York City, theater has always been notably dependent on press reviews to attract audiences. For many years Brooks Atkinson's theater reviews published in the *New York Times* had been preeminent in a field of ten metropolitan newspapers covering new plays and musicals. The *Times'* closest competitor was the *New York Herald-Tribune*, where Walter Kerr had been its theater reviewer since 1951.

All of this began to change in 1962 when the city's newspaper unions representing 17,000 workers went on strike for 114 days to protest low wages and the automation of the industry. They went on strike again in 1965, this time for 140 days. As a result of these two events, one newspaper after another went out of business, until New York City's daily newspapers had been reduced from ten to just three: the *New York Times*, the *New York Post*, and the *New York Daily News*.

The impact on the theater was significant. After the *New York Herald-Tribune* folded in 1966, the *Times* hired its drama critic, Walter Kerr. His opinion, in a field stripped of serious competition, now became as potentially deadly to the survival of a new play or musical in New York City as Octavius Caesar and Marc Antony deciding the live-or-die fates of their fellow Romans on a list, with Antony saying, in the words of Shakespeare, "These many, then, shall die; their names are pricked."

Variety had once called Walter Kerr "the lead slugger among the review-ers for the New York dailies." The fact that he was also a legendary wit and wordsmith made his negative verdicts all the more formidable because in deflating the value of what he didn't like or didn't understand in the the-ater, his mischievous reviews had always been wickedly fun to read. He was, not-so-parenthetically, the same critic who had opposed free Shakespeare in Central Park, an issue that Joe had previously debated with him in the pages of the *Tribune*.

Mr. Kerr's first major piece about the Public Theater in the *Times* was a purported overview of its first two seasons called "Were You There All the Time?" (*New York Times*, Sunday, March 30, 1969).

When I read it, I was appalled to see that his overview failed to mention three important productions: *Hair*, the groundbreaking rock musical by Gerome Ragni, James Rado, and Galt MacDermot; Charles Gordone's *No Place To Be Somebody*, which had won the first Pulitzer Prize for a Black playwright; and Václav Havel's *The Memorandum*, which had won an Obie for Best Foreign Play. How in God's name, I wondered, could a responsible critic omit these three acclaimed new productions from an evaluation of the Public's first two seasons? And how could a responsible critic fail to mention that Joe had produced new works by seven Black playwrights (Kerr's only nod to this being a tepid sentence alluding to "the yet inconclusive work of Adrienne Kennedy.")?

Mad as hell, Joe banged out an angry riposte to Kerr on his Remington Standard, titled "Walter Kerr Never Liked Me (Joe Papp's Complaint)." It began:

Walter Kerr never liked me. Please don't ask me to prove it. I can't. But I was always suspect to this critic. The "free bit" and all just didn't seem to sit right with him. All I know is that when I began to read his column in the *New York Times* headlined "Were You There All The Time?"—and I saw the phrase "Mr. Papp's Public Theater, *which we all wish well*"—I thought OI VAY [oh my], here it comes. As my father used to say "From such well-wishers, *mir ken geharget veren*" [one could get killed]. And Mr. Kerr proceeded to work us over with his journalistic rubber hose—the innuendo, the sluro, the double reverso.

Several more angry pages followed before Joe took a break to call Seymour Peck, the astute and kindly Sunday Drama Editor of the *Times*, under whose aegis Kerr's article had appeared, to let him know that he was writing a piece in response to it.

Back at his typewriter, Joe resumed:

To examine why Mr. Kerr felt compelled to do a hatchet job on "Joe Papp's Public Theater, WHICH WE ALL WISH WELL" might shed some light on his ambiguous feelings.

We can approach the examination with a sociological postulation: A critic's attitude toward the theater does not originate in a vacuum, nor do his values operate in a void. They are shaped in a specific milieu, and in Mr. Kerr's case, that milieu happens to be the commercial theater, Broadway . . . The Off-Broadway movement was of little interest to Mr. Kerr. It took Brooks Atkinson, former *New York Times* critic, to break the rule which confined first-string crit-ics to the Times Square area. (I suppose part of the reason was to make it easy for the critic on opening nights to walk over to the Times to write his review.) But Mr. Kerr would not go downtown for anything.

The world has changed, and although Mr. Kerr now manages to cover plays in out-of-the-way places, apparently he is still not at home in the milieu. This is a world which he evidently resists and resents, and one which he seems to wish would somehow disappear. One can detect his discomfort and alienation . . . with changes that have taken place in the theater—particularly those changes which insist that the theater is not merely a showcase for hits but a continuous expression of ideas, served in a particular way by particular groups at a particu-lar time in history.

This version included Joe's lengthy faux-sardonic rebuttals to Kerr's criti-cisms of the plays. He then messengered it to Sy Peck, impatient to see it in print as soon as possible.

Later that day he and Sy Peck talked on the phone again after which Joe did a rewrite, making the same points in fewer words and adding a new final paragraph:

This is not an attack on Mr. Kerr's integrity, his stylistic gifts and his right to call them as he sees them. But those of us who strive to create the products of the theater have the right to expect courtesy, responsibility and concern from those who make their living off these efforts. The framework of the theater has changed and the criteria must undergo changes as well.

He messengered the rewritten response to Sy Peck with a covering note:

Dear Sy,

Let me put in writing what I said to you on the telephone. Walter Kerr is incapable of objective evaluation of new works. The Public Theater is constantly engaged in producing new plays which he constantly baits and sneers away. This has become intolerable and in all conscience to the new writers I cannot permit the executioner Kerr to enter our house. Joe

The *Times* finally published it with the title "How Shall A Critic Judge?" on Sunday, April 30—marking not the end but the beginning of Joe's struggle against Walter Kerr's supercilious (and newly monopolistic) put-downs of the diverse and talented work that Joe chose to produce at the Public Theater.

Over the course of the seventeen years that Kerr held sway at the *Times*, Joe converted his initial rage about Kerr's reviews into a significant advocacy for new and previously disregarded voices in the theater. In these early days, however, he just wanted to keep the man away from the Public Theater, and two years later he didn't consult with anyone before writing directly to Walter Kerr at his Spanish-Tudor castle overlooking Long Island Sound in Larchmont, New York:

Dear Mr. Kerr:

The game playing is over. It is quite clear to me what you are intent on doing, consciously or otherwise, and this is to notify you that you are not welcome at the Public Theater for any of our new presentations. My conscience does not permit me to allow you to annihilate young writers who are the mainstay of this theater. So please stay away. Don't come. Keep out. I don't want you here. You are incapable of judging and evaluating new works.

Joseph Papp

Of course, there was no way that Joe could prevent Walter Kerr from reviewing plays at the Public Theater. If Kerr wasn't on the free press list, he could simply buy a ticket.

The fundamental problem here was the new influence that the *Times* critic wielded due to the newspaper's unique stranglehold on the fortunes of theater in New York City after the calamitous newspaper strike had removed much of its competition.

As the Public Theater's producer, Joe couldn't take issue with every unreasonable review that made him angry because his job was to deal with the artists affected by such a review and to plan the strategy necessary to keep a wounded show running with enough audiences throughout its limited eight-week engagement.

However, Joe wasn't constitutionally disposed to keep his grievances secret, and so there were, I admit, a few times when I saw his anger override his professional decorum. One of them was his necktie-grabbing clutch on *New York Magazine*'s John Simon in the lobby of the Public Theater. I forget which play Simon hadn't liked, but Joe's move had been provoked by one of Simon's anti-woman, anti-gay, anti-Black, or anti-Semitic remarks, which, it seemed to me, erupted from his reviews like Dr. Strangelove's notoriously uncontrollable Nazi-saluting arm in the Kubrick film.

Joe's most bellicose interaction with a critic was with the *New York Times*' Clive Barnes about his disrespectful review of David Rabe's *In the Boom Boom Room* with which Joe opened his first season as producer of Lincoln Center Theater in 1973. Before the critics came to see it, Rabe's play about the soul of a go-go dancer had had a difficult launch, with firings and Joe taking over its direction two weeks before the opening.

In those days, long before the Internet, to get advance notice of the *Times* review we hired a man in the newspaper's Composing Room to read it to us over a speakerphone before the papers hit the newsstands. And so, honoring this time-encrusted tradition, after the show a few of us had gathered in the glass-walled Patron's Lounge in the Beaumont Theater lobby, where we listened to the Composing Room man read Barnes' snarky opinion that "*Boom Boom Room* is full of chic filth . . . Let us hope the Shakespeare Festival will have better luck next time. There is nowhere to go but up."

Outraged, Joe immediately called Barnes at home and began cursing his disrespectful review with a stream of obscenities which, if you didn't listen too closely to them, had the Falstaffian fluency of archaic insults akin to "Fusty nut with no kernel" or "Clod of wayward marl," though that isn't what he said.

Meantime we got word about other reviews coming in that said the play was a "near-masterpiece" and a "strikingly staged, magnificent exploration into a woman's soul."

Barnes was so angry at Joe about his phone call that, as he confessed to *New Yorker* writer Phillip Hamburger, he planned to expunge Joe's name as producer in all of his reviews of the Public Theater's productions.

Living with him, I knew that Joe's heart, mind, and even the health of his body were bound to the two theaters that he had created—the Delacorte Theater in Central Park and the Public Theater in Greenwich Village. A "killing" critic was therefore a multidimensional threat. Associating his own mortality with the fate of the socially driven Public Theater when it was under what he experienced as repeated attacks, Joe sought a principle for its continuity, writing in a note to himself: "I know why despite failures we stay afloat. Whether it is conscious or not, it is understood in some unspoken way that the Public Theater has meaning over and above the production of a single play . . . Rather than decrease the importance of a particular play, this view connects it with a life process, and there's nothing more important than that."

In the end, Joe outlasted eight *New York Times* drama critics: Brooks Atkinson (whom he greatly respected), Howard Taubman, Stanley Kauffmann, Walter Kerr, Clive Barnes, Mel Gussow, Richard Eder, and Frank Rich.

Managing editor Arthur Gelb deserves a special place of honor on the list because it was Gelb's personal coverage of a half-rained-out performance of *The Taming of the Shrew* at the East River Amphitheater in 1956 that, with the added support of Brooks Atkinson, brought the first favorable attention of the *Times* to the struggling New York Shakespeare Festival. Unlike Joe's stormy interactions with Kerr and Barnes, he always enjoyed a cordial relationship with Arthur Gelb, as well as with Abe Rosenthal, the executive editor of the *Times*. As different in personality as Joe and these two men were, the three of them had a personal rapport that lasted throughout their lifetimes.

Born in the early 1920s, they were all sons of Jewish immigrant parents—Rosenthal's from Byelorussia, Gelb's from a Czech border town in today's Ukraine, and Joe's from Kielce, Poland and Kovno, Lithuania. They were each deeply attached to New York City whether by birth or residency; and they cared passionately about the world. As a result, Joe didn't hesitate to complain to Arthur Gelb about the newspaper's drama critics, as in a letter to him in 1980 excoriating Walter Kerr for his review of Wallace Shawn's *Marie and Bruce* at the Public Theater: "He missed Beckett by a mile and Pinter too . . . He absolutely missed Wally Shawn's play. Where is the Times' culture? Where is the alert eye and mind in your Drama Department that is capable of recognizing real writing talent? Kerr's eye is dim and his mind is made up of old hairy roots of some other time. Joe."

I sometimes felt like the fly-on-the-wall of Joe's feuds with the critics because he'd show me the different drafts of his rebuttals to them, and I'd follow their transformations from pages of unbridled indignation to publishable articles.

In the 1980s some critics began to publish think pieces "draped around a phantom authority" in which they unloaded their concerns about Joe's malfeasances. Their sweeping allegations ranged from Joe's supposed espousal of "a misguided esthetic philosophy" to his ostensible complicity in "the malign effects of celebrity." I groaned when I read them because it always upset me to read outrageous criticisms of Joe. I imagine it's like seeing your loved one under fire in a political campaign. Though one may seethe with personal outrage about it, being related to the candidate, or in my case the producer, you have to learn to handle it.

Since I had seen Joe go "inscrutable" when someone around him became overly incensed about a bad or stupid review, I usually refrained from making intemperate remarks about the critics. But there was one morning at home when I couldn't help myself as I finished reading a critic's review of Caryl Churchill's *Fen* at the Public Theater, a play that had deeply moved me.

"I can't *believe* this!" I exclaimed to Joe at the breakfast table, knuckle-rapping the offending paragraph I'd just read. "He doesn't get the point of the *generational tableaux* at the end of her play! That there's an important generation *MISSING* in the picture! And it's the WOMAN! How in God's name could he NOT have *SEEN* that?"

"Yes," Joe said quietly. "I noticed that."

Generally, however, I was careful not to let my own anger interfere with Joe's quarrelsome responses as they began to flow from his pen. Joe was superbly equipped for the task. He had the essential tough skin to answer apocalyptic charges against him with think pieces of his own, fueling the life in print of these so-called controversies that certain critics liked to stir up. Although I was angry about them at first, in time I realized that they actually served everyone's purpose: the critics and their publications because readers were always interested in anything by or about Joe; and Joe because they gave him a forum for his ideas and kept the Public Theater in the public eye.

Besides, it simply wasn't in Joe's DNA to let a challenge go unanswered.

36

In the Public Eye

Having come of age in the 1950s, I thought that particular decade had to be the bottom of the barrel in denying decent recognition to women in public and private life. But since we've recently reached a new low in that respect in the early twenty-first century, I thought I'd look back to the way it used to be in the 1970s and 1980s expecting to find a more enlightened reflection, based on my own experience. In this case, however, memory did not serve and I was in for a surprise.

In 1978 *Working Woman Magazine* interviewed me and five other women who it said had "succeeded in business without really trying to dress for it." The article ran two pictures of me at work in my office. One showed me on the phone, the other reading a script. The caption for both was: "Merrifield takes special pride in her oxford riding boots from Miller's, N.Y."

Back then I was always identified as Joe Papp's "fourth wife." Joe didn't like this any more than I did, but the numbering of a man's wives added interest to his biography, whereas a wife so numbered merely achieved the fleeting status of a trophy scalp, unless she was already famous or wealthy herself.

Negative clichés popped up in unexpected places. *Parade Magazine*, reporting Joe's effort in the eighties to raise money from the Board of Education, wrote: "He's been sweet-talking the Mayor, too. You suspect Papp can sweet-talk anyone. Except maybe his wives. He's had four of them."

Of course he still had one of them, me, to whom he'd been happily married for ten years. But no doubt mentioning a happy marriage would have put a crimp on the item's trophy-scalp humor.

I was grateful to the journalist Patricia Bosworth who interviewed me through a different lens in *Working Woman* seven years after the magazine had spotlighted my boots. In her article in the November 1985 issue ("Gail Merrifield: New York Theater World's Best Kept Secret"), she wrote, "This season looks exceptionally promising, which reflects Gail Merrifield's wide-ranging interests and fresh approach to theater." Bosworth observed that when the *New York Times* had profiled Joe, there were descriptions of "his high visibility, his fund-raising techniques, his power as a culturebroker in America—but no mention of Gail Merrifield's contribution. When asked if she resented this, Gail laughs. 'My style is different than Joe's. He is definitely a public personality; I'm private about what I do. And I happen to like it that way.' . . . More and more of their life together seems public. Even the family's annual Passover seder (Papp has 5 children by previous marriages) was filmed by a TV crew for the MacNeil-Lehrer News Hour. Gail isn't complaining though. 'This is a one-of-a-kind job and I love it.'"

Three months before Bosworth's article appeared, Joe was interviewed for a "Close Up" in the *Daily News*. Feeling good about my work with writers, he asked me to join him. When I arrived at his office, I could see that the reporter was pressing Joe for personal stuff that he didn't want to talk about, and it came through in the story.

"The 23-time Tony Award winner has no desire to elaborate on his personal life. He ticks off the names and ages of his five grown children, but when asked about their mothers, barks: 'I'm not gonna break it down for you.'"

So Joe was already annoyed when I joined them, and even though his intention had been to say positive things about my role as head of the Play Department, the reporter's insinuating questions were now eliciting gruff responses from him.

Accordingly, in the article the *Daily News* reporter wrote: "Papp says, 'I can select plays, but she finds them.' Merrifield is in his office, and as if to put their professional relationship in perspective, Papp notes, 'She's an employee: I'm the boss here.'"

This was, of course, a cringe-worthy remark that was awful to see in print. It falsely implied a reductive attitude toward me that Joe never had and that I didn't deserve. I blamed the scandal-seeking reporter for provoking it.

37

"The Great Theater Massacre of 1982"

New York City remembered the appalling act of corporate vandalism that had demolished the magnificent Pennsylvania Station in 1963. The civic outrage and trauma caused by the destruction of that world-famous architectural jewel gave rise to the creation of the Landmarks Preservation Commission in 1965 and new laws protecting the city's historic buildings.

However, nineteen years later, in 1982, New Yorkers were again threatened with another irresponsible destruction of the city's heritage, this time of priceless theaters in the heart of historic Broadway to make way for a huge, fifty-story Portman-Marriott Hotel. Several theaters had already been bulldozed to clear the site for it. Scheduled next for demolition were the Helen Hayes Theater on West 46th Street and the Morosco Theater on West 45th Street. But strong public opposition had been mounted by citizen, architectural, and cultural groups who intervened with lawsuits, petitions, and lobbying efforts in city, state, and federal corridors of power to stop it.

In 1982 the last-ditch effort of these preservationist groups was focused on the Morosco Theater, a unique dramatic house for plays because it had "an intimacy not found in new theaters." Built in 1917, the Morosco's acoustics were like a Stradivarius instrument, the irreplaceable product of the materials and workmanship of a bygone era that had enriched the premieres of prize-winning American plays by Eugene O'Neill, Arthur Miller, Tennessee Williams, Thornton Wilder, Edward Albee, and others.

"It was almost a perfect house," actress Colleen Dewhurst said, "where you could knit the whole audience into one person and hold them like in a womb."

Although various groups had been campaigning to save the Morosco and Helen Hayes Theaters, unfortunately Joe didn't learn about the theaters' impending demolition until the chances were very slim for modifying a real estate deal that had already been wrapped up at New York's own City Hall, and in Albany, Atlanta, and Washington, D.C., over the previous years. Joe nevertheless decided to join the fight to save them, establishing a headquarters at the Piccadilly Hotel, a block from the Morosco, with a staff from the Public Theater and other organizations.

He recruited a squad of volunteer "deputies" to handle action on the street, as well as in the empty lot next to the Morosco Theater where a huge wrecking machine was positioned and ready to go into action. He encouraged protesters to occupy the lot, telling them, "We'll have an honor guard of fifty people on duty at all times so they won't be able to start demolition in the middle of the night. We'll lie in front of the demolition equipment if necessary."

Many staff people, including me, slept in chairs at the Piccadilly Hotel on readiness alert.

Meanwhile, Joe organized readings of the famous plays that had premiered at the Morosco, presenting them on an outdoor platform on the street in front of the theater. Their famous casts stopped pedestrians dead in their tracks as they recognized actors like Colleen Dewhurst, Jason Robards, Irene Worth, and Estelle Parsons performing them.

These readings went on for more than a week. Before and after them Joe stood at a microphone urging passersby to sign a petition to Mayor Edward Koch demanding that the hotel chain's Atlanta-based architect, John Portman, build *over*, rather than demolish, the Morosco Theater, an alternative supported by a coalition of architects trying to save the playhouse.

However, John Portman, like Robert Moses, refused to see or even speak to Joe, being unwilling to reconsider any aspect of his paint-by-numbers tropical atrium hotel. Mr. Portman had been successful in other states and cities with his template for hotels featuring glass elevators, sunken cocktail banquettes, and rotating rooftop restaurants. But in Manhattan's historic Broadway district, where the lighted marquees of theaters had welcomed people to its narrow streets and slender sidewalks, there was now the threat of them being

Staff assistant Emmett Foster, me, and Joe demonstrating against
the demolition of the irreplaceable Morosco Theater in 1982.
Papp Estate

replaced by the street-level eyesores of the fortress hotel's blank exterior wall and load-in ramps. An eleventh-hour petition to City Hall to save the theaters signed by 150,000 people was to no avail because every legal challenge had already been defeated in the lower courts. At the last minute, U.S. Supreme Court Justice Thurgood Marshall granted a temporary stay of the demolition, but it was only good through the weekend.

At 10:45 a.m. on Monday, March 22, a large crowd gathered on West 45th Street as Joe spoke to them over loudspeakers that could be heard many blocks away.

"I'll tell you frankly," he said, his voice booming eerily in the streets, "these theaters are going to come down. The Supreme Court has lifted the stay."

Cries of anger met his announcement from New York City's artistic and civic community which now had to face the final hours of a long fight they had lost.

I wondered how Joe was going to lead this angry and crestfallen crowd that could no longer dream of snatching victory from the jaws of defeat.

What he did was to orchestrate a classic act of civil disobedience. Two hundred prominent citizens—including famous actors, directors, and writers—swarmed onto the lot next to the Morosco Theater and stood in the way of the monstrous wrecking machine parked next to its eastern wall. When ordered by the police to leave, they refused. Standing among them Joe led chants of "Shame on Koch!" through a bullhorn.

But that wasn't all. He had worked it out with city police that after the civilly disobedient protesters on the lot had been arrested, loaded into the paddy wagons waiting for them on West 45th Street, and booked at the precinct, they'd all be permitted to return to 45th Street to bear witness to the shameful destruction.

Joe also made sure that the arrests of New York's famous citizens would be televised and that the scheduled demolition would be sufficiently delayed by their resistance so that it would take place at the optimum time for television and press coverage.

As planned, the demolition of the Morosco Theater saturated national television news and front pages across the country with pictures of the theater's proscenium and crystal chandeliers crashing down in clouds of dust and shattered glass.

Joe angrily described the scene in radio interviews that day:

On Monday, March 22, 1982, a 40-ton Caterpillar Traxcavator stood poised before the east wall of the now demolished Morosco Theater. As spectators looked on in horror, this monster machine—named "Godzilla"—opened its massive jaws and rammed its 80,000 pounds against the building. Women screamed, a Police Lieutenant wept. Others stood in shock—No . . . No . . . It was a moment in life that those who bore witness will never forget!

A few hours later "Godzilla" struck again, chewing a 30-foot hole through the backstage wall of the beautiful Helen Hayes Theater. The atrocity was now complete. Two great New York theaters had fallen.

It was a wiping out of a whole tradition. Portman's hotel, which could have been built over the theaters, should not have been built at the expense of these two landmark treasures, which had to do with the roots of the city. When we start tearing ourselves out by the roots, what have we got? These big, fat, ugly buildings that don't mean anything and destroy the whole nature of a particular environment.

I know it will not happen again. I think it'll be a terrible political risk for anybody that's running the City. I think they'll think twice. The Landmarks Commission will think twice. The City Planning Commission will think twice. The Mayor of New York will think twice.

That's all we wanted to do. Think twice.

38

A Gondolier in Brooklyn

At the beginning of 1979, during a short-lived thaw in the Cold War, Joe wrote to the Soviet Union Minister of Culture, Pyotr Nilovich Demichev, proposing a joint production of *A Chorus Line* with American and Russian dancers that would tour Moscow, Leningrad, and Kiev. It was no accident that Joe's proposal coincided with the upcoming Olympics to be held in Moscow in 1980, as well as with the ratification of the S.A.L.T. II Agreement between the United States and the U.S.S.R., which limited nuclear weapons on missiles.

The Minister of Culture, an important figure who was a member of President Leonid Brezhnev's Politburo, responded very favorably to Joe's letter, inviting him (and me) to the Soviet Union as his guests to discuss the proposal.

At home I said to Joe, "I'm surprised I'm included in the invitation. Why do you suppose that is?"

"Because you're my wife, that's why," Joe said, fully aware that his faux-gruff answer would annoy me since he knew how sensitive I was about privileges based on "wifedom" and my touchiness on the subject always amused him.

"No, I mean it," I protested.

"Well maybe the Kremlin has found out you're head of the Play Department," he joked.

I rolled my eyes. "C'mon, it's a serious question."

"Why not?" Joe said. "They actually value that sort of thing."

I experienced our long flight to Moscow in May 1979 with the composure of a person who finds herself slung athwart a winged Tyrannosaurus Rex on *Walpurgisnacht*. As always, Joe was sympathetic to my airborne terror and tried to divert me from it. Before we landed I slapped cold water on my face, then stepped out with Joe from the Aeroflot jet into the frosty air of Moscow, where the immense "MOCKBA" sign looming over Sheremetyevo International Airport afforded me a beginner's lesson in the Cyrillic alphabet.

Two men and a woman bundled in winter coats stood at the bottom of the stairway holding flowers and a bottle of vodka to welcome us to Russia's arctic springtime. Flashing credentials, they cleared us through customs in a very rapid manner by which time Joe and I learned that we were a "delegation." A short while later the same group checked us into the Sovietskaya Hotel, a huge establishment decorated in lavish Czarist-imperial style.

"It was Stalin's favorite" they told us with a knowing wink. At that time, it was the only hotel in Moscow where you were able to get room service.

"We may be the only Americans here," Joe whispered to me.

The next day a shiny black government car drove us to our appointment at the Ministry of Culture, where Deputy Minister Georgi A. Ivanov received us in a large, wood-paneled office on behalf of the minister who was out of the country. After Joe recapitulated his proposal about the joint Russian-American tour of *A Chorus Line*, he brought up a controversial aspect of it.

"I realize full well that homosexuality is a forbidden subject in your country," he told the Deputy Minister in his usual forthright manner. "However *A Chorus Line* is not about homosexuality. It's a play about dancers trying to get a job. It's just that homosexuality in the particular work is a *fact* of life. Here's a case in point that I think we'll have to deal with."

For Joe, nothing was ever pro forma. No matter where or with whom we found ourselves—whether in an elevator with a stranger or in a meeting room with an officeholder—he always needed to get through to the essence of things, often pushing questions past the point of comfort.

I never ceased to be startled by this propensity of his. Out of the blue Joe might say to a difficult reporter who was interviewing him, "So this contumelious attitude of yours towards me is because you hated your father, is it?"

Joe's political straight-talking was equally guileless. For example, when we met the Cuban Minister of Culture, Armando Hart Davalos in his office in Havana in 1984, Joe had no sooner shaken the hand of this leading figure in the Cuban Revolution against the Batista dictatorship, than he said, like a blunt-speaking fellow, "I'm concerned about ideological control in Cuba."

Here we go again, I thought, but to my surprise the Cuban Minister of Culture was seriously enchanted.

"We're trying to freshen things up a bit and provide more cultural opportunity," he told Joe, offering him a choice cigar from his humidor.

On our trip to the Soviet Union in 1979 I couldn't imagine how the deputy to the Minister of Culture, a high-ranking commissar, would respond to Joe raising the explosive subject of homosexuality in *A Chorus Line*. After all, it was still classified as a crime in the U.S.S.R. He was attentive, however, considered it for a moment, then wagged one hand in a no-problem gesture, and said to Joe, "Horo*sha*. [Fine] It's dealable." He was following the lead of his überboss, the Minister of Culture, who had strongly favored Joe's proposal.

During our stay in Moscow, we assumed that our deluxe room at the Sovietskaya Hotel was bugged so we turned up the volume of the music on Radio Moskva whenever we felt the need to talk confidentially.

Whispering like spooks in a graveyard, Joe and I discussed the situation of a Jewish director, the former head of a Moscow theater, who had been demoted to a black box in the suburbs because, his colleagues told us, he'd gotten "on the wrong side" of an anti-Semitic party functionary.

The next morning, as sunlight filtered through the heavy lace curtains in our room, Joe seemed restless. He had never been able to tolerate the feeling of being closed in, and in 1979 the atmosphere of Stalin's favorite hotel felt decidedly claustrophobic, with dour matrons stationed at desks on every floor to keep track of the comings and goings of the hotel guests.

I had just pushed back the curtains in our room to let in more light when Joe said to me, "Start packing. We have to get out of here."

He was in one of his headstrong don't-ask-me-why moods as he swept his wallet and change off the top of the flame mahogany dresser in preparation for leaving, but then froze as if possessed by a dybbuk.

In a voice that was recklessly audible in our bugged room, he said, "Here I am, in an anti-Semitic country where everything is controlled by the government . . ."

I immediately lunged for the radio on our bedside table to turn up the volume on the music being broadcast by Radio Moskva. Underneath the deafening sound that now filled the room, I could just barely make out Joe saying ". . . by the government and I know that there's repression, that ideas aren't tolerated, that certain kinds of demands are made on individuals which I couldn't survive . . ."

Aggravated by a sense of imminent danger, Joe's speech had lost its usual crispness and he was breathing heavily. I had never seen him this way before. During the next feverish minutes, I sat beside him on the edge of the bed as he mumbled through the story about his father's flight on foot through the forests of Poland and Germany to escape conscription into Czar Nicholas II's army . . . I heard him saying something about the great actor Solomon Mikhoels, the head of the Moscow State Jewish Theater, who had been murdered on Stalin's orders in 1948. Throughout this disjointed stream of consciousness, I listened and held Joe's hand.

When it ended as abruptly as it had begun, I turned down the deafening volume of the radio.

After a pause in the suddenly quiet room, Joe said to me, "Guess what they were playing?"

"I don't know," I replied. "I wasn't really paying attention to the music."

"American songs!" Joe exclaimed. Then he started humming a snatch from each one as he wrote their titles on a Sovietskaya memo pad:

> *If I Were a Rich Man*
> *Pennsylvania Six-Five-Oh*
> *San Francisco, Open Your Golden Gate*
> *Hold That Tiger*
> *I'll Be Loving You Always*
> *Sing Sing Sing*

"They also played *Piccolino*," he said and sang it to me.

> By the Adriatic waters
> Venetian sons and daughters
> are strumming a new tune
> upon their guitars.

It was written by a Latin,
a gondolier who sat in
his home out in Brooklyn
and gazed at the stars.

I laughed. "Where did you learn that one?"

"It's an Irving Berlin song from the Astaire and Rogers movie *Top Hat*," Joe said. "I saw it as a boy in Brooklyn in 1935. I remember the date because it was the year after my bar mitzvah." Miraculously he'd also remembered the lyrics.

We ate a light supper in the hotel's restaurant that night before going to a play at the innovative Taganka Theater. Usually we didn't drink before the theater, but in the aftermath of the personal drama that had transpired that morning in our hotel room, tonight seemed to call for a relaxation of that practice, and we ordered four straight shots of vodka, two each.

39

A Musical I Wish We'd Done

Like other high-achieving people, Joe was able to compartmentalize himself and could tune out distractions when the need arose. I felt this had figured in his attraction to a comedy we saw in Leningrad called *The Nest of the Woodgrouse*. The Nest in the title was the troubled, unlistened-to family of a Russian diplomat, who was the title's Woodgrouse, "an animal that goes deaf during mating." The playwright, Viktor Rozov, invited us for dinner at his home in Moscow, where we joined his wife and adult children at the table. Afterward, back at the hotel, Joe said to me, "Did you see that? Rozov is just like the character in his play! He didn't listen to any of them at dinner!"

Joe was so keen on *Woodgrouse* that he had it translated and then directed it at the Public Theater with Eli Wallach perfectly cast as the attentive diplomat but tuned-out paterfamilias.

In Moscow we also met with Andrei Voznesensky—the great poet of the post-Stalin era famous for declaiming his works "in sports stadiums to overflow crowds." With a sly half-smile, Voznesensky told us, in English, that he had written a rock opera called *Juno and Avos*.

"It's a very sad love story between a Russian naval explorer and the Spanish Governor's daughter in California," he said. "Alexei Rybnikov has done the music. You must hear the recording."

Voznesensky invited us to an evening party at his *dacha* in the wooded outskirts of Moscow. By the time Joe and I arrived, the playwrights, actors, and directors converging at his cottage had transformed it into *La Bohème*'s Café Momus, replete with camaraderie, big-voiced hilarity, emotive toasts, and a bottle of Russian red wine on the country table.

Oleg Yefremov, the tall, charismatic actor-director of the Moscow Art Theater, greeted us warmly, as did Yuri Lyubimov, the founder of the Taganka Theater, who wore a red bandana around his neck. Somewhere in the tumultuous room a deep male voice thundered, *"Za-NÁ-shoo-DRÓO-zhboo!"* (To our friendship).

Later that evening Joe surprised everyone by singing "The Internationale," the anthem of the world socialist movement ("Arise, ye prisoners of starvation! Arise, ye wretched of the earth!")—it being one of Joe's idiosyncrasies that he always knew every refrain and stanza of any song he sang be it "Tit Willow," "The "Star Spangled Banner" or, as now, "The Internationale."

When Joe and I returned to New York, the *Times* sent its Off-Broadway critic, Mel Gussow, to the Public Theater to interview us together about our trip to the U.S.S.R. After an hour of nonstop exposition and questions, Joe fell silent for a moment to light up a Montecristo No. 2.

"Let's see," he said to Gussow, studying his cigar like Yorick's skull. "What else do I have to tell you about *Rossiya*? We saw three to four plays a day for ten days. I fell asleep during *Dead Souls* at one theater in Moscow. So did Gail and so did the translator. We all nodded off. I said let's get out of here! That was the *only* time I nodded off during a performance there."

Joe turned to me.

"Let's put that Russian record on. Can you play a little bit?"

He explained to Gussow: "This is a young Russian composer who's working with the poet Voznesensky. He's into a kind of rock and a Byzantine sound. It's Byzantine rock and I'm interested in doing it."

The chance to hear a bit of this thrilling Russian rock opera again would be the most exciting moment of my day. As I began to search for it among the LP records stacked on the floor beside Joe's desk, he said to me, "Gail, who did the composer Rybnikov say was his greatest influence?"

"Pink Floyd," I answered from the floor.

"Yes, Pink Floyd he said he liked best of all," Joe averred to Gussow. "He was a very serious composer. Studied at the academy under—Gail, who is that great Russian composer, contemporary—?"

"Khatchaturian," I replied, seated now on the carpet.

"Yes, Khatchaturian," Joe affirmed, "but he broke away from that." At last I found the LP record of *Juno and Avos*—its title being the names of the Russian naval explorer's ships in the story.

"We had a marvelous lunch with Rybnikov and his family at their apartment in Moscow," Joe continued. "Gail, what was that wonderful dish they served us?"

"Boiled garlic," I said, sliding the Russian record out of its sleeve.

"Boiled garlic!" Joe told Gussow. "But it was delicious and so sweet."

I started *Juno and Avos* on the record player.

It's hard for me to do justice to the symphonic tsunami that Alexei Rybnikov's magnificent music unleashed in Joe's office at that moment: of supersonic electric guitars set against the plangent reverberations of Gregorian chants . . . of nasally Machiavellian singspiel recounting narrative twists of the tragic story . . . of coloratura orgasms piercing the sonic booms of an all-bass Russian male chorus.

If anyone in the vicinity of Joe's office felt in a slump that afternoon, this music definitely woke them up.

Having to stop it after hearing only the few minutes that Joe had specified triggered something akin to withdrawal symptoms in me and, I had to assume, also in Mel Gussow. I dutifully stopped the music, however, as Joe rose from his chair to usher him from his office.

"All right, *Comrade Tovarich*," he said, clapping a friendly hand on Gussow's shoulder when they reached the doorway. "Did you get everything down?"

As a result of Joe's intricate negotiations with the All-Union Ministry of Culture and a host of ancillary agencies, the Soviet government agreed to pay half the cost of a joint *Chorus Line* tour if Joe came up with the other half. Since Joe had no government behind him, this meant he would need to personally raise the other half, which was estimated in 1979 at $1.5 million, or about $6,132,469 in 2023 dollars.

Joe said, "The main principle at stake here was this. Rather than these old-fashioned exchanges, I felt it was now time to do something on a scale that was commensurate with the importance of the signing of the SALT agreements." Accordingly, he began to contact American corporations who did business in the U.S.S.R., such as Armand Hammer's Occidental Petroleum, and organizations that were members of the U.S.–U.S.S.R. Trade and Economic Council.

In July he sent General Manager Robert Kamlot to Moscow to begin a survey for the tour, followed by a technical staff of four in November, who wrote a lengthy report detailing the difficulties involved, such as, "In the Electric Department the only thing that will be familiar will be the cable. They do not have any equipment that even closely resembles what we will be setting up."

In the back of Joe's mind was the thought that since the U.S.S.R. was building many structures for the Olympics in 1980, "Some sort of structure could be put together within this period of time, which would be about a year, for a house which would be a sort of international theater where the runs were not limited." *A Chorus Line* could play there. This kind of capacious thinking with unfettered possibilities in the early stages of an idea was quintessential Joe. So was his stoical temporizing when he announced on December 19 that he'd been unable to find financing for the American side of the venture but projected mid-January as a final deadline.

Six days later, on December 25, 1979, the Soviet Union invaded Afghanistan. Soon after, President Carter announced the withdrawal of the U.S. Olympic Team from the 1980 Games and Joe's year-long effort toward artistic rapprochement with the Soviet regime came to an abrupt end.

40

"TzefarDEYah!"

I had set our table at home for the Passover Seder, the ceremonial family dinner that celebrates the biblical story of the ancient Hebrews' liberation from slavery. I was proud of the way the table sparkled with silver Kiddush cups, white candles, and my parents' wedding tablecloth. The preliminary food was in place: shmurah matzahs from a Lubovitch friend, bottles of kosher wine, and an antique seder plate—a sampler of symbolic foods representing sacrifice, mourning, the bitterness of slavery, the clay and mortar of pyramids, and renewal. Also a dipping bowl of salt water representing tears. Behind each symbol lay a wealth of tradition and interpretation.

Sitting at the head of the table, a fringed black-and-white tallis gathered around his shoulders, Joe ceremonially washed his hands before reading aloud in Hebrew the story of the Exodus of Moses and the Israelites from Egypt, as retold in an ancient rabbinic compilation called *The Haggadah* ("The Telling"). The rest of us followed in a bilingual paperback edition of *The Haggadah* that was set at each place.

There was nothing Reconstructionist in our Seder. For example, we had no feminist rituals like the "Miriam's Cup" of water to honor the sister of Moses, or selections from modern poets, or prayers for peace in troubled parts of the world. Instead, Joe conducted the service in the Orthodox way he'd learned from his father, interrupting his reading of the Hebrew text only when it was time to cue family and friends in English to participate in the service.

Looking up from his Haggadah, Joe said, "O*kay*, here's where we make a sandwich of bitter herbs, *maror*—the horseradish—with the matzoh. Pass the seder plate around."

When he got to the story about the Ten Plagues that Yahweh inflicts on Egypt, Joe told us, "Now here's the part where each time I say the name of a Plague, you finger-flick a drop of red wine from your Kiddush cups onto your plates."

These biblical Plagues are disgusting infestations of Lice, Flies, Locusts, Frogs, Diseased Livestock, as well as Blood, Darkness, and the Death of the Firstborn. They're fearsome enough in English, but they were positively terrifying the way that Joe rendered them in Hebrew, accompanying, for example, his pronunciation of the word for "Frogs"— "TzefarDEYah!"—with a stabbing hand gesture like the *sforzando* of an orchestra conductor's baton. It sent chills down my spine.

His only departure from tradition was when he came to a section called "The Four Questions." They're usually recited in Hebrew by the youngest male child present who asks why do we eat only unleavened bread, only bitter herbs, and so forth, on this night, whereas we do something different on all other nights?

Joe said to our guests in English, "Now here I always include Yiddish in the seder I conduct at home. I don't do it all in Hebrew because as a boy I used to ask The Four Questions—*Die Fier Kashes*—in Hebrew *and* Yiddish. Growing up I said them in an East European way, and Tony here is going to do the same thing."

Twelve-year-old Tony, who had learned the Four Questions in Yiddish and Hebrew to perfection by rote from Joe, then piped up in his little boy's voice:

> "Papishee, Papishee,
> ich vill dich dragn Fier Kashes?
> Di Ershte Kashe vill dich fragn:
> *Sheb'khol haleilot . . .* "
> ["Papa, Papa,
> I want to ask you Four Questions?
> The First Question I want to ask you:
> *Why on all other nights . . .* "]

When the last the question was done, Joe's teenage daughter Miranda interrupted the flow of the ceremony with an urgent question of her own.

"Why can't a *girl* ask The Four Questions?" she objected in her clear rational voice. "It isn't fair. Girls should be given a chance."

I agreed with her. I also felt that the time was long overdue, after thousands of years, for the mother of Moses to be mentioned at last by name in the Seder service.

"Jochebed was her name," I volunteered, further interrupting the ceremony. "I also think that the Egyptian stepmother of Moses should be mentioned because she's the one who rescued him as a baby out of the bulrushes in the river and then raised Moses in the palace of her father, the Pharoah. *Her* name was Bithya."

My advocacy for Bithya was prompted by the fact that I was now a relatively new stepmother myself and had a growing respect for the challenges of the relationship. Joe was more than willing to mention Jochebed and Bithya, but somehow we never got around to it in future seders.

While Joe had long ceased to be observant, he retained a deep connection to his Orthodox upbringing. He told me that as a boy he had believed in the coming of the *moshiach*, the Jewish messiah.

"I still have those beliefs now and then," he said.

It must have been wonderful to be that way as a child, I thought, with a flutter of regret that I had grown up without religion. As a little girl I had been amazed to learn that other children at school believed in a male god who lived somewhere above the clouds, a notion that seemed crazy to me. I had arrived at this juvenile judgment without any coaching from my agnostic parents.

Later I became interested in their religious leanings.

One was my mother's affection for her late grandfather, a distinguished Methodist minister, and for his brothers who were the first and fourth founding presidents of the University of Southern California in Los Angeles. She had honored them by giving me their French Huguenot name of "Bovard" as a middle name.

The other was my father's curiosity about his Sephardic (Spanish) Jewish ancestry, which may account for my DNA results showing a ghostly connection to the Iberian peninsula. It's my father's curiosity about his unproven Jewish heritage to which I attribute my lifelong interest in reading Jewish history.

One night, the week after the aforementioned Seder, I stayed up very late reading a new book about the history of Judaism. In it I had just learned that Jewish sages in the Hellenistic diaspora had borrowed the ritual and literary "form of the Greek symposium or banquet" for the Seder, although they had "drastically changed its content." I continued reading about this with addictive fascination until a noise in the living room broke my concentration.

Looking up, I saw Joe.

Setting aside the fascinating book, he gently took my hand and indicated without words that I should come to bed before sunrise, which was only an hour away.

41

"WAIT! Go Get the Pictures to Show Them!"

I had always wanted to know more about Joe's family, but he had little information beyond a few stories about Poland that his father had told him, and almost nothing from his mother except that she was a Lithuanian orphan who had sailed alone to the United States in 1909 when she was fifteen years old to join relatives in Brooklyn. Joe's parents had died in separate nursing homes in Brooklyn in the 1960s.

There was one potential family historian left, however—Joe's uncle, his father's youngest brother who lived in Israel—so I was excited when Joe said that we would visit him during a theater-related trip there in 1981.

I knew something about Joe's uncle, Zisme Papirovski, because four years earlier the *Jewish Forward* had published a reminiscence about the Papirofsky family in Poland by a former schoolboy acquaintance of the uncle. The author of the reminiscence, Yitzakh Shmulewitz, wrote that on a trip to Israel in 1976 he had met with his "old chum, Zisme Papirovski":

We had occasion to reflect on the past, on our boyhood and on the Cheder of Moshe the Melamed, a hometown teacher from pre-war Poland who taught an entire generation of Jewish youngsters in the town of Keltz. These conversations were particularly significant since Moshe the Melamed was Zisme Papirovski's father.

And conversing thus Zisme tells me that the son of his brother Shmuel is the well-known theatrical producer Joseph Papp. I did not know this. Not only did I not know that Joseph Papp was the grandson of a famous teacher, but as it turns out, that teacher was my teacher more than fifty years ago. All this I learned quite accidentally during my last visit to Israel . . .

Moshe the Melamed was loved by all. He and his wife Baile had several sons and daughters. We, the students in the Cheder, would often speak of Moshe's son Shmuel who went to America before the outbreak of the First World War. I recalled how the neighbors envied Moshe the Melamed having a son in America.

I remember full well as a student in Moshe the Melamed's Cheder that the majority of students coming from poor homes did not pay any tuition. Moshe the Melamed died in Keltz at the age of 78, the last day of Passover 1928. His entire family were victims of the Nazi murderers. Miraculously his son Zisme escaped.

Moshe Papirovski in faraway Keltz raised an entire generation of Jewish youth. Today in the free United States his grandson is bringing culture and enlightenment to the masses of people with equal dedication and determination.

Joe's uncle, who had changed his name from Zisme Papirovski to Sol Pepper, lived now in the residential suburb of Ramat Aviv in an apartment building surrounded by pink bougainvillea bushes. More than thirty years had passed since Joe and his uncle had last met in New York City, and they greeted each other with outstretched arms in the doorway of Sol's apartment.

"Come in! Come in!" Uncle Sol exclaimed.

"Come in! Come in!" Sol's wife Ruth repeated from a dinette table on the other side of their small living room. Apologizing for not getting up, she informed us in a bright chatty voice that she was disabled.

Sol Pepper, a short, dignified man, positioned two dinette chairs for Joe and me to sit near his wife. However, he himself remained standing throughout our visit, as if on alert.

Seconds after our arrival the Peppers urged us to help ourselves to the generous buffet they had laid out in our honor consisting of rye bread, pastrami, gefilte fish, chopped liver, horseradish, pickles, macaroons, and pound cake.

"Go ahead! Eat! What are you waiting for?"

Joe began to layer a Dagwood sandwich for himself at the buffet, as the Peppers, eager for news of the American branch of the family, inquired about his younger siblings—his sister Anna and his brother "Murray" (unaware that he had long ago changed his name to Phillip Martel).

"And how is Rhoda?" Sol said from his standing position in the middle of the living room. He and his wife were especially grateful to this older sister of Joe's because she'd always kept them informed about his theatrical career.

"She's fine, she's fine," Joe said, putting in place the final slab of his layered sandwich and then walking over to stand next to Sol to eat it. Soon, between a few jokes and many fine compliments about the food, Joe announced that we would have to leave in forty-five minutes because we had an appointment at the U.S. Embassy in Tel Aviv.

The Peppers were stunned. So was I, because I knew the Embassy date wasn't until later that afternoon.

But I had noticed from the moment that Joe entered his uncle's apartment that he had seemed restive, behaving, I thought, like a dutiful son who secretly wished to be somewhere else. It startled me because I had never seen him act this way before, definitely never like a *son*. But then I realized that of course his Holocaust-survivor uncle bore a family resemblance to his father and it was undoubtedly difficult for Joe to be within the orbit of the Papirofsky family's tragic twentieth-century history any longer than necessary.

When Joe announced our imminent departure, Sol had dug his hands in the pockets of his cardigan sweater. After a pause he said, "Do you know that Ruth and I are almost first cousins?"

Preoccupied with his sandwich, Joe said no he didn't know that.

Ruth sang out, "It's true! I'm part-Papirofsky!"

Sol and Ruth then began to speak over each other at the same time, sometimes agreeing but more often vociferously correcting each other's recollections that they wanted to share with us about members of the Papirofsky family.

Sol said to Joe, "Did you know that Ruth's mother brought your father over to the United States from Poland in 1914?"

"No, I didn't know that," Joe said.

Sol continued excitedly, "And it was Ruth's mother who got your father his job as a trunkmaker in Brooklyn?"

Ruth exclaimed, "You left out that she introduced his parents to each other!"

Joe had never heard any of this. He seemed skeptical.

"It's true!" Ruth Pepper cried out.

"No! It's true!" Sol agreed.

I sat up at attention. I said I wished I had brought my tape recorder because their information was so valuable. I asked the Peppers would they mind if I took notes? They didn't mind at all. In fact they were pleased and eager for me to do so.

"Get her a pencil! Get her some paper!"

Joe's mood brightened. He was happy to see me in what he called my "research mode" and he told the Peppers how important it was to him.

Racing against time, Sol and Ruth talked nonstop as they related never-before-heard stories about Papirofskys who had lived exclusively in large cities like Warsaw and Kielce (Vahr-SAW-vah, KELL-tzeh) in Poland, Vilna in Lithuania, Dubrovnik in Austria-Hungary, and Hamburg in Germany.

They told us about members of the family who had worked as a baker, photographer, klezmer musician, real estate owner, concert singer, teacher, dressmaker, and, of course, mothers with many children.

Mindful that their forty-five minutes were ticking away, Ruth suddenly shouted to Sol, "WAIT! Go get the pictures to show them!"

Sol hurried to the bedroom and returned with an album of Papirofsky photographs.

Opening the precious album on the dinette table, he tapped a picture in it with his index finger.

"Dubrovnik 1919," he said.

Joe and I leaned over a photograph of a group of adults on a summer porch in that former Austro-Hungarian city on the Adriatic Sea. The young women on the porch were dressed in Gibson Girl outfits and the young men wore high collars. They were all posed standing around an old man with a long white beard. This was Joe's paternal grandfather, Moshe Leib Papirofsky, the *melamed*, the teacher of young boys, with his wife Baile and several of their eight grown children, who were Joe's aunts and uncles.

Next, Sol flipped to a large sepia-tinted studio portrait taken, he said, in the 1920s. It showed a young man with a pencil-thin mustache, wearing a rakishly angled fedora, with his overcoat collar turned up theatrically around his handsome face.

"That's Asha," Sol said. "He was a professional photographer in Krakow."

Asha was Itzakh Papirofsky, one of the four Papirofsky brothers, who, besides Sol and Joe's father Shmuel, had also included Shimon, the eldest, a baker in Hamburg. They had all been born and raised in Kielce, Poland.

Pulling the album toward her at the table, Ruth turned to another studio photograph taken, she said, in Warsaw in the 1910s. It showed an elegant woman in a statuesque full-length pose, dressed in a beaded drop-waist evening gown accessorized with ropes of pearls and a shimmering headband.

"This is my mother Rebecca Mernitsky in her concert attire," Ruth said proudly, her eyes glistening behind her heavy eyeglasses. She slid one hand across the dinette table in Joe's direction.

"She was the half-sister of your grandfather Moshe Papirofsky. She was a professional singer. She sang with the famous Goldfaden Company, you've heard of it?"

Although Joe had never heard of Rebecca Mernitsky, he certainly knew about Avram Goldfaden, the celebrated Russian-born "Yiddish Shakespeare" who had founded the first professional Yiddish theater company at the end of the 19th century. Joe had reviewed a book about him for the *New York Times*.

I forced my mind to take hold of the significance of what Ruth and Sol Pepper had just told us: The photograph of the woman in the beaded evening dress was Joe's great-aunt Rebecca, a singer with the famous Goldfaden Company, who had brought his father to America. I was thrilled by this extraordinary new information.

We were shown many more photographs in the Peppers' album. As their provenance, names and relationships flew by in a blur, they seemed to cover a period from the turn of the twentieth century through the 1930s.

I lingered over a snapshot taken in Kielce in the late Thirties. It was of a young woman wearing a "Robin Hood"–style hat, kneeling on a city sidewalk with her arms wrapped around a little boy and girl dressed in matching coats and hats. She was coaxing them to look at the camera, just as my mother used to do with me. From the quaint style of their outfits, I judged that the children were the same generation as myself.

"My first wife and children," Sol said.

Almost offhandedly then he told us that he had been in "lagers"—camps—during the War: Auschwitz, Bergen-Belsen, Lublin. Not revealing how he had survived them, he said that except for himself, Joe's father, and a sister in Brooklyn, all of their siblings, and Sol's first wife and those two little children in the snapshot, had died in the Holocaust.

"The Papirofskys are inscribed at Yad Vashem," he said, referring to the Holocaust Martyrs' and Heroes' Memorial in Jerusalem.

Joe now made motions to leave but Sol wanted him to stay a little longer so he could tell us a story about Eidel, his youngest sister, of whom he had been especially fond.

The story was that Eidel had saved enough money from her earnings as a dressmaker to go to New York City, but her dentist in Kielce wanted her to put off booking passage on a ship so that he could finish the dental work he'd begun on her. Although Eidel didn't want to delay her departure for the United States, she eventually gave in to the dentist's advice and postponed the trip. Sol bitterly blamed him for her death.

"If Eidele hadn't listened to that lousy dentist," he said, "she wouldn't have been rounded up by the Nazis!"

"Ginger ale? Would you like some tea?" Ruth said. "How about a macaroon?"

"I'll have a macaroon," Joe said and asked Sol where he could find our coats. The time had come for us to leave.

I stalled to ask the Peppers about some names that I wanted to include in my notes.

"Have to go now," Joe announced after a few minutes, pulling on his coat and handing me mine. "It's been wonderful to see you."

The Peppers protested.

"How can you be leaving so soon? You just got here! You haven't eaten anything!"

Joe explained again that we had an important meeting regarding cultural exchange that had been set up by the U.S. ambassador.

Despite their distress about our leaving, Sol and Ruth Pepper were pitch-perfect in their comprehension of Joe's priorities.

"Of course if it's the ambassador, you have to go. You shouldn't be late for the ambassador. Take some cake."

Sol wrapped two slices of pound cake in a paper napkin for us to eat on the way to the U.S. embassy in Tel Aviv.

Turning around in the back seat of our taxi, I waved goodbye to Sol Pepper, who had come down with us and was standing on the sidewalk in front of his building watching our car as it drove away.

42

A Magisterial View

The day before our return to New York from Israel, Joe and I struck up a conversation with a veteran of the Israel Defense Forces at a roadside café on the outskirts of Jericho. Young Israeli soldiers with guns slung over their shoulders patrolled the empty highway in front of us, beyond which there were endless acres of orange groves.

"Have you been to the Sinai?" the veteran asked. No we hadn't. "Listen to me, you can't leave Israel without seeing the Sinai!" he exclaimed. "After we return it to Egypt next year, the desert tours will never be the same again."

We needed no further persuasion. We postponed our departure and signed up at a desert tour agency in Jerusalem for a three-day camping trip called a "Sinai Safari." The next morning after a short flight to Eilat at the north end of the Red Sea, Joe and I joined a small group of French, German, and American campers who had rendezvoused there in an army truck that resembled a covered wagon.

Our two guides were a stocky, red-bearded Israeli who had recently served in the army, and a slender, clean-shaven Bedouin named Ahmed Abou Ayesh in chinos and a T-shirt. They told us that we would be entering the Sinai through a dry ravine called Wadi Watir (VAH-dee-vah-TEER) en route to the Ein Khudra Oasis.

Wadis! Oases! I could hardly believe Joe and I were going on this adventure. We'd never done anything remotely like it before.

This was in 1981—before Hamas, the intifadas, and suicide bombers. However, two weeks earlier when we'd landed at the Tel Aviv Airport, Israeli Security had been on high alert due to the assassination of Egyptian President Anwar Sadat the previous month by Muslim fundamentalists.

The army truck set out on a smooth stretch of new highway before it turned off onto a bumpy local road. After rumbling noisily through several Egyptian villages, it suddenly began to heave sideways and slide around as if we were skidding on ice. Then—like a sleight of hand—the last village disappeared and we were in an unmarked universe of sand with an immense red disc bulging on the horizon. The change was so sudden that it took me a second to realize that the disc was the sun setting in the vast expanse of the Sinai desert.

That night, after dinner, Joe and I dragged our sleeping bags to a dune within sight of the campfire's fading embers. Zipping ourselves into them on the body-molding sand, we stared at the Milky Way shimmering in the night sky until the starlight and the fresh air cooling our eyelids lulled us to sleep. It seems incredible now, but we slept well and had no fear for our safety.

The next day the truck paused at a tiny oasis in the Sinai, a vest-pocket pond shaded by palm trees, so that Ahmed Abou Ayesh could climb out to greet some Bedouin friends in flowing white robes and shemagh headgear who were watering their camels.

After that, the landscape began to change as rocky formations rose up from the desert and rippled dunes morphed into ravines. These topographical changes preceded our stop at a monastery nestled in the foothills of a small mountain. From its backyard we climbed 3,750 stone steps (laid by a penitent monk in the sixth century) to the top of Mount Sinai where the three Abrahamic religions believe that Moses received the Ten Commandments. On our way up we waved to a little girl herding goats who paused each time she skipped by us to return our smiles with a shy one of her own.

When Joe and I reached the summit (shamefully littered with a few candy wrappers and a can of soda), we saw the mountain ranges and jagged ravines of the lower Sinai Peninsula spread out before us as far as we could see, a magisterial though somber panorama that made the beginning of our year on the receiving line at the glittering Reagan White House seem as insubstantial and remote as a trace memory from a previous incarnation.

43

Guess Who's Coming for Cocktails?

VARIETY

"A Chorus Line Dancers Perform at White House"
Variety, February 25, 1981
"Dance will be the featured entertainment at the White House this week during two black tie dinners to be held by President and Mrs. Reagan. The cast of *A Chorus Line* is slated to entertain at a reception for the nation's governors tonight."

"Papp Reacts to Reagan's Proposed Arts Budget Slash"
Variety, February 25, 1981
"A combative response to the Reagan Administration's proposal to slice the Federal arts budget in half."

After the rollercoaster years of the 1970s, Joe and I found ourselves at the beginning of the 1980s on the red-carpet line at the White House shaking hands with newly elected President Ronald Reagan and his wife.

Nancy Reagan, who like her husband had once been an actor, said to Joe gaily, "We're all in the same profession, aren't we?"

"Yes, but you're on the *world's* stage now," Joe answered gallantly, channeling Jacques in *As You Like It*.

As the president shook Joe's hand, Reagan said to him affably, "Where are the new musicals?"

"That's a very intelligent question for a President to ask," Joe said to me later. "Most Presidents wouldn't ask a question like that."

Why were we there? A few weeks ago, Mrs. Reagan had asked Joe to present a special performance of *A Chorus Line* at the White House to celebrate the president's first state dinner. Joe was reluctant to do it at first because her husband had just slashed the federal budget for the arts by a draconian 50 percent, but he finally agreed on the condition that a meeting be arranged for him with someone high up in the administration to discuss the president's threatened withdrawal of support for the National Endowments for the Arts and Humanities.

"I don't expect to change anything," Joe told me. "I just want my point of view heard at the highest level."

Accordingly, Nancy Reagan arranged for Joe to meet with her husband's then chief of staff and future secretary of state, James A. Baker III.

Joe said later that when he suggested to Baker that 50 percent was a crippling cut for programs that were, like the theater, revenue-producing stimulants to the economy, Baker had replied that the administration felt that if it withdrew from supporting the arts, in a flourishing economy the private sector would pick up that support. Joe countered that such a premise was "theoretical and had yet to be demonstrated." Then, having obtained his part of the agreement—to be heard at the highest level—Joe fulfilled his part of the bargain and brought *A Chorus Line* to the White House.

It was somewhat surreal to find ourselves in its glittering State Rooms among so many recently empowered Republicans wearing red satin cummerbunds and beribboned medals. We sat at Secretary of the Treasury Donald T. Regan's dinner table, adjourning afterward with the president and his guests to the chandeliered East Room to watch Michael Bennett's expertly abridged version of *A Chorus Line*, at which the dancers changed into their beautiful costumes for the finale of the show in a stairwell.

Although a decade is an artificial division of time that doesn't necessarily correspond to the real flow of events, that demarcation suited the 1980s because those ten years bookended the presidency of Ronald Reagan, starting with the empowerment of his conservative ideology in Washington and closing with the politicization of the National Endowment for the Arts.

However, when Ronald Reagan was swept into office in 1981, Joe had felt at first that a politically conservative government wasn't necessarily bad news for the arts. After all, he pointed out, President Nixon had given more money to the arts than any of the Democratic presidents since Franklin Roosevelt.

But although Reagan was a popular *viveur* of the entertainment world, he wasn't Richard Nixon, and Joe had been immediately outspoken in his criticism of Reagan's retrograde arts policy which was to reduce federal funding of the arts and eventually to eliminate the National Endowment for the Arts.

In spite of this, the president later invited Joe back to the White House for a private screening of Laurence Olivier's *King Lear*.

In this freshly minted conservative era, Joe and I were invited by Samuel (Sr.) and Mitzi Newhouse to join them for cocktails at their New York City townhouse. Mr. Newhouse was the founder of the Newhouse magazine and newspaper dynasty. We were puzzled by the invitation because their donor relationship to Joe had peaked ten years ago with a $1 million gift to name the Mitzi E. Newhouse Theater at Lincoln Center Theater when Joe was still running it, and although Mitzi had always liked him, there was no reason we could think of for their renewed interest now, a decade after Joe had left it.

Our hosts greeted us warmly in their opulently cozy parlor, introducing us to the only other guest who had arrived so far, their personal lawyer and, they said, long-time friend, Roy Cohn.

Joe and I barely managed to conceal our astonishment.

At the peak of the anti-Communist hysteria in the 1950s, Roy Cohn had served as the Chief Committee Counsel to Senator Joseph McCarthy's infamous red-baiting army hearings in Washington. He had also been a prosecutor in the trial of Julius Rosenberg and his wife Ethel on charges of espionage, for which they were executed by electrocution. I still remembered my horror the day their sentences were carried out.

Now here was the notorious man close at hand, small-statured, with the hairpin mouth and penetrating eyes set in a sort of bruised look that had become familiar to millions of viewers of the hearings on television.

We engaged in small talk as we waited for the other guests to arrive, but after a while it dawned on Joe and me that no one else was going to show up—that Cohn was the only other guest besides us.

The reason became apparent. He was a Shakespeare lover. He had always wanted to meet Joe, and his influential clients had obliged him. Cohn confessed that he had loved the bard since his youth and, setting his drink down on a glass-top coffee table, recited a speech from one of the plays for Joe's benefit. When he finished, he asked Joe about *his* favorite speech from Shakespeare.

Of course, Joe could have chosen from dozens of speeches that he knew by heart, but he offered instead a single line from *King Lear*, explaining that he had just seen Laurence Olivier's film of it with President Reagan at the White House, which, of course, impressed our conservative hosts and their special guest.

"It's the line when the Earl of Gloucester meets King Lear on the heath," Joe said to Roy Cohn, who leaned forward now in rapt attention.

"Gloucester wants to kiss Lear's hand," Joe went on, "but the mad king withdraws it, saying, 'Let me wipe it first; *it smells of mortality*.'"

44

When the Downtrodden Become Uptrodden

The Public Theater ran out of office space in the early 1980s due to our institutional expansion that had been fueled by the theater's income from the profits of *A Chorus Line*. There just wasn't an inch left to put another desk anywhere within the old Astor Library, so Joe leased a floor in the building next door to it at 419 Lafayette Street where he relocated four of the Public's nineteen departments.

The four departments that took up residence at the new address in 1982 were: Joe's office with Chief of Staff Barbara Carroll and administrative staff members Emmett Foster, John Moscone, and Kate O'Neal; the workspace of Artistic Director Wilford Leach; the office of Associate Producer Jason Steven Cohen and his associate Chris Fleming; and the Play Department situated in an open area adjoining the corridor to the elevator, consisting of me, Literary Manager Bill Hart, Music Associate Tom Ross, and Literary Associates Morgan Jenness, Robert Blacker, and Elizabeth Holloway.

This wasn't the first time that the Public Theater had spread out into other buildings in the neighborhood. In the 1970s Joe had leased industrial floors in a building across the street to house our costume, scenic, and prop shops. He had also leased what we called the Annex, which occupied the ground floors of all the buildings on the south side of Astor Place from Lafayette Street through to Broadway. We used them for rehearsals, an art gallery, and special projects like Al Pacino's workshop of Brecht's *The Resistible Rise of Arturo Ui*.

Situated now on a floor at 419 Lafayette, Joe liked his small new office where rows of colorful theater posters by Paul Davis caught the sunlight on the wall behind his chair, and Datchery, the resident cat, slept in the warm circle of light under his desk lamp. Joe's sunny windows faced Lafayette Street, a welcome change from his former office at the Public Theater which had been dark and without a view.

Although I missed the ambience of the Public Theater next door, I grew to like the intimate layout of the leased floor with its "Studio A" that we used for auditions and play readings, and the proximity just down the hall of Artistic Director Wilford Leach, whom I had introduced to Joe in the 1970s.

I had admired Wil Leach's multiskilled directorial and designing talent at Ellen Stewart's LaMama Theater ever since seeing his ingeniously gothic production of *Carmilla* in 1972. Joe also admired Wil Leach's work, and by the time we moved to the leased floor, he had engaged him as the Public Theater's artistic director.

"Wil has a very strong conceptualization of things and creates lots of room for the actors," Joe said. "And being of a gentle nature, he's always amused by people who are tempestuous. I guess that's why he likes me."

Back in the Sixties, when I was reading articles about Joe for the first time, I noticed that he was frequently described as "peripatetic," which means traveling from place to place. Twenty years later, the word was still often used to describe him, conjuring an image of the way he tended to show up at protests, or on the steps of City Hall, or in parks in the city's boroughs—here, there, and everywhere for a multitude of reasons, like a multitasking Robin Hood or Til Eulenspiegel.

As Joe headed now into his fourth decade in theater, looking, as he always had, ten years younger than his actual age, he hadn't changed these roving habits of engagement with the city that he loved, and at the personal intersection of an interview, he remained, as always, frank, open, fun, funny—and an incorrigible punster. ("If you park a car in a car lot, where do you park a camel? In a camel lot.")

When he turned sixty in 1981, *New York Magazine* ran a fanciful article dividing his life into three acts. Act One was the triumph of Free Shakespeare in Central Park. Act Two was the creation of the Public Theater, the success of *A Chorus Line*, and running Lincoln Center Theater. Act Three was blank except for the question: "Joe Papp's Third Act in which the hero seeks . . . *what?*"

Rolling Stone magazine followed suit with an ambitious attempt at summation and forecast in which its author contended that "Joe Papp is the most profiled personality in American theater—yet he's the most elusive, most mysterious, most unknown." The story then offered "Three Endings for Yet Another Profile of Joe Papp."

What these articles reflected was the media's fascination with the fact that Joe, a native son from a poor and humble background in Brooklyn, had singlehandedly and indisputably created one of New York City's major cultural institutions.

For others, however, this presented a conundrum that was hard to digest.

The indigestible conundrum had been on display in an article called "The Stages of Joseph Papp" by the seasoned cultural critic Stanley Kauffmann, published in the 1974–1975 winter issue of *The American Scholar*. In it, Mr. Kauffmann had written, evidently in honest perplexity, that "Papp is the only person who has made a considerable mark in the theater—in any American or European theater that I have seen or read about—without extraordinary talent, without exemplary taste, without an esthetic imperative, without intellectual distinction." Baffled that a person from Joe's poor working-class background could have achieved what he achieved, Mr. Kauffmann then suggested that a large part of Joe's "considerable mark" must therefore have been due to "luck."

When I read this I was reminded of what Joe had once told me about certain newspaper and magazine writers. "Their writers' hearts can bleed for the downtrodden," he'd said, "but just let one of those downtrodden become uptrodden, and watch the ink fly!"

Around this time a new generation of reporters started to record their first impressions of Joe. Since they were usually free of baggage from the past, I found them refreshing:

"He was seated with a kind of tense relaxation in his office."

"He spoke with conviction and possessed a curious intellectual integrity as well as audacious manner."

"His voice was smooth, with a smoky quality, but the words pelted out at computer speed."

"He was essentially intimidating."

"He was intense, impatient, gruff, coarse, impolitic, kind, polite and friendly."

As Joe's biographer Helen Epstein astutely noted, there was always "a shifting balance within a conversation" with Joe, "like with a fencer."

Despite the fact that he impressed some people as intimidating or arrogant, no one ever accused Joe of being jaded or indifferent as he ranged over his constant flow of ideas and plans. Even when he answered timeworn questions about his legendary early fight with Robert Moses, Joe would do so with animated geniality for the benefit of a new questioner, bringing fresh spontaneity to the details of the old saga.

Although Joe brushed aside the recent articles describing him in the "third act" of his career, they had been somewhat jarring to me because I was aware of his private existential distress in the notes he was writing to himself at home. In one of them he'd said:

> I no longer feel that my own individuality is at the center of my life's work. In the beginning of the Festival, what I was and what I did were one and the same: my goals and physical output were of a single piece, my philosophy of theater contained in the lightboard I lifted and the seats I installed. I fought for art and turf, and the mix was perfect. Now I still lead the battle, but I seldom fire a gun. I supply, I teach, I support, but when I get a rush of ideas and energy for a particular job, I take the job away from myself and give it to someone else. This is a condition that my being contradicts.

A few years before this Joe had decided to quit directing in order to concentrate on his producing responsibilities which had increased exponentially since the Seventies. Although he'd been fervently engaged in his work as a director, he was candid about his talent, telling me once that he considered himself somewhere in the "middle range." Nevertheless directing had always served as a creative point of engagement for him, a chance to recharge his batteries, and after several years without it he began to feel the drain. I thought that Joe's sensibility about dispossessing himself from his own creativity had doubtless been aggravated by the media's questions about the "third act" of his life, and it seemed to me they had also begun to trigger a spate of harrowing thoughts about his mortality. In a note to himself at this time he wrote:

> How can you be reconcilable about pain, old age and death? You have to be crazy to believe that rational thinking offers any kind of significant support. There are people starving to death, diseased to death, shot to death, accidented to death, dying young or at birth or in middle age. So what does my voice mean in such gargantuan slaughter?

Since Joe's terrors mirrored my own, there was no comfort to be found in our shared belief that divine instrumentality did not exist in the real world and that it had obviously never been at work in the universe. This is essentially "a tragic view of life," as the physicist Steven Weinberg has written, which says that "we are here without purpose, trying to identify something that we care about."

However there were significant differences between Joe and myself in this shared view. One was that, as a child, Joe had believed in the existence of God and although the substance was gone, he could recall the feeling, and the feeling was rooted in a deep connection to his Jewish heritage. I had neither an early belief in God nor a communal identity, which I regard as the primary benefit of religion. All of this, I venture to say, was a silent undercurrent to our lives in the theater.

Joe's job was to produce meaningful theater, and, as he said about himself, "My job is my life." Mine was to find writers. At the beginning of the 1980s, however, we had just entered a new conservative era empowered by Ronald Reagan's election. Joe's wariness about its impact on the country, as well as on the arts and the Public Theater, was like that of a creature who senses the underground signs of an earthquake before it bursts into the landscape.

Playwright David Henry Hwang with actors John Lone and Tzi Ma in *The Dance and the Railroad* at the Public Theater in 1981. The play tells the story of a former Chinese opera star working as a coolie laborer in the nineteenth-century West.

Martha Swope/Billy Rose Theatre Division, The New York Public Library

Offstage at *Alice in Concert*, a musical based on Lewis Carroll at the Public Theater in 1981. (L–R) Composer Elizabeth Swados, Meryl Streep who played Alice, and Joe who directed it.

Photofest

Choreographer Graciela Daniele rehearsing a scene from *The Pirates of Penzance* with (L) Rex Smith as Frederic, Kevin Kline as the Pirate King, and seven Pirates at the Delacorte Theater in 1981.
Martha Swope/Billy Rose Theatre Division, The New York Public Library

Joe greeting Mike Nichols and Jacqueline Kennedy Onassis who came to see *The Pirates of Penzance* at the Delacorte Theater in 1980. (L rear) Director Wilford Leach on his way to join them.
Images Press/Getty Images

Joe and me arriving at a
reception in 1980.
Carol Rosegg

At home in 1975.
Frederic Ohringer

Joe and me on the receiving line of newly elected President Ronald Reagan and
Nancy Reagan in 1981 before his first state dinner at the White House. Joe had
agreed to bring *A Chorus Line* to the East Room that evening, providing he could
discuss proposed cuts in the arts with someone high up in the administration.
Billy Rose Theatre Division, The New York Public Library for the Performing Arts

Joe and me at a party
in January 1978.
Adam Scull/MediaPunch Inc/
Alamy Stock Photo

Joe rehearsing his singing
debut at a small nightclub
called The Ballroom in
1978. The musical director
was composer-arranger
Stanley Silverman
(behind the piano).
Billy Rose Theatre Division,
The New York Public Library
for the Performing Arts

Joe and me at a synagogue in Moscow on our theater-
related trip to the Soviet Union in May 1979.
Papp Estate

Joe visiting an orphanage in Vietnam in 1982 when he accompanied a delegation of Vietnam Veterans to Saigon and Ho Chi Minh City as their cultural representative.

Papp Estate

Joe saluting fellow protesters on March 22, 1982, after they had all been arrested for blocking the demolition squad at the Morosco Theater.

AP Photo/David Bookstaver

Joe's birthday dinner with staff at home in 1987. (R–L) Emmett Foster (staff assistant), Tom Ross (music associate), Barbara Carroll (chief of staff), Joe, me, and Jason Steven Cohen (associate producer).
Courtesy of Barbara Carroll

Mandy Patinkin as Hotspur (center) with Ralph Byers as Richard Scroop (L) and Robert Westenberg as Sir Richard Vernon (R) in *Henry IV, Part 1* at the Delacorte Theater in 1981.
Martha Swope/Billy Rose Theatre Division, The New York Public Library

JOSEPH PAPP PRESENTS

HAMLET

THE PUBLIC THEATER

Poster by Paul Davis of Diane Venora as Hamlet at the Public Theater in 1982.
©Paul Davis

(L–R) Iconic modern dance choreographers Alwin Nikolais and Murray Louis with Joe in 1983, the year they staged the musical *Lenny and the Heartbreakers* at the Public Theater.

Wilford Leach, the Public's artistic director, with the principals of two alternating casts in his production of Puccini's opera *La Boheme* in English at the Public Theater in 1984. (L–R front row) Howard McGillin, Cass Morgan, and director Wilford Leach. (L–R second row) Gary Morris, Linda Ronstadt, Patti Cohenour, and David Carroll.

45

"Who *Cares* If You Do Another Season?"

An aunt, describing me at the age of four, once exclaimed, "You were such a lively one!" making me wonder whether all these years later she saw any trace of that spark in the grown woman who had come to visit her. Being called "a lively one" in the past tense made me feel odd, sort of like a palimpsest of myself—the definition of palimpsest being *"a piece of writing material on which the original writing has been effaced to make room for later writing, but of which traces remain."*

After I had independently applied this notion to myself, I was humbled to discover that Gore Vidal had used it as the title of his memoirs.

With a stretch of the imagination, "palimpsest" can be applied not only to writing materials as in its definition, or to an aunt's memory of one's preschool personality, but also to architectural spaces—like those at the nineteenth-century Astor Library that we now inhabited, of which we had seen only the ghostly vestiges remaining of the library after its occupancy by the Hebrew Immigrant Aid Society.

Since our own occupancy of the building, I have also become aware of the "palimpsest" nature of the Public Theater itself in the twentieth and twenty-first centuries. On the physical premises, for example, Joe's large office, which had once been the theater's artistic hub where so many human interactions had taken place, was later turned into a carpentry shop with tall racks for the storage of wood planks. Only the arched windows of Joe's office remained recognizable. What had once been the exquisite floor of the Public Theater's lobby, crafted in hand-laid Italian stonework, later became an expanse of modernist black tile. And what was once known as "The Little Theater" became a storage room.

In terms of the creative use of the physical premises, my memory summons stages and spaces in the building that had been early centers of artistic work by Black and Latino playwrights such as Ed Bullins, Charles Gordone, Pedro Pietri, Miguel Piñero, and many others. (I've listed everyone, to the best of my ability, in the appendix.)

This palimpsest phenomenon had been occupying my thoughts in 1982 when Joe called the Annual Staff Meeting in the Anspacher Theater. Arriving for it with my Play Department colleagues from the rented loft next door, we took our places in the audience, joining over a hundred staff members there from the Public Theater's nineteen departments. Yes, there were *nineteen* departments now—a far cry from that day in 1966 when only twelve of us had moved into the ramshackle building, and the Anspacher Theater had been just a gleam in Joe's eye.

Joe called these Annual Staff Meetings to review the past year and to talk about his future plans for the Public Theater, but I sensed there was something different afoot at this one. Looking trim and handsome in a yellow turtleneck sweater as he stood at the edge of the Anspacher stage, Joe simply started talking to the staff, as if resuming a conversation with them.

"The thing that makes this theater different is that it shows that a major institution doesn't have to become institutionalized. It can still function as a small storefront theater in the way it experiments. The thing that makes us large is only in terms of cost, but in terms of art, we're still functioning on a very small scale. No big bureaucracy, only as much as is necessary to operate a theater of this size, and it's always for the benefit of the artist and the public."

Joe's voice sounded determined and fervent.

"Some of the principles on which the Public Theater is founded are important and I think will continue—the fact that we were built on the notion of free Shakespeare and the orientation of the theater for the most part toward new plays of some social meaning, yet still, in a peculiar way, not divorced from the 'razzmatazz' of show business. The Public Theater will have staying power because the forces that are involved are not just myself, but all the people who have been attracted to this kind of theatrical life."

I had noticed that as some theatrical institutions aged, they ran the risk of losing their original creative spark, but I felt that hadn't been the case at the Public Theater because Joe had somehow managed to embed his beliefs in the DNA of the organization itself. His current message therefore came across as fresh and positive. However, whenever Joe referred to the continuance of the Public Theater without him, as he seemed to be doing now, it triggered in me the premonition of an unbearable personal loss at precisely the same time that everyone else listening to him felt cheered by his optimistic vision of the Public Theater's future.

It was a peculiar occupational hazard of my working at the theater, where I sometimes couldn't avoid feeling as if I had been prematurely caught in the fifth act of *The Tempest* when Prospero, contemplating the end of his magic powers on his island, says, "And thence retire me to my Milan, where every third thought shall be my grave."

"As far as the present is concerned," Joe continued, "the mood is very conservative now. There's no question the country has seen a diminution of the kind of energy a place like the Public Theater draws on. We flourished in terms of our social consciousness in the Sixties and Seventies when most of the plays were about Vietnam, civil rights, Black plays, some Latino works. But the consciousness is different now and it shows in what we do."

Joe then freely acknowledged recent criticisms he'd received from the staff about his activity on behalf of many causes on the grounds that they had been distracting him from his work at the Public Theater. It was true, he said, that he'd been preoccupied with problems concerning Cambodian refugees, Soviet Jewry, Vietnam veterans, and an array of domestic issues exacerbated by Reaganomics and the burgeoning culture wars.

"But there's a reason I'm so goddamned caught up in these issues," Joe told the staff with a defiant rise in his voice. "It's because the theater today is not satisfying me in terms of what it's doing. And when the theater gets less of life than what is on the outside, I have to infuse it with what *I* get from the outside. I've got to be out there doing something."

This Annual Meeting had taken place in the morning. At the end of the day four or five of us on the staff had drifted to the threshold of Joe's office. With the late afternoon sun streaming through his windows, we found Joe with his feet up on his trestle desk and a glass of scotch in hand. He'd just finished telling a joke to Barbara Carroll, his high-spirited chief of staff.

When he saw us in the doorway, Joe quipped, "What's this? A delegation from the Commissariat?"

Taking this as an invitation, we settled on the sofa and chairs in his small office, where Joe seemed to welcome an opportunity to continue his remarks from the morning staff meeting about the challenges entailed in becoming a "major" institution.

A reasonable person may ask what my colleagues felt about the "boss's wife" being there with them. My presence among them was due to the fact that I had worked beside them for many years long before Joe and I were married, and after we were married my work relationships had remained pretty much the same—friendly and collegial in the intersecting responsibilities of our various jobs in administration, casting, production, promotion, and play development.

Somewhere in the back of my mind, however, there was always the memory of a previous job I once had where I worked for a married couple in an organization. It had given me a firsthand sense of the personal and professional difficulties involved in that arrangement, both between the parties themselves and in their work relationships with everyone else. I remembered me and staff members limiting ourselves at meetings to ludicrously tactful language and feeling cut off from an essential flow of information.

Because of that experience, during my seventeen years so far at the Public Theater, I'd held myself to a fine line that required a wary balance of discretion, integrity, circumspection, prudence, probity, scrupulosity, and other saintly attributes that I deemed essential to functioning properly in my job despite being married to everyone's boss. Beyond that sensitivity, I never felt that I shouldn't be there or that I hadn't earned my place.

I can't pretend to know exactly what my co-workers felt about my role at the theater. After 1991 when I no longer held a job at the Public Theater, I enjoyed the kind of frank personal friendships with several of my former colleagues that I couldn't have had when I was still employed there.

My position would probably be impossible in this day and age of accusations, reckonings, and corporate codes of conduct, but it was doable then in the unconstrained aftermath of the Sixties and in the cultural context of creating a new theater.

Meanwhile Joe continued his time-honored habit of taking staff members out to Japanese dinners in the neighborhood before previews, or hashing out problems with them in his office over drinks at the end of a very long day.

Picking up the thoughts he'd expressed at the Annual Staff Meeting in the morning, Joe now chatted with the aforementioned "delegation from the Commissariat" that was sitting in a relaxed manner in his office.

"It's so easy in an institution to create structures and then you become a slave of that structure," he said. "So every year or two I say, Why am I in the theater? What am I doing that's really important? There are so many things happening outside, and look, here I am, putting on plays. Who *cares* if you do another season?"

Removing a matzoh from the box on his desk, Joe said, "I was just telling Barbara here that the problem we have now in the 1980s is playwrights writing in their own heads and bellies. The focus seems to be very narrow, and that tires me. I'm not interested in what I call middle-of-the-road plays,

Joe at his desk in 1985. "Who *cares* if you do another season?"
Gail Papp

domestic or bourgeois encounters, where the emphasis is placed on the minutiae of relationships and recognizable situations we all know about. I'm interested in *unrecognizable* situations." (This was a reference to some current plays then on Broadway.)

"Anyway, my notion is that you have to be doing something important to justify your existence. I've always felt that responsibility. I feel that I have to constantly demonstrate that we have a *reason* to exist."

As he broke the matzoh in half, he added, "Once you stop doing that, go somewhere else, do something else."

This declaration by Joe was accompanied by the sound of clinking ice cubes in the glasses from which the four or five of us had all apparently just taken a sip at the same time. Joe paused to study the Commissariat seated in front of him, taking in the fact that we each now had our own scotches in hand.

Beyond the windows of his office the sky was growing dark and the street lights in the city had switched on. The room suddenly felt more cozy and cheerful.

As if to erase the cares of the day, Joe began singing to us in full performance mode from Cole Porter's *Broadway of 1940*:

> So move Grant's tomb to Union Square
> And put Brooklyn anywhere,
> But please, please,
> I beg on my knees,
> *Don't monkey with Old Broadway!*

46

for colored girls

Director Oz Scott, a former stage manager at the Public Theater, brought a manuscript to me in 1976 that was unlike anything I had ever read. Titled *for colored girls who have considered suicide/when the rainbow is enuf*, it was a collection of declarative poems described as a "choreopoem" for seven women. Although I didn't know what to make of them as a theatrical piece at first, the words leapt off the page with unmistakable vitality and urgency.

Oz Scott told me that this work was by the poet Ntozake Shange, who had developed it in performances in the San Francisco Bay Area, brought it to a bar in the East Village, and then to Producer Woodie King Jr. at his New Federal Theater on Grand Street, where it had been a great success during its limited engagement. Oz was suggesting an extended run of it at the Public Theater in a co-production with Woodie King Jr. He left the manuscript with me, but said that *for colored girls* had to be experienced in person rather than just read. He was absolutely right about this and accordingly a full-cast presentation of it at the Public Theater for Joe, me, and a few other people was arranged.

To this day I remember the superb performances and the power, beauty, and anger of Ntozake's soaring poetic voice. I also remember thinking to myself that we absolutely had to do it, even though in this early phase of the Public Theater, I knew that Joe wasn't particularly keen on co-productions, preferring that new work be hatched at the Public Theater rather than elsewhere. Nevertheless when he saw the special performance of *for colored girls*, Joe responded wholeheartedly to the unusual work.

When twenty-seven-year-old Ntozake Shange—accessorized in hoop earrings and wearing a head scarf—walked into Joe's office for the first time, she seemed wary both of him and of the off-Broadway milieu of the Public Theater, whose mission was similar to but different from the neighborhood-based New Federal Theater where she and the other six women in the cast had been performing her show. Joe sensed this, but he had studied the script and as a result had a reorganization of it to propose, with different dramatic juxtapositions than the ones in the version she'd been performing. In future years Ntozake remembered that "Joe helped us refine it so we got rid of all kinds of extraneous things. He gave us enormous support in just saying, 'I want this thing heard. I want to see it.' I have a really great daddy of my own, but I used to call Joe my 'art father' because it was through him that I got ushered into a new way of looking at my work."

In 1978 I was praying that a co-production would go forward, but like everything in the theater, nothing is preordained. A host of seen and unseen factors can either advance or thwart the path of a dramatic work to its proper life in the theater. As Joe always said, "You cannot predict it."

Privately, I had been wondering about the source of my strong emotional response to *for colored girls*. Ntozake had written it from her personal sensibility and experience in America, which obviously wasn't mine. Nor was there anything in my relationship experience with men that was equivalent to what she wrote about in *for colored girls*. Back in that ultra-sensitive day, I felt obliged to question my emotional response, even though I knew my feeling for the work was genuine, and later on decided that Ntozake's power as an artist had simply reached me on a universal level—the same as Emily Dickinson's New England poems had, or Frida Kahlo's Mexican paintings, despite the fact that their words and images came from unfamiliar worlds of personal and cultural experience.

When *for colored girls* opened at the Public Theater, it struck a nerve in the body politic, becoming the most unanticipated "hit" show in anybody's experience, and Joe moved it to a successful run at the Booth Theater on Broadway. In liner notes to a cast recording of the show (Buddah Records), he wrote,

I was struck, first of all, with the honesty of the piece, and then impressed with its high flights of pure poetry intermixed to such a marvelous degree with down-to-earth, folk, Black material. Her imagery is fantastic. She has a power and strength which makes it dramatic. I felt very moved by the material. When someone speaks something, says it out loud, and you're moved by it, that's the first law of the drama.

I thought there was an audience for it. The ability of something of this nature to fill the Booth Theater, 800 seats, each night, only speaks for its eloquence and dramatic power. Its cry is a universal one. That's what makes it so appealing. Zake has no prejudice. That's one of her great qualities. She recognizes the difference between white and Black. She recognizes the imposition of white culture and economy on Blacks. She is, in one sense, as militant as anybody can be. But she's an artist, which means that she will never avoid certain truths to make another kind of point.

Ntozake Shange wasn't happy about performing on Broadway, her prejudice against the commercial theater being as virulent as Joe's had recently been. She went on to experiment with other works downtown at the Public Theater. One of them was a theatricalized poetry recital written and performed by herself and fellow poets Thulani Davis and Jessica Hagedorn. Called *Where the Mississippi Meets the Amazon*, I remember how these three young women performed it with all of the expressive brio and fine-tuned reciprocity of an exciting chamber ensemble composed of consummate musicians.

Fast forward to 1985. Joe and I learned that Thulani Davis of the *Amazon* trio had written the libretto of a new opera called *Malcolm X* composed by her cousin, Anthony Davis. We went to see its first premiere at the Walnut Theater in Philadelphia and were profoundly impressed by the work.

Around this time Joe and I also attended a small cabaret where Ntozake was performing a new program of her poetry, accompanied by composer Anthony Davis on the piano.

As Joe and I settled ourselves on floor cushions facing the cabaret's tiny stage, I became aware of a gentleman three cushions to my right who was leaning forward.

"Miss Merrifield, I presume?" he said in a deep resonant voice.

I immediately recognized the unforgettably rich, commanding voice of Dr. Charles T. Davis, who somehow remembered my face and name from a freshman class in American literature that I had taken with him twenty-five years earlier when he was a young professor at New York University. His influence on me then was deep and lasting, and I had saved his comments on all the papers I had written in his class.

Since that time long ago, I knew that Charles Davis had become the founding chairman of Afro-American Studies at Yale University and the Master of one of its colleges. Seeing him again in the cabaret brought back a surge of my youthful admiration for this extremely brilliant and generous man who had encouraged my freshman writing efforts, and who had also advised me and my first husband in producing the campus literary magazine.

"The pianist is my son," he now said to me.

Thrilled by the interconnecting thread of my long-ago student past with Charles Davis extending to the present with Ntozake Shange, I introduced Joe to Dr. Davis just as the cabaret's dimming house lights heralded her performance. Dr. Davis' surprise and delight in meeting Joe in this way was unmistakable. Soon afterward he extended an invitation to Joe to speak to his residential students at the subsequently renamed Calhoun College at Yale.*

In 2008 his famous protégé, Henry Louis Gates Jr., paid tribute to Charles Davis as the man who had "ignited his passion for the study of African-American literature." In an article in *The Journal of Blacks in Higher Education* ("Charles Twitchell Davis: The Seminal Scholar of the African-American Literary Tradition"), Professor Gates wrote that Dr. Charles Davis "was the first African American to be granted tenure in the English Department at Yale University. Davis was also the first Black master of Calhoun College—John C. Calhoun College—an irony he never tired of noting, with that inimitable gleam in his eye. Davis was a man of style, as dapper in spirit and dress as he was dapper in mind." Gates called him a "true giant of our field."

Joe and I drove up to Yale in New Haven in our Jeep Wagoneer, parking it in an asphalt-covered lot at the university. As I disembarked, I saw Dr. Davis striding across the asphalt toward us with a big smile and outstretched arms. Without a moment's hesitation I ran toward him and was immediately engulfed in his welcoming embrace.

Joe held an animated seminar about the theater with the residential students of Davis's college in a large New England style living room. He and

---

* John C. Calhoun, a white supremacist and owner of slaves who was vice president of the U.S. from 1825–1832.

Davis matched connoisseur notes about the cigars they liked to smoke, although Davis hinted that he'd recently been obliged to "forego the pleasure." On the drive back to New York City, Joe and I were both exhilarated by the visit, unaware that it would be the last time we saw Charles T. Davis before his untimely death in 1981.

The following year, his book, *Black Is the Color of the Cosmos: Essays on Afro-American Literature and Culture, 1942–1981*, was posthumously published (Garland Publishing Company), edited by Henry Louis Gates Jr.

47

"Hic et ubique"– *Hamlet* in Eastern Europe

Our foreign travel on theater-related business increased dramatically, from fifteen trips in the 1970s to fifty trips in the 1980s. The main reason was Joe's interest in broadening the horizons of the Public Theater, along with his growing dissatisfaction with theater in the United States in the conservative Eighties. Though Joe's mind was set on new plays, we found *Hamlet* haunting our trips to Communist bloc countries at that time. The play seemed to be "hic et ubique"—here and everywhere, as Hamlet says of his dead father's voice in Act I, Scene 4. Two instances of its ghostly reach across the chasm of four hundred years still linger vividly in my memory.

In November 1981 Joe and I had been handed a phone message at our London hotel from the Polish director Andrzej Wajda (*VYE*-dah) saying that he hoped we could see his production of *Hamlet* in Krakow. There was no callback number.

Wajda had become an international celebrity earlier that year when he won the Palme d'Or at the Cannes Film Festival for *Man of Iron*, a fictionalized account of the rise of Poland's anti-Communist trade union movement.

Interested in seeing Wajda's stage work, we applied for visas at the Polish Visa Office in London, giving as the reason for our trip "To see Andrzej Wajda's *Hamlet* in Krakow." The next day, we learned that our request had been denied.

"It is not now possible," the visa clerk informed us without giving any explanation.

Outraged, Joe demanded to speak to the visa director. When the visa director emerged from his inner sanctum, Joe told him that this action stood in appalling contrast to the official welcome we'd just received in the Soviet Union. Joe's furious rebuke—with the specter of a displeased U.S.S.R. hovering behind it—immediately got us an appointment to see the Polish Ambassador at his townhouse in a fashionable part of London.

Urbane and charming, the ambassador motioned us to richly upholstered wing chairs in front of a crackling fireplace. He listened attentively as Joe spoke about the urgent need for communication among artists and his belief that creative connections in the arts promote bonds of peace and mutual understanding. Summing up, Joe told the ambassador, "They're acts of grace, I think, at a time when there is tremendous tension."

The ambassador nodded in agreement. Then, uncrossing his legs, he said, "Mr. Papp, do you ski? There is very good skiing in Poland. Poland is noted for its excellent Alps."

"Yes, I've heard about the Alps," Joe said. "We'd like to see them."

The ambassador rang for his butler to show us out. As we left, Joe said *"Dziekuje"* and *"Do widzenia,"* the Polish words for *thank you* and *goodbye* that he hadn't used since his childhood. We returned to the Polish Visa Office, applied for visas to go skiing in the Alps, and got them right away.

I knew that Joe's grim taciturnity on the eve of our departure for Poland reflected his mixed feelings about visiting the country where most of his father's family had been murdered.

Equally grim was a Cultural Attaché assigned to us in Poland when we joined the theatergoers who had packed the large Teatr Stary ("Old Theater") in Krakow to see Wajda's *Hamlet*. We waived the services of a translator since we knew the scenes so well we could guess what the corresponding lines in English would be. During the performance both Joe and I noticed the audience's super-vigilant attention to the play, which on the surface didn't seem to be a significant departure from a classical standard in its performances and production. The next day we had an officially arranged lunch with Wajda and his wife, our conversation necessarily circumscribed due to the presence of the dour Cultural Attaché.

Two days later when we were back in New York, we read a front-page story in the *Times* about martial law having just been declared in Poland. It said that Wajda had been detained because "Mr. Wajda had refused to sign a statement supporting measures taken to suppress 'counterrevolution.'"

Despite the imposition of martial law, we learned that Wajda's *Hamlet* had continued playing to packed houses in Krakow, because before and since then the audiences had found reflections of their political situation—students' strikes, imprisonment of Polish trade union members, and the violence of the police and army—in aspects of the play. This accounted for the atmosphere of super-vigilance in the audience that Joe and I had both felt. It also accounted for Joe's political savvy in accepting Wajda's invitation to see *Hamlet*. Later we heard that at one performance in the scene where Hamlet chastises his mother Queen Gertrude, the actor playing Hamlet had said the following lines out front to the audience instead of to her—

> "Forgive me this my virtue
> For in the fatness of these pursy times
> Virtues itself of vice must beg pardon"

—upon which the audience had erupted in a *standing ovation*.

***

Playwright Václav Havel, a thirty-year-old rock 'n' roll–loving dissident from Prague, had made his first trip to the United States in 1968 to see his play *The Memorandum*, which Joe directed in our opening season at the Public Theater. It won the Obie for Best Foreign Play but unfortunately Havel couldn't stay to collect his award in person.

Fast forward to 1984, three years after our visit to Poland. In that year Czechoslovakia's long-entrenched Communist regime, which had jailed Havel for several years, commuted his sentence to house arrest due to his failing health. He was now being detained at his family home in Hrádeček in the Krokonose Mountains near the Polish border.

Learning that Havel would be able to receive visitors, we decided to visit him there and bring his large, framed-glass Obie Award from 1968 with us. I had placed it in our suitcase, padding it on all sides with our clothing.

We were to be met at the Prague airport by his brother, Ivan Havel, a theoretical computer scientist with a PhD from the University of California in Berkeley.

"How will I be able to recognize you at the airport?" Joe asked him on the phone before we left New York City.

"I'll be the only person carrying a book," he replied.

Ivan Havel drove us to the family home about two hours from Prague, where the playwright had invited us to stay overnight. Václav Havel was still the casually dressed man I remembered meeting in 1968 with a manner that was a distinctive mixture of courteous formality and genuine warmth. Havel's English, though not fluent, was entirely serviceable for conversation. Greeting us at the door, he introduced Olga, his wife, a lovely, statuesque woman with a sad air.

"Václav, we've brought you something!" Joe exclaimed in the entrance hall, which was a signal for me to unpack the Obie Award while we were still in the foyer. As the Havels' dog Golda sniffed around our suitcase with determined canine interest, I unpacked it, a little embarrassed to reveal it swaddled in our clothing, but when Joe handed Havel the framed Obie, he was completely surprised and very touched that we had brought it with us.

We got a chilling firsthand sense of what his "house arrest" meant when Havel said that a policeman was on twenty-four-hour duty checking who went in and out of his front door. To facilitate this, Havel said that a small chalet had been built for the policeman at the top of the hill facing Havel's house and all the trees formerly on the hillside had been cut down to clear the view for him.

"Look!" Havel said with a chuckle. "You can see him right now at one of the windows up there." And sure enough, there he was with his binoculars trained on us.

We had dinner with the Havels in a cozy room with beige curtains and a sign on the wall, in English, that said, "All you need is love."

Havel told Joe, "I don't know who I'm writing for anymore." Although he was able to smuggle his plays out of Czechoslovakia, it was many years since he'd been able to see any of them performed for an audience.

Joe noted "a ruefulness about him, and a sadness about the whole place. He's very gentle but very angry." I snapped a disposable-camera picture of Joe and Václav at the dining table, which has proved to be the only photo of them together.

Joe and I stayed overnight in the guest room whose white stucco walls were decorated with the psychedelic posters Havel had bought on his 1968 trip to the United States. A photograph of Pope John II hung above the bed.

As we were about to leave the next day, Havel said, "Wait! I want to show you something before you go."

Rummaging in his desk, he brought out a sheaf of pages typed on the letterhead of the Trutinov District Police. Havel said it was a list of personal possessions the police had seized during one of its periodic raids on his and Olga's home. I noticed that the list he showed us was dated August 16, 1984, just three weeks before our visit. There were hundreds of possessions itemized on it, each one numbered and described with the punctiliousness of the Nazi record keeping I had seen on display at Auschwitz.

"Guess what this one was?" Havel said to us, pointing to an item on page 2. "This one will specially interest you."

We couldn't guess because it was in Czech.

"It's my copy of *Hamlet!*" Havel exclaimed with a laugh. "Can you believe it? They took *Hamlet!*"

"Well I could have warned you about that," Joe said. "I've always known it was a dangerous play."

We had no inkling of the Velvet Revolution that would shake off the Communist yoke five years later in 1989, or of Václav Havel's future role as the first president of the new Czech Republic. When it happened, Joe saw fit to mark the Velvet Revolution by commissioning a poster from Paul Davis with a picture of Havel and the motto "Pravda Vitezi" ("Truth Is Victorious"). Joe had always felt that Havel was a blood brother. "We're of a similar kind," he told me.

In a letter from prison to his wife Olga, Havel had written, "When a person chooses to take a certain stand, when he breathes some meaning into his life, it gives him perspective, hope, purpose. When he arrives at a certain truth and decides to 'live in it,' it is his act and his alone. It is an existential, moral and ultimately a metaphysical act, growing from the depths of his heart and aimed at filling his own being."

That, I believe, captures the connection that existed between Joe and Václav Havel. It was political, but beyond politics.

48

"Woo't drink up eisel?"

I always felt a sense of renewal when Joe and I were at a play at the Delacorte Theater. The open air, the free admission for all attending, and its democratic audiences never failed to lift my spirits with affection for and allegiance to this "blessed plot" of land in Central Park and the opportunities it enshrined.

I was in that mood as Joe and I watched James Lapine's enchanting production of *A Midsummer Night's Dream* in the park in 1982, where the entire stage of the Delacorte Theater had been transformed into a beautiful landscape of real greensward with real trees by Scenic Designer Heidi Landesman. It was a living picture garden, like something Monet might have created.

During the play's first scene Joe drew my attention to the actress playing Hippolyta, the Queen of the Amazons.

"She has a tremendous presence on stage," he whispered. "The next time she should play a major Shakespearean role for us."

I understood what he meant. Although Hippolyta has few lines and isn't a leading character, you couldn't take your eyes off the young actress playing her when she was on stage. I looked at the program. Her name was Diane Venora.

I wondered what role Joe might be thinking of for her. Desdemona in *Othello* and Kate in *The Taming of the Shrew* had been acted too recently to be repeated again so soon, I thought, but the field was wide open for a new Rosalind in *As You Like It*, Beatrice in *Much Ado About Nothing*, Viola in

Twelfth Night, Portia in *The Merchant of Venice*, Isabella in *Measure for Measure*, Cleopatra in *Antony and Cleopatra* . . . She could probably do any of them. Since Joe saw "potential in people who didn't fit the traditional mold," I was immensely curious about which of those roles he'd want to see Diane Venora play.

It turned out, however, that he had something completely different in mind than the roles I'd thought of. Joe offered her Hamlet, and he decided to direct it himself.

I couldn't have been more delighted when after an absence of six years, our huge facsimile edition of Shakespeare's *1623 Folio*, the earliest anthology of all his plays, reappeared on our dining table at home. This was like the return of an old friend because whenever Joe had directed Shakespeare in the past, the *Folio* had always been open alongside his scruffy paperback edition of the play whose margins would be crammed with Joe's penciled directorial notes. (My favorite was one he'd penciled in the margin of *Measure for Measure*: "ANTONIO TOO SLOW WITH DAGGER AT HER THROAT.")

I had a keen interest in his idea of a woman playing Hamlet. I'm not entirely sure why. Perhaps it was because I'd always identified with boys in the books I grew up reading, such as young Oswald in E. Nesbit's *The Bastable Children*, and later on when I graduated to classics like *Wuthering Heights* and *War and Peace*, I had immediately bonded with Heathcliff and Pierre Bezukhov, rather than Catherine Earnshaw or Natasha Rostova.

By the time I read *Hamlet* in my teens, my identification with boys and men in literature was firmly rooted and I passionately embraced the Danish prince as someone who gave voice to my own thoughts and feelings. Later I experienced the same uncanny affinity with Samuel Beckett's androgynous bums in baggy coats.

Joe was as keyed up about directing Diane Venora in *Hamlet* in 1982 as he'd been about his hellzapoppin version of it with Martin Sheen in 1967. Having produced *Hamlet* ten times and directed it himself twice before, Joe was on intimate terms with the play. He'd also had a longstanding interest in casting a woman as Hamlet and from time to time had made some notes about it. However now that his production of *Hamlet* with Diane Venora was in preparation, Joe discarded his previous ideas and instead asked me to see what I could find out about the tradition of women who had played the role.

Delving into this subject long before a book had been written about it, I discovered the fascinating four-century-long history of women playing Hamlet. It looked to me as if the seeds of it had been sprouted in 1660 when women were allowed to perform on stage in England for the first time. At last they could act the female characters in a play which up to then only boy actors had been permitted to portray. Part of this boy-actor convention had been that, for urgent reasons devised in the plot of a play, a female character (played by a boy) needed to disguise herself as a boy. Examples of this are Viola/Cesario in Shakespeare's *Twelfth Night* and Julia/Sebastian in *Two Gentlemen of Verona*. Later, when women played these parts, they were called "breeches roles."

I didn't think it was such an implausible leap for an actress impersonating a boy in the service of such a plot to covet playing the part of a university student like Hamlet.

Sarah Siddons is the first actress known to have starred as Hamlet when she went on tour in the role in the 1770s. Over the next 150 years, hundreds of actresses followed her, not only in England but also in Ireland, Spain, France, Germany, Sweden, Denmark, Italy, Poland, Finland, Turkey, Russia, Japan, Australia, the United States, and Canada. This tradition of what used to be called "travesti" Hamlets reached its peak in the United States in the nineteenth century but petered out in the twentieth century.

Eva Le Gallienne, a British actress devoted to the art of theater who became the producer of the Civic Repertory Theater in New York City from 1926–1936, had played and directed *Hamlet* at the age of thirty-eight in 1937 at the Cape Playhouse in Dennis, Massachusetts. She happened to be in New York City at the time that I was researching the tradition of travesti Hamlets, and I was able to arrange an interview with her. In words that were almost identical to those in her autobiography *With a Quiet Heart*, she told me in her authoritative voice, "I think psychologically one feels Hamlet was a youth, and therefore because a boy of that age might not be technically equipped to play the role, this is why many women in their thirties who can look like a youth, and had the technical skills to play this great role, have played it."

Joe agreed with Le Gallienne about Hamlet being a very young person— "He's an adolescent, a student," Joe said—but Joe carried the notion of a woman's suitability for the part a step further.

"I have always felt that there is a strong female side to Hamlet—not feminine so much as female. To me that has to do with an easier capacity to express emotion. The person playing Hamlet should be able to weep unabashedly and unashamedly."

I told Joe that I thought the reason so many actresses had wanted to play Hamlet was simply their desire to act a great role that offered complexities of thought and feeling not otherwise ascribed to or written for them.

Before rehearsals began, auditions of understudies for Venora's Hamlet were held in a studio room just around the corner from my office. I was moved when I saw a seated line of young women in boots waiting in our hallway to audition for this great role, free of the speciation of being female.

As director of the production, Joe dedicated himself to supporting the distinctive qualities that Diane Venora brought to playing Hamlet as a *young prince*, convinced that she could distinguish herself with a classically legitimate performance in the role.

Joe said, "Diane is a strong Hamlet, but not a macho Hamlet; vulnerable, but not hysterical. I've seen forty Hamlets but I've seen things in Diane's Hamlet I've never seen before. She illuminates parts of the play you would never see if a man were playing the role. When you take a major classic and change the terms of it, you immediately force people to really look at it again."

When the play was in dress rehearsals, Diane, in a moment of frustration about something, kicked the hard wall of the theater with her black-booted foot. I saw her crumple to the floor in pain as someone rushed to call an ambulance. In the incredible aftermath that followed, medics placed Venora on a stretcher in her Hamlet costume and slowly carried her out through the Public Theater's lobby—just like the dead Hamlet at the end of the play when Prince Fortinbras says, "Let four captains bear Hamlet, like a soldier, to the stage."

The opening had to be postponed for a couple of weeks for her injured foot to heal, but Diane returned to the role better than ever.

I loved this Hamlet!

Looking every inch the part at age thirty (and at times bearing a startling resemblance to Joe's twenty-one-year-old son Tony), Venora was a passionate young prince in a state of shocked bereavement—betrayed, bewildered, disillusioned, diabolical, revengeful, vulnerable, and brave. The emotional honesty and virtuosic range of her performance deeply moved me.

For instance, in the scene where Hamlet accidentally discovers Ophelia's funeral in progress and sees her brother Laertes weeping at her grave, he's both shocked by her death and furiously competitive with her brother's grief. Hamlet jumps into Ophelia's grave, crying out to Laertes, "Woo't weep? Woo't fight? Woo't fast? Woo't tear thyself? Woo't drink up eisel [vinegar], eat a crocodile? I'll do 't."

To this day I remember how Venora's rich voice cracked on the word "eisel" in her vainglorious, half-crazed protestation. She broke your heart.

49

Undying Hatred of Nazis at Tea Time

Joe once told a reporter, "The thought of relaxing never crosses my mind. When you work really hard, it naturally relaxes you. I get tense when I'm not working. I never take vacations. If I go someplace there has to be a purpose."

Our foreign travel on theater-related business, which had increased dramatically in the 1980s, was always on a tight schedule that left no room for personal excursions.

However a week before our departure for London on one such trip in 1984, I was mystified when Joe said, "Why don't we drive out to Penzance and back?"

"*Penzance?*" I said.

"Yes, Penzance," Joe said. "Why not?"

"What's there that you need to see or do?" I asked.

"Well there's the sea," Joe said. "But mainly I thought it would be nice for you and me to go on a scenic trip in the English countryside. We've never done that."

And so a week later we were motoring along the hedgerowed highway to Penzance in a green Rover driven by an Anglo-Irish guide. Following Joe's instructions, he avoided all the sightseeing detours to museums and churches, delivering us at night to lodgings in thatched-roof villages.

The only person on our agenda during our driving excursion to Penzance was A. L. Rowse, the celebrated Elizabethan historian. For the past fifty years

236

he had been an openly gay scholar at the research-oriented All Souls College at Oxford University. He was also its first endowed Fellow with a working-class background and the author of a hundred books about the Elizabethans, Shakespeare, Rowse's Cornish boyhood, and the groundbreaking *Homosexuals in History*, which I had always wanted to read.

Joe and I had never hobnobbed with a Shakespearean savant like Rowse, but we were attracted by his kind invitation to visit him at Trenarren House, where he lived in rural isolation in a tiny village at the tip of the Cornish boot of England that juts out into the Atlantic Ocean.

When we arrived in sparkling Penzance, Joe read aloud the directions that Rowse had sent us in a letter. "My house," he wrote, "is located three miles out of St. Austell towards Black Head."

Frowning over his road map, our driver complained that this didn't tell him the street that Rowse lived on, and for some time we dithered around the unmarked byways of this hamlet making hapless turns at every chicken crossing and cow lane until we found ourselves bumping with alarming speed down a footpath toward a cliff with a view of the azure blue ocean beyond it.

I imagined the green Rover hurtling into the sea from the cliff's edge like a movie stunt, but a stone wall stopped us and the driver got out to knock at a door in it for help. He returned triumphant. Willy-nilly, we had stumbled onto Trenarren House—and A. L. Rowse was at home.

The bespectacled, sharp-nosed scholar graciously received Joe and me for tea on his stone terrace overlooking the sea. He was garrulous and opinionated as he chatted about his late friend "Dear Tom"—the poet T. S. Eliot—and Eliot's first wife Viv, whom he called a "witch," erupting with this epithet when Joe told him that he would be producing a new play by Michael Hastings called *Tom & Viv* in association with Max Stafford-Clark's Royal Court Theater.

Rowse reminisced about his many other illustrious, long-dead friends, citing in particular the German scholars and scientists he'd known who had been driven into exile or murdered by the Nazis. Swatting at the wasps that had begun to swarm over the bowl of home-grown figs that his housekeeper had placed on the patio table, Rowse then exclaimed in great emotional agitation, "I *hate* this century! I *hate* democracy!"

This outburst, in the context of what Rowse had just told us about the murder of German scholars by the Nazis, I mentally attributed to the twentieth-century's god-awful place in history as an era of unprecedented mass slaughter. Rowse's outburst about hating democracy took me an extra moment of mental calculation (and later checking), but he seemed to be citing the fact that Hitler and the Nazi Party had received a whopping third of the votes in Germany's democratic parliamentary elections in 1932.

Joe and I listened in flummoxed silence as he also fulminated against a rival scholar's claim that Shakespeare's sonnets had been written to a gay patron.

"What egregious nonsense!" Rowse exploded, insisting, as he had done in his writing several times, that Shakespeare was "a strongly sexed heterosexual who was faced with an unusual situation when the handsome, young, bisexual Earl of Southampton fell in love with him."

When we were about to leave, it was obvious that our host had been pleased by our visit. Walking us to his gate, Rowse said, "You know, when I was a poor boy growing up in nearby Tregonissey, I used to gaze at Trenarren House from a distance and dream of living here someday."

Before our Green Rover backed out of his stone-walled cul-de-sac to return to Penzance, Rowse confessed to us through its open rear passenger window that he felt a special kinship with Americans because, he said, "The first English-speaking settlers in America, you know, were *Elizabethans*."

On the drive back to Penzance, I was aware that Joe didn't feel as stimulated by our visit to Trenarren House as I did and guessed that Rowse's Labour-turned-to-Tory politics had soured him, the unfavorable impression only somewhat ameliorated by Rowse's undying hatred of the Nazis.

Possessed with an eagerness to read Rowse's books, I was delighted to find *Homosexuals in History: A Study of Ambivalence in Society, Literature and the Arts* at a bookstore in the seaside town. Because I had been meeting back home with Larry Kramer regarding *The Normal Heart,* his play about the AIDS epidemic then ravaging the gay community in New York City, I was especially drawn to the subject of Rowse's book, which had been published in 1977.

"It's an astonishing survey of important gay men in history up to modern times," I said to Joe after I'd finished reading its preface back at our hotel. "Rowse also writes about what he calls 'the psychological rewards of ambivalence.'" I had to put the interesting book aside for the time being, however, because we had a six-hour drive back to London the next day to see a play at the Royal Court Theater in the evening, and we intended to leave at the crack of dawn.

That schedule got us back in London with some free time in the afternoon, so we decided to visit the Middle Temple, the only place still in existence where a play by Shakespeare—it was *Twelfth Night* in 1602—had been performed during his lifetime. But when Joe and I arrived there, we were disappointed to find a sign on the Middle Temple's massive door that said, "NOT OPEN TO THE PUBLIC."

Amazingly, however, the massive door was slightly ajar, and we could see through its towering breach that the place was empty. We walked in, and there before us was the resplendent Elizabethan hall in all its refurbished glory. A carved oak beam ceiling vaulted high above its wainscoted walls and stained-glass windows emblazoned with escutcheons. Joe and I tried to picture Shakespeare's original cast of Viola, Olivia, Orsino, Sir Toby Belch, and Malvolio performing in the long rectangular space of the enormous hall, and where the audiences might have sat. But our illegal presence had been detected and a Dickensian beadle suddenly rushed in shouting, "No, no, NO! NOT OPEN TO THE PUBLIC!" and chased us out into the street.

Still having free time, we stopped by the archaeological excavation of the Elizabethan Rose Theater that was then in progress. The remains of the Rose Theater, a rival of Shakespeare's Globe Theater, had been recently discovered during an urban construction project. It aroused much excitement because Shakespeare's *Henry VI, Part 1* and *Titus Andronicus* had been performed at the Rose and Shakespeare himself had acted there. A successful campaign had been launched to preserve the vestiges of the Rose Theater underneath the modern building that would soon be rising above them. Fortunately Joe and I saw them when the site was still open to the sky and we could make out the ground contours of the 400-year-old theater, where excavators had found its audience areas littered with hazelnut shells.

Shakespeare's Globe Theater had been almost next door to the Rose, but unlike the Rose, its footprint wasn't preserved because there'd been no stay of construction of the modern building above it to allow time for an archaeological investigation. However, we did find public access to a dimly lit cellar in the modern building, where we were able to view the soggy imprint left by a few Elizabethan timbers on the Globe Theater's original site.

Stimulated by what we'd seen during the day, I asked an usher at the Royal Court Theater that night if anyone had ever come across a *bourne*—as

Joe (second from right) across the street from the archaeological excavation
of the Elizabethan Rose Theater in London in 1989. Shakespeare's
Globe Theater was its neighbor in the area of the overpass.
Gail Papp

in Hamlet's famous description of death being "That undiscovered country from whose bourne no traveler returns."

"Why yes, luv," she said. "We've got one here at the corner."

And sure enough, at the corner Joe and I found the bourne. It was a small earthen opening from which you could hear the faint gurgling of a deep underground stream. We each put an ear to it.

50

The Normal Heart

I had become involved with *The Normal Heart,* Larry Kramer's now-famous play about the beginning of the AIDS crisis in New York City in 1984, after the work had been rejected by numerous agents, directors, and producers. Kramer had then turned for help to Emmett Foster, Joe's personal assistant at that time, who was also a solo performance artist revered for his deadpan expression of eternal perplexity and vexation with human affairs.

Many years later, after Joe's death in 1991, Emmett reminisced in my living room about Larry Kramer's outreach to him at the Public Theater.

"Larry wanted to know how to get his play to Joe," Emmett told me. "I didn't know about his personality and tactics at that point. If I did, I probably would have said '*All right, whatever you want, just spare me the years of aggravation.*'"

In this imagined aside, Emmett was acknowledging Larry Kramer's reputation as a notoriously critical and castigating personality.

Emmett continued, "So I told him I thought he should go about it the proper way, and give the play to Gail and the Play Department and have it read. But he wanted Joe Papp to read his play and he really didn't want to go through the usual circuits."

Emmett squinted as he tried to recall the precise details of his past history pertaining to *The Normal Heart.*

"Then Larry was at me and calling me and asking me questions. I've blocked it out like a really bad dream, but I remember him trying to manipulate me into things that I didn't really want to do. He went on the attack and wrote Joe something like, 'You don't want to do this play because you're homophobic.'"

"Oh my gosh," I said. "I never heard that part before."

"And I remember *exactly* what I said to Larry," Emmett continued, going on to chastise the guilty playwright as if he was in the room with us. "I said, 'I will be *happy* to give this letter to Joe from you. I will be *more than happy* to take it in there and put it on his desk. But I just want to tell you, if Joe reads this letter, you will not have your play produced at this theater. Joe doesn't go for that kind of tactic. But I'll be *real* happy to go in there right now and put the letter on his desk.' So he came to his senses and said 'All right, don't.'"

Eventually Larry Kramer allowed Emmett to give *The Normal Heart* to me and the Play Department.

In the meantime, Emmett read it himself.

"I didn't know how to tell Larry that I didn't think it was a well-written play," Emmett said. "Of course, if you're a gay man in the middle of the AIDS crisis, yes, it's got some resonance. But it was hard for me to tell Larry things. Once he came to the theater and was right outside of Joe's office, and was saying to me 'Well, what the *fuck*, he's doing that *Cinders* thing up there in that hall' and I said, 'Larry, Janusz Glowacki's *Cinders* is a well-*written* play.'"

I had been unaware of these machinations when Bill Hart, the Public Theater's Literary Manager, placed *The Normal Heart* on my desk saying, "I think you should read this. It's about AIDS. The text is *interminable*, but there are all these little veins of interest—a little bit of gold here and there in all the sludge. I think it has possibilities."

On Bill Hart's recommendation, I set about reading *The Normal Heart* but found that its numerous characters, locales, flashbacks, soliloquies, and pages of mind-numbing medical statistics didn't provide easy access to the substance of the work itself. On superficial examination it seemed to be a political story about the members of a gay service organization competing for space with an unrelated family story about a gay and a straight brother.

I felt there was a disconnect between the personal and political stories in *The Normal Heart*—unlike the brilliant plays that Joe had produced by Eric Bogosian, Caryl Churchill, Charles Gordone, David Hare, David Henry

Hwang, Tony Kushner, Miguel Piñero, David Rabe, Dennis Reardon, Nto-zake Shange, Wallace Shawn, Elizabeth Swados, and George C. Wolfe—play-wrights who had achieved an imaginative fusion of life experience with social themes and politics.

Written with noble fire in a time of cruel silence about AIDS, *The Normal Heart*'s dramaturgical chaos was complex, suggesting a whole history of over-whelming prejudice and aversion, of things that had either been denied by other people to the characters, or had not been faced by the gay community itself. By the time I finished reading the play, I had been swept off my feet by the protagonist's biblical rage as he grappled with the mysterious illness of his friends and finally the death of his lover from AIDS.

I called the playwright and arranged a meeting with him.

Emmett had warned me about Larry Kramer's confrontational personality as well as his irritation about the handling of his script at the Public because it hadn't been given directly to Joe, so I had steeled myself for a difficult first meeting when Larry Kramer, a grizzled man in his late forties, walked into my office with his dog.

"I was incredibly moved by your play," I began, and then told him all the things that I admired about *The Normal Heart*. His comparing the neglect of the AIDS crisis to the media's neglect of the Holocaust in World War II was a powerful indictment, I said. His depiction of the tortured confusion of the characters in the play was devastating. Their inability to reach a consensus for political action was riveting. The death of the protagonist's lover was heartbreaking.

When I paused for a moment to ask him a question about something that I hadn't understood concerning one of his characters, Kramer whisked a large notebook from his briefcase and began writing furiously.

"Yes!" he exclaimed. "That's because he's a *composite* character."

Returning the following week with rewrites I hadn't asked for, he sat down again in my office and, to my surprise, wanted more questions. I had the advantage of knowing nothing about his recent expulsion from the board of the Gay Men's Health Crisis, of which he was a co-founder, so I wasn't able to read the details and personalities of that real-life drama into the play. Larry liked the informal methodology of my asking questions because, when he tried to explain something to me, it became clearer in his own mind. He demonstrated a great facility and eagerness to rewrite.

At this time in 1984, I was acutely aware of Joe's dissatisfaction with the playwriting of that decade which he felt paralleled the conservative swing following President Reagan's election at the beginning of the decade. I winced in agreement when Joe said that the country had seen a diminution of the kind of energy a place like the Public Theater drew on.

"We flourished in terms of our social consciousness in the Sixties and Seventies," he told the staff at an annual meeting in the Anspacher Theater, "when most of the plays here were about Vietnam, civil rights, Black plays, some Latino works. But the consciousness now is different and it shows in what we do."

I remembered all too vividly the recent era Joe referred to when the circumstances of contemporary life had been closer to what was being done in the theater than they were now, when writers had been writing plays that reflected what was happening on a major scale.

The Normal Heart is in that tradition, I thought, but what good will it do to give the play to Joe in its present unwieldy and confused version? I know he'll reject it, and I don't want that to happen.

Meanwhile Larry grew impatient for Joe to read it, convinced that the only hope of bringing attention to the ignored AIDS epidemic was through his play being produced at the Public Theater as soon as possible.

"When are you going to give it to Joe?" he would nag me.

I heard that Larry was sending the script to other theaters. I didn't know if that was true—it could be, because the Public didn't have an option on the play—but it forced me to think harder about what I should do. Sensitive to the fact that I was both the gateway and the impediment to Larry's script reaching Joe, I felt a stark crunch of priorities—the specter of AIDS all around us among our friends and co-workers, about which there was still an appalling official silence on the part of the federal, state, and city governments, weighed in the balance against my sense of what kind of draft of the play I could persuade Joe to consider, or even to read.

I had been brooding about this matter when Larry stopped by my office with his dog one day. He didn't sit down. Triumphantly cheerful, he told me "I've cut *all* the stuff that I love BEST—all the flashbacks about the two brothers. I'll make another play of them."

I looked at what he'd done. In his new version the shape of *The Normal Heart* became visible for the first time.

It was set in New York City from 1981 to 1984 during the outbreak of the first cases of AIDS. A gay journalist, estranged from a straight brother, writes scathing indictments of the *New York Times* and Mayor Edward Koch for ignoring the AIDS crisis. His intemperate political confrontations with public figures outrage his co-founding partners on the board of a gay health service organization, which ousts him, as his lover dies from AIDS.

"Okay," I said. "I'll give the script to Joe."

When I first began to read scripts for Joe I discovered that we had similar tastes in plays. I really can't account for it. We were dissimilar in so many ways. There was a thirteen-year age difference, a difference in backgrounds, and our personalities were polar opposites. Nevertheless we were both attracted by powerful language and subjects inspired by what Joe called "the terror and pity" of human existence. I shared his conviction that art was "fighting energy and an affirmation of the struggle to live."

But I knew that persuading him to read *The Normal Heart* wouldn't be an easy task because, despite my privileged access to Joe, I had learned that there was never a good time to ask him to read a play. Regardless of the circumstances, it spoiled his mood and interrupted something that had a greater claim on his attention. In addition Joe was habitually doubtful that recommendations ever proved to be worth their salt, and I was in no way exempt from that standard, so there were many reasons for me to severely test my judgment before recommending a script to him.

Although Joe was often passionate about the plays he produced, at the beginning of the process he was seldom enthusiastic about producing any play, as if the last thing on earth he wanted to do was to take on the responsibility of bringing yet another play to fruition in one of his theaters.

Since *The Normal Heart* was too long to read in one sitting at the office, I brought it home. Taking a deep breath, I said to Joe, "Here's a play that deals with a really important issue. It needs a lot of work, but it's full of passion and I think you should read it."

"What's it about?" Joe asked me.

"AIDS."

"Gail, you know I don't like plays about illness," Joe said. "I've never done them, and I never will do them."

"I know," I said, "but this one is different."

I left the script on our dining-working table, but a week passed before Joe picked it up. The first twenty pages were a disaster.

"Gail, I can't go on with this," he said, pushing the script away as if he'd just tasted spoiled milk. "This is one of the worst things I've ever read."

"I know, I know," I said, "but if you read a little further, you'll see that it has something."

Putting myself on the artistic line with Joe was a nerve-wracking business. I wasn't shielded from his stern verdict about the worthiness of a play anymore than anyone else was. However, I felt confident about *The Normal Heart*, not because it was timely or political, but because it had made me cry, something that rarely happened when I read a play.

Reluctantly, Joe picked up the imperfect opus again, protesting every time he turned a page, alternately on strike or grumpy about going on with it, but he finally got to the end and when he did he was in tears, as moved as I had been.

When Larry walked into Joe's office for the first time, Joe didn't give him a chance to sit down before he said, "I want to produce *The Normal Heart* but I expect you to do more work on it."

This wasn't music to Larry's ears because it meant a further delay.

"But it's a *wonderful* play," he complained. "Why won't you do it right away?"

After he left, Joe called Bill Hart to his office. "Someone has to get control of the play's structure," he said to Bill. "Meet with Larry. See what you can do."

Literary Manager Bill Hart was a chain-smoking intellectual who was engaged at that time in curating a play called *Cuba and His Teddy Bear* by a teenage Cuban-Russian playwright named Reinaldo Povod. Joe, knowing nothing about Bill as a director but sensing his special relationship with Povod, had chosen him to direct the play at the Public Theater with a brilliant cast headed by Robert De Niro, after which Joe moved *Cuba* to Broadway for a sold-out run.

Despite that current assignment, Bill was excited to work on *The Normal Heart*.

"You had something very unusual," he recollected when we got together years later to talk about it, "which was Larry Kramer, the writer himself, who's a homosexual moralist—outspoken, righteous, dealing with right and wrong and what has to be done—in a culture of *playboys*, which has a whole list of laws like 'Leave us alone to our vices, we've barely had a chance to enjoy them.' It's unusual to have a person say '*I accuse*.' This is not what we're used to saying about ourselves. It's usually against the right wing."

Bill flashed his mischievous smile at me.

"But Larry was invested in being truthful, in a sense in being '*straight*.' There's a robustness, a vigor, a directness in the writing, rather than cleverness and charm. Here's a guy who in all his fury is coming right at you. Well, I thought to myself, this is actually refreshing!"

There was no temper or ego flying around at all when Bill and I worked with Larry, but that was not the case in Larry's dealings with other people on the Public Theater's staff.

Rosemarie Tichler—Casting Director at the time of *The Normal Heart* and later Artistic Producer of the Public Theater in the 1990s—confided to me, in her characteristic stage whisper, that "Larry had a critical edgy stance always. He would joke about his dog, and other things, but there wasn't a real sense that we were in this together. He maneuvered in outrageous ways and didn't trust anyone to do their job professionally. In the end, however, we came out of the work with a great deal of respect for each other."

Meanwhile, Emmett Foster heard through the grapevine that Larry had thrown a pair of costume shoes—saying "These are *ugly!*"—out a third-floor window, and that the production manager wouldn't let him in his office. Soon the rumors about Larry Kramer being "an impossible man who threatens, cajoles, wheedles, and does anything to get you" reached the producer's office. When they did, Joe joked, "I wouldn't want to have him for an enemy, but fortunately he's a friend."

Larry offered to show us his file of newspaper clippings that documented his accusations against his two designated villains in *The Normal Heart*: Mayor Edward Koch and the *New York Times*.

This was a touchy matter because both were fulcrums of power in the city with whom Joe had sensitive relationships. First of all, Mayor Koch was our landlord. The city owned the Public and the Delacorte Theaters, and the Mayor controlled the leases and purse strings for their upkeep. Furthermore, Mayor Koch's Corporation Counsel and Cultural Commissioner were ex-officio trustees who sat on the Public Theater's board and attended our meetings.

Of equal importance was the *New York Times* where Joe valued his cordial relationship with Managing Editor Arthur Gelb, who, despite Joe's feuds with a long succession of the newspaper's theater critics, had always been supportive of him.

I was in Joe's office when he telephoned Koch and Gelb to inform them that he was producing a play that hung their institutions out to dry, saying, "I have a play that is going to severely criticize your institution—and you personally, Ed—and I'm going to go ahead with it. I can't censor my writer."

Koch said, "Fine, Joe. Thanks for telling me."

But Gelb protested on the phone that Kramer's allegations about the *New York Times* were incorrect. Joe replied that the author's documentation seemed to be in order. We had in fact vetted it with the theater's law firm and verified the accuracy of Larry's specific complaint—i.e., that the *Times*' reportage of the AIDS epidemic from 1982 to 1983 had been meager compared to its prolific coverage of deaths caused by deliberately poisoned Tylenol in the same time period.

Citing the evidence, the protagonist in *The Normal Heart* (Ned Weeks) says, "Have you been following the Tylenol scare? In three months there have been *seven* deaths, and the *Times* has written fifty-four articles. The month of October alone they ran one article every single day. Four of them were on the front page. For us—in seventeen months they've written seven puny articles. And we have a *thousand* cases!"

I was both excited and nervous when Joe, gambling on the combined talents of the playwright, director, and literary manager to get *The Normal Heart* in shape, set the wheels in motion for its production. The team did a fantastic job. By the time previews began, the script had gone through many rewrites, an hour had been cut from the play, and an important new scene added at the end. Director Michael Lindsay-Hogg had fine-tuned an outstanding ensemble of thirteen actors, including Brad Davis in the leading role of Ned Weeks, and Eugene Lee had designed a powerful set displaying the names of hundreds of people who had died of AIDS, reminiscent of Maya Lin's Vietnam memorial wall in Washington, D.C.

Emmett Foster remembered crying through the whole thing when he saw *The Normal Heart* for the first time.

"I went up to Larry after the play," Emmett told me. "I was still crying, and I said 'Larry, it was so powerful. What an incredible piece of theater. Please don't misunderstand these tears. I still think that you're a big asshole, but the play was so incredibly moving.'"

Emmett wasn't alone. Every night at the end of *The Normal Heart*, as the audience left the Anspacher Theater, there would be groups of theatergoers who didn't leave, mostly men who remained in their seats, unable to move. Sometimes Joe and I saw people in the audience go over and sit with a group. Some wept. Some comforted them. A few just stared at the empty stage. Ushers never hustled them out. When they did leave the Anspacher Theater, many of them lingered in the lobby downstairs, talking in low voices. Joe and I saw this moving ritual night after night, a kind of testifying and witnessing.

Years later when Bill Hart and I reminisced about the impact of *The Normal Heart*, Bill told me, "What the play had to do with AIDS was one thing. What it had to do with homosexual consciousness is quite another. *That* is what it really changed."

He reminded me that Leonard Bernstein had come to see *The Normal Heart*.

"He was really quite impressed," Bill said, "and was particularly interested in the play's recitation of all these famous artists, writers, and respected thinkers in history who were homosexual. And he said to me 'Oh, this is great! *Am I going to be on there next?*'"

As though confirming the adage that if everything seems to be going well, you have obviously overlooked something, another "first" play about AIDS opened off-Broadway in 1985 at the Circle Repertory Theater twenty days before our opening of *The Normal Heart*. In his review of *As Is* by William Hoffman, *New York Times* critic Frank Rich wrote that it "turned a tale of the dead and dying into the liveliest new work to be seen [at Circle Rep] in several seasons."

It read like a "money review," meaning the kind of notice that launches a play from off-Broadway to Broadway where national attention is paid, Tony Awards are given, future productions around the country are boosted, and money can be made.

Frank Rich praised playwright William Hoffman for dealing with the "squeamish" subject of AIDS with "both charity and humor." He noted that the play's protagonists "recall fond memories of past anonymous liaisons in leather bars . . . but in mocking obsessive promiscuity with light wit, the playwright can gracefully bid such behavior a permanent farewell without adopting a hectoring, moralistic tone."

The Circle Rep play moved to the Lyceum Theater on Broadway in time for a Tony nomination for Best Play.

As the date of *The Normal Heart*'s premiere at the Public Theater drew near, Larry was pessimistic, predicting that the *Times* would not favorably review a second play about AIDS a mere two weeks after the first one.

On the night of our press opening in April, I joined the cast and crew in the greenroom, an informal space ringed by mirrors and dressing rooms, to hear Joe read the review in the *New York Times* which someone had dashed out to buy at a local newsstand.

As Joe read the review to us, it was clear that Frank Rich hadn't liked *The Normal Heart* very much. He characterized it as "a parochial legal brief," objecting to its "unflagging, at times even hysterical, sense of urgency." He voiced his irritation with the "galloping egocentricity" of its protagonist and criticized the play's "pamphleteering tone." Although he acknowledged "powerful vignettes sprinkled throughout," he said that its characters were "flatly written" and that the dramaturgical deficits of the work "blunt the play's effectiveness." He was strangely unmoved.

As if this thumbs-down review wasn't enough, an unprecedented, black-framed, unsigned editorial box appeared next to it objecting to the play's allegations about the newspaper's coverage of AIDS. The *Times*' editorial box took issue with Larry's charges of neglect, saying that the newspaper had assigned a member of its scientific staff as early as 1981 to cover the AIDS pandemic, making the *Times* "one of the first—if not the first—national news media to alert the public to the scientific recognition and spread of the disease."

All that was true. But Larry's point in the play had not been that the *Times* failed to report the early stages of the AIDS epidemic, but that the *Times* had run only a handful of articles about it in comparison to dozens of stories about the significantly less fatal and isolated occurrence of the poisoned Tylenol scare.

There was an eerie silence in the greenroom after Joe finished reading the review and editorial box to us, like the hush when a coffin is lowered into a grave. I felt angry and sick at heart thinking of the enormous personal and professional effort that had gone into bringing *The Normal Heart* to the stage, of Larry's long and difficult journey with the script, and our belief in its power.

Removing his tortoise-shell reading glasses, Joe looked at the circle of downcast people around him.

"Every so often," he said to us, "maybe once in a decade, if even that, we have a play that can make a difference and affect the world we live in. I believe *The Normal Heart* is that kind of play, and I'm going to run it in this theater as long as I possibly can because its presence on the stage is so important."

Everyone burst into cheers.

The Normal Heart became the longest-running play in the history of the Public Theater. The same year that the *Times* gave it a lukewarm notice in New York, it won the 1985 Olivier Best Play of the Year Award in London. The British National Theater named it one of the "hundred most important plays of the twentieth century." By the end of the decade, it had had more than six hundred productions in eighteen countries. Twenty-five years later it opened on Broadway for the first time and finally won the Tony Award it had so long deserved.

To do him justice, the critic of the play in 1985 later amended his view to a more favorable opinion, an unusual instance of fair-minded hindsight.

Looking back on the culturally conservative landscape of the United States in the 1980s, I was proud that Joe had been able to say, "Larry's play put us in touch with the world again."

.51

Life, Loss, and Redress in 1986

After listening to the songs of the British-American singer-songwriter Rupert Holmes on LP records, I went to see him perform at a nightclub. Since no one from the Public was free to go with me, I went alone, feeling a little Eeyore-ish sitting at a table by myself, but I soon forgot about that when Holmes' wonderful performance began and I came under the spell of his exceptional music and lyrics. After the show I wrote a note on my card and left it at the front door, asking if he might be interested in doing something in musical theater. His answer came the next day. It was Yes!

When Rupert Holmes, a convivial man in his thirties wearing oversized aviator sunglasses, arrived at my office, I responded right away to his enthusiasm about a musical he had in mind based on Charles Dickens' unfinished last novel, *The Mystery of Edwin Drood.*

He told me that he'd invented a framing device to render the story as a British music hall entertainment (Holmes was half-British) with multiple whodunnit and romantically paired musical endings to Dickens' suggestive unfinished plot. The audience would vote on them, he said, and depending on how the vote went, there would be different ways both dramatically and musically that the show could end at each performance.

This was more fun than I'd ever bargained for in my work, and as Rupert set about writing his musical, it seemed to emerge almost perfectly formed like a full-blown Venus on a half-shell. He would send me cassette tapes of the songs as he wrote them, with him singing and accompanying himself on his synthesizer. Already, there were hints of the orchestrations that he would later compose—an unusual feat in musical theater where the talents of songwriter, lyricist, book writer, and orchestrator are seldom found all in one person.

"I can compose in any style you want," he told me one day, and the next day sent me a cassette tape of a symphonic movement he'd just composed on his synthesizer in the style of Mozart.

The music of *Drood* was so accomplished and irresistible that it was easy to get Artistic Director Wilford Leach involved. Meantime I had introduced Rupert to Joe and could hardly wait to hear Act I of *Drood* in a sing-through that Wil had organized with the amazing cast of Betty Buckley, George Rose, Cleo Laine, Howard McGillin, and Patti Cohenour, all of whom pledged to sign on for the still unfinished *Drood* if Joe produced it. A response like that tells you something about the exceptionally high quality and fabulous talent of this work-in-progress.

When we had a sing-through of the just-finished Act II, we heard for the first time the triumphant return of the missing, mysterious Edwin Drood in an anthem thrillingly sung by Betty Buckley:

> If you hear my voice, then you're alive.
> What a bloody marvel we survive,
> When you think of every risk we face
> In our mad human race!

Joe produced this musical first at the Delacorte Theater and then on Broadway, where it won five Tony Awards including Best Musical in 1986.

But tragedy set in that year when Rupert and his wife Elizabeth lost their little daughter Wendy to a brain tumor. And in a series of incomprehensible disasters, Larry Shue, the peerless actor-playwright in the cast, was killed in a plane crash and the consummate British actor George Rose was murdered in the Dominican Republic.

How to reconcile such terrible events with recollections of a different happier time seemed unattainable to me. Nevertheless there appears to have been something in the evolution of the human heart and brain that makes it possible for antithetical experiences and memories to coexist, and so my heart still aches over the tragedies associated with the production of *The Mystery of Edwin Drood*, but I still treasure my once-carefree and joyous memory of the magical creation of Rupert's musical.

That fall my stepson Tony Papp asked Joe and me to meet him for dinner at Knickerbocker's Restaurant in Greenwich Village. Already recognized at the age of twenty-five as an outstanding designer of marriage-of-metal artware (jewelry devised from different metals seamlessly soldered together), Tony had just opened his own gallery on Fifth Avenue and had been written up in *New York Magazine*. From a rebellious, openly gay teenager, he had become an activist for gay rights and a serious artist who now taught at Parsons School of Design.

"The situation is really *gross*," Tony said to Joe and me over appetizers, using his favorite expression of contempt as he told us about the status of New York City's proposed Gay and Lesbian Rights Bill that would prohibit discrimination in hiring, housing, and public accommodations.

Jabbing at his shrimp cocktail, he groaned, "The bill has been defeated for the past fourteen years by a coalition of the Catholic Church and Orthodox Jewish groups and they're campaigning against it again this year."

Tony asked his father to testify in support of the reintroduced gay rights bill at an upcoming public hearing at City Hall on March 11, 1986. Joe readily agreed.

On arriving at City Hall on the appointed day, however, Joe found a near-riot in progress between the bill's supporters and its opponents with so much angry yelling going on, it didn't seem as if Joe or any other speaker would be able to make themselves heard above the din of the polarized melee.

Ultra-Orthodox Hasidim from Brooklyn were in attendance, highly visible in their distinctive black Prince Albert tailcoats, black fedora hats, and long beards. As Mayor Edward Koch began to testify in favor of the bill, they booed him and showed their backs.

When it was Joe's turn to speak, he had to push his way through this heckling religious gauntlet to get to the podium. Then, as one reporter wrote the next day, "Producer Joseph Papp, who testified in favor of the bill, stunned the audience by reciting a long list of artists, writers and respected thinkers throughout history who were homosexuals."

Joe had liked my suggestion that he quote the list of famous gay men in history that the protagonist of *The Normal Heart* recites in a passionate speech.

Some of these famous names were the same ones I had read about in A. L. Rowse's *Homosexuals in History.*

Intoning the list like an Honor Roll at the microphone in City Hall, Joe gave each name a measured pause before he pronounced it:

"Marcel Proust
Henry James
Tchaikovsky
Cole Porter
Plato
Socrates
Aristotle
Alexander the Great
Michelangelo
Leonardo da Vinci
Christopher Marlowe
Walt Whitman
Tennessee Williams
Byron
E. M. Forster
Herman Melville
Federico García Lorca
W. H. Auden
Francis Bacon
Henry Stack Sullivan
John Maynard Keynes
Dag Hammarskjold
Bertrand Russell
George Santayana
King James I of England . . . "

At breakfast the next day I asked Joe if he'd seen the *Daily News* story about the gay rights hearing.

"No," he said.

I held it up. Its large boldface headline said "Uh, Mr. Papp, about your 'gays'. . ." Below it were pictures of five of the men whose names Joe had intoned at the hearing: Bertrand Russell, Herman Melville, Henry James, George Santayana, and Somerset Maugham. There was also a photograph of Joe, plus two more pictures. One was of John Lennon—because he'd been named in a *Daily News* list of "48 Heterosexual Role Models." The other was of Keith Hernandez, the St. Louis Cardinals' first baseman—because a *Daily News* reader was upset that his name hadn't been included in the list of "48 Heterosexual Role Models."

I said to Joe, "There are a few Letters to the Editor here from some disgruntled people. One of them strongly objects to your inclusion of Herman Melville."

"Okay," Joe said. "Let them write Larry."

"Listen to this!" I said. "Here's a reader complaining '*What Mr. Papp failed to mention is that these men, if they indeed lived a gay lifestyle, are burning in the eternal hell-fire. What kind of role model is that, Mr. Papp?*' Can you believe that?"

But it didn't matter. New York City's Gay and Lesbian Rights Bill finally passed into local law in 1986, and we celebrated its passage with Tony.

52

The Belasco Project

In 1987 Joe was interviewed by the acclaimed British actor Ian McKellen for a celebration of Shakespeare's birthday on National Public Radio. Responding to McKellen's questions about his American perspective on this occasion, Joe reminisced about his early experiences producing Shakespeare for school audiences in the 1950s.

Joe told McKellen, "When George C. Scott went out to the schools as *Richard III* in the early days, he scared the hell out of them and they paid attention, particularly in tough vocational schools. When he got up there, he'd swing one of these huge fourteenth century weapons and they would pay attention. It's the actor's responsibility to hold the attention of the audience. It must have been true in Shakespeare's time as well."

Joe also told McKellen about his own teenage experience of seeing *Hamlet* for the first time.

In 1938 when I was in high school they invited a bunch of us kids to go to Broadway and to see in one week *two* productions of *Hamlet*. One was with John Gielgud and the other was Leslie Howard. And you know we *all* had taste of some kind. You always have it on the street. You know a good dancer. You know a good piece of music. You know a good baseball player. So you have taste in this area as well.

"First of all, I thought the speech was artificial. Everything was so affected and sort of pompous to me. Sir John—before he was Sir John—was a young, handsome, very attractive, beautiful figure on the stage. He just was wonderful and some of the words affected me, but mostly I thought "Why does he have to speak in that fancy way?" I had already studied *Julius Caesar* in school and I knew you could say the lines in an American way, even in a Brooklyn way, and still understand them if the passion was there.

There was a very pretty girl sitting in front of me at the time and she was really getting most of my attention, so I missed a few things here and there. Probably all the soliloquies.

Forty-eight years later in 1986, Joe had put together a repertory company of actors, mostly young, who were Black, Hispanic, Asian, and white to perform Shakespeare for high school students.

"The stage will have the same kind of population that is in the schools," Joe had said when he announced it. "We'll do *Macbeth, As You Like It* and *Romeo and Juliet.* Estelle Parsons, the director, has a good sense of popularizing—not vulgarizing—Shakespeare, and here and there Spanish will come into the lines."

Most important, unlike his Shakespeare productions for students in the past which had been performed in school auditoriums, in 1986 these plays were to be done at the Belasco Theater on Broadway.

And instead of just one or two performances of a single play for the students in any given school, the Shakespeare plays at the Belasco on Broadway were to be performed *twice a day, six days a week, for nine months!*

Students now packed the 1,042-seat Belasco Theater twice a day, arriving in chartered buses, accompanied by teachers who had prepped them for the event in class. Most had never seen a play or been in a theater before. In this respect they were similar to our Mobile Theater audiences, albeit more distractable because they were teenagers. Nevertheless they were exceedingly quick and 100 percent interactive with the play, the players, and the characters, and unlike a regular theater-going audience, the teenagers got all the humor.

Since this $2.2 million program wasn't remotely within the regular budget of the Public Theater or within the scope of its normal fundraising capabilities, Joe set about raising the extra money himself from the Board of Education, the American Federation of Teachers, the mayor, the chief of police, and a consortium of newspapers, banks, and oil companies.

He persuaded the Shubert Organization to give him the use of the Belasco Theater, a lovely old dramatic house on Broadway, free for the duration of the program. Because there was no box office income involved at the Belasco (since all tickets were free), he was also able to obtain waivers from the eleven Broadway unions so that less-costly non-union labor could be hired to work on the shows.

We had to add temporary staff for a special unit at the Public to handle the complicated logistics and various agencies involved in running this program. The staff's nickname for it was "S.O.B." (Shakespeare on Broadway).

Joe explained the project's importance to them: "I selected a legitimate theater in order to give the kids a full theatrical experience rather than putting a play on in a noisy school auditorium where the first thing that happens is a teacher gets up and says 'SHUT UP!' and the next thing you hear is, 'If music be the food of love, play on!' That's not the proper atmosphere. You want to get them out of that atmosphere so that there's a sense of a festive occasion."

On the other hand, Joe had reservations about filling the Belasco Theater twice a day with students.

"I would prefer that they become part of a general audience. I don't like a bunch of kids thrown in together because their interests waver and they kid around with one another. But for the most part when you *do* get their attention, it's a remarkable achievement."

Joe's point was that when a young person is put in touch with the stimuli of art, either as a spectator or as a participant, a new world opens up. It demonstrates to a young person already cultured by her/his own music, dance, or a preacher's rhetoric, that they possess valuable and useful knowledge "in their bones," and that awareness gives them a feeling of confidence and a desire to learn.

"The Black, Hispanic, or Asian child begins to understand that his own culture is not something to be concealed or wiped out," Joe said, "but, on the contrary, it is part of a world culture and, as such, is to be nurtured and valued."

Actually his feelings about the ownership of culture had always embraced a much wider view—one without any age limit—and Joe reaffirmed it now in the new context of Shakespeare on Broadway.

"My connection has always been with the people who don't go to the theater. I mean, people who don't even know the theater exists. Ordinary people.

Since I come out of that myself, I feel that some forms should be evolved on an educational basis—from youth to old age—so that the arts become a way of life rather than just putting shows on in theaters. It means a different way of looking at the arts in the U.S."

At the end of the nine months of Free Shakespeare on Broadway, more than half a million students—and their parents (who were admitted free on Saturdays if accompanied by a student)—had seen our Shakespeare plays at the Belasco Theater.

53

Hoping against Hope

In retrospect, the exhilarating accomplishment of The Belasco Project in 1986 seemed to presage the nonconformist stride of the Public Theater's subsequent seasons, which included George C. Wolfe's audaciously satirical *The Colored Museum*, consisting of "exhibits" of stereotypes about African-American culture . . . Eric Bogosian's tour-de-force as playwright and performer in *Talk Radio* . . . Caryl Churchill's dazzling feat in *Serious Money* about the British stock market rendered as a murder mystery in rhymed couplets (starring young Alec Baldwin) . . . and director-choreographer Martha Clarke's *Vienna: Lusthaus*, a feast of musical dream images depicting "a civilization sleepwalking to the edge of doom."

We'd also developed and produced *Cuba and His Teddy Bear*, a play about a drug dealer and his rebellious son by Reinaldo Povod, the teenage Cuban-Russian playwright who was a protégé of Literary Manager Bill Hart. Directed by Hart, the relationships depicted in this work persuaded Robert De Niro to return to the stage at the head of an all-star cast in our 99-seat Shiva Theater. After Joe moved the play to the 1,091-seat Longacre Theater on Broadway for a limited run, long lines of teenagers queued up to buy tickets. The lines extended from the box office, down along West 48th Street, and wrapped around the corner and out of sight onto 8th Avenue—an unprecedented sight for any play at that time. The teenagers on the line didn't have credit cards; they paid cash. When Joe saw this, he decided to sell a third of the house at a steep discount.

In Central Park there had been *Much Ado About Nothing* with Kevin Kline and Blythe Danner in superlative top form as the quarrelsome lovers Benedick and Beatrice, worthy successors to Sam Waterston and Kathleen Widdoes in the Public Theater's 1972 production.

Few people were aware that Joe had also produced a delightful chamber version of Mozart's *The Magic Flute* with talented young actor-singers on the second floor of the building just north of us near Astor Place.

Next season? There would be *Julius Caesar* at the Public with Al Pacino as an electrifying Marc Antony that challenged Marlon Brando's movie achievement in the role.

Meanwhile Joe had pitched the idea of an oral history of the New York Shakespeare Festival/Public Theater to a publisher who had responded positively and helped to launch the ambitious project. The oral history was to be told, Rashomon-style, by Joe and more than a hundred actors, playwrights, directors and other people who had worked at the Public in a staggering number of taped interviews conducted by Kenneth Turan, the film critic of the *Los Angeles Times*. He also interviewed Joe, the future co-author of the book.

Their project got underway in January 1987 with Joe's first interview. At this point he and Kenneth Turan didn't know each other very well and they began on an awkwardly joking note:

Turan: Okay. I'm going to start from the beginning. That's just the way I find it easier to work.

Joe: What do you think, you're God?

Turan: He started before me.

Joe: No, he said, "As it was in the beginning . . ."

After that, they were off and running in a narrative decathlon that would eventually yield 1,107 pages of Joe's transcript, plus 5,581 pages from 159 other interviews. Honed to a 574-page book called *Free for All: Joe Papp, The Public, and the Greatest Theater Story Ever Told* by Kenneth Turan and Joseph Papp, it was later published by Doubleday in 2009.

The following month in this busy year Joe and I flew to Moscow to attend a Soviet-sponsored International Forum for a Nuclear-Free World. Hundreds of guests had been invited to this huge conference of world leaders in science, business, and the arts at which General Secretary Mikhail Gorbachev was to give the keynote address in a great hall at the Kremlin. There was a lot of buzz in that hall about the man sitting directly across the aisle from Joe and myself—the dissident nuclear scientist, Andrei Sakharov, who had been furloughed from his forced exile in Gorky to attend the event. Gorbachev spoke at very great length in a formally reasoned and historically contextualized speech in which he pleaded for "a nuclear weapon-free and non-violent world—for the sake of the immortality of human civilization."

It was now spring 1987 and Joe was confirming the line-up of plays that he planned to produce in Central Park that summer. Wilford Leach, the Public's Tony Award-winning Artistic Director, was going to direct *Henry IV, Part 1*, the great Falstaff play, as soon as he returned from London where he was directing the West End production of our musical *The Mystery of Edwin Drood*.

And Joe had persuaded Charles Ludlam, the flamboyant founder of the Ridiculous Theater, to direct his first Shakespeare at the Delacorte Theater in a wildly anticipated version of *Titus Andronicus*.

On his month-at-a-glance calendar, Joe had drawn a line through April 3 to 6 for a trip to the state of Yucatán in Mexico with the directors of our International Latino Festival, Oscar Ciccone and Cecilia Vega. The trip was to see the work of an indigenous theater company they wanted him to bring to New York. In a rush at the last minute Joe went to his internist for the necessary shots and had his annual checkup. He felt good, his only issue being a minor bursitis-like sensation in a shoulder. Since we were used to being together all the time, I knew I had to make plans to offset the emptiness I'd inevitably feel even during the brief four days that he'd be away.

On Joe's return, he was full of fresh energy and could hardly wait to tell me about what he'd seen in the Yucatán: "We had to go by boat and helicopter to watch this marvelous Indian peasant group perform an outdoor production of *Bodas de Sangre, Blood Wedding*, by Federico García Lorca," he said. "Their performance was quite unusual—most of it was done on horseback by 136 people!"

Joe also told me that when he disembarked from the helicopter after it had set down in a field that was the actual site of the performance, two hundred children rushed out from the surrounding woods and had run toward him, tossing flower petals as they shouted greetings in Spanish and Mayan.

"It was amazing!" Joe said. He was jubilant about the experience, and about Director María Alicia Martínez Medrano's powerful production of *Blood Wedding* performed by the indigenous company she'd founded in the tiny pueblo of Oxolotán. He said that despite some logistical challenges, the company was absolutely worth bringing to the Latino Festival in New York.

Later that week Joe's internist called us at home with his report on the physical that Joe had taken before his Yucatán trip. The doctor said that one of the tests he'd done indicated the possibility of prostate cancer but, he quickly added, since lab results were often quite different, he'd sent it out for retesting at another facility. Unfortunately it had confirmed the diagnosis. After a strained pause he said, "I'm sorry, Joe." Later that week a second doctor informed us that the disease was in an advanced stage and was inoperable. On the taxi ride home from that appointment, Joe and I gripped each other's hands, too stunned to speak.

In 1987 we had known each other for twenty-two years. At ages sixty-six and fifty-three we thought we had a reasonable slice of shared existence left to us, and Joe had assumed he still had a few good years to lead the Public Theater. At home we were immobilized at first in shock. However through our friends, Patrick Mehr and Helen Epstein (Joe's future biographer), we were put in touch with one of the few prostate cancer specialists in the country at that time, Dr. Marc Garnick, at the Dana-Farber Cancer Institute in Boston. We went up there for baseline tests that he ordered for Joe, checking wearily into a hotel on Boston Commons when, to our utter surprise and delight, the actors Kevin Kline and Phoebe Cates rang us from another floor. They'd come up from New York to keep us company, they said, and for the rest of that week they hung out with Joe and me, sitting cross-legged on the carpet in our hotel room as we talked about life, death, and Shakespeare.

After Dr. Garnick, who knew everything there was to know at that time about hindering the progression of advanced prostate cancer, took charge of Joe's treatment, we returned to New York in a somewhat better frame of mind. On our arrival at home, we received a phone call from Artistic Director Wilford Leach. He spoke to us from London, where he was directing *The Mystery of Edwin Drood* in the West End. Unaware of Joe's illness, the usually unflappable Wil sounded emotionally distraught on the phone as he told us that he wouldn't be able to direct the first play in Central Park.

"I've developed a bronchial condition caused by this darn weather in London," Wil said. "I can't tell you how sorry I am to let you down, Joe."

Besides being too sick to direct in the Park, Wil said that he'd been obliged to turn the London previews of *Drood* over to its brilliant choreographer, Graciela Daniele. Joe and I were expecting his return to New York, but Wil then disappeared. Only when his health deteriorated further did we learn that he had been diagnosed with AIDS, and that after being informed of it, Wil had sequestered himself in a Manhattan hotel for a couple of despondent weeks before checking into New York Hospital. We began to visit him there.

Wilford Leach had always seemed like Joe's natural heir—a talented director with producing expertise, taste, the ability to choose the right people and get things done. Though Wil didn't share Joe's love of Shakespeare (and didn't much like to direct his plays), Joe trusted Wil as an accomplished peer and a "dear, dear friend," and I had looked to Wil as a kind of surrogate brother. It was very painful now to think of the road ahead without him.

Joe's immediate problem as a producer now in May 1987 was *Henry IV, Part 1*. Since the play would have to be cast and go into rehearsal by the end of May if it was to be the first production in the Delacorte season, Joe needed to find a director to replace Wilford Leach who would be able to take it over right away.

"I'll only be able to get someone to do it as a professional favor," he told me.

At this moment we received more tragic news: Charles Ludlam had suddenly died of AIDS at Saint Vincent's Hospital.

There were now no directors for two of the Park's three summer productions. At this late date Joe concluded it would be impossible to find last-minute replacements for both Wilford Leach and Charles Ludlam. Without them there was still *Two Gentlemen of Verona* at the end of the season to be directed by Stuart Vaughan, a highly accomplished though prickly colleague of Joe's, who had been significantly, though intermittently, associated with him since the early Shakespeare Workshop days. As a director he was entirely capable of mounting two Shakespeare plays on short notice, but Joe knew that Vaughan wasn't free to direct anything before his scheduled play at the end of August.

Joe now faced the prospect of a Delacorte Theater that would be vacant during the months of June, July, and most of August. Since he couldn't let that happen, he decided he'd have to direct the first two plays himself. Although privately conscious of the fact that he was subject to the unpredictable course of a potentially lethal disease, he was feeling fine.

He decided to keep *Henry IV, Part 1*, but substitute *Richard II* for Ludlam's *Titus Andronicus*. In addition to his reputation as a prodigious producer of Shakespeare, Joe was also well-seasoned as a director of many of Shakespeare's plays, having directed eighteen of them in twenty-six productions. However, he had never directed these two particular plays before, although he had produced both of them twice.

Assuming directorial duties now under these tragic circumstances that were unknown to the public, he threw himself energetically into preparations for *Richard II*.

"I love Shakespeare," Joe told a radio host. "I just love his work. I'm directing *Richard II* this year, which is a play all in verse and rhymed couplets. And I'm also doing *Henry IV, Part 1*, which is the sequel to *Richard II*. They're two gorgeous plays for different reasons. Why do I get excited about a play all over again? You'd think by this time you wouldn't be talking about it. You'd say, well, you know, you've been around a while and you become kind of cynical about things. Not at all."

Joe began rehearsals of *Richard II* in June in an exuberant mood that reminded me of earlier years when he was still directing regularly in Central Park. It was wonderful to see him like that again.

He wrote,

> I learned something new about *Richard II*. Something about the central relationship between King Richard and his cousin Bolingbroke, who displaces Richard and becomes king (Henry IV). I had always thought of Bolingbroke as a villain and a treacherous usurper. But when I began to look at the speeches and work on the scenes, I realized that Bolingbroke is not the villain of the piece . . . [and] Richard isn't necessarily a martyr. Indeed, he is always the master of Bolingbroke because he's so good with words, and his cousin isn't. It's this verbal dexterity that allows Richard to dominate the play so thoroughly. Although he may lose in politics, he unquestionably wins in the theater—for in Shakespeare the character who controls the language is the character who controls the play. On any stage, and particularly on the Shakespearean stage, language is power, and language is life.

Shortly before *Richard II* opened in Central Park in July, we received a call at home from Michael Bennett, the genius who had conceived, choreographed, and directed *A Chorus Line*. He spoke to us from Tucson, Arizona, where he had been receiving treatment for lymphoma associated with AIDS. He was unaware of Joe's diagnosis.

"I'm calling to say goodbye," Michael told us in his boyish voice.

He thanked Joe for his friendship and recalled the Oath of Integrity we three had sworn twelve years earlier. He said, "I'm going to tap dance my way to heaven" and predicted that he and Joe would meet there again some day. He laughed when Joe replied, "Your place is assured but there's some doubt about mine." Michael Bennett died later that week.

In one sense late summer that year seemed almost normal because Joe didn't look, act, or feel ill. Sometimes his diagnosis seemed like a nightmare that had passed and I must have been in error to think it was real.

He had just started rehearsals of *Henry IV* when Tony, now twenty-six with a career as a recognized designer of artware, asked us to meet him at the office of his dermatologist. He was not at all his usual talkative self. When we sat down with him, his doctor informed us that Tony had been recently diagnosed with symptomatic AIDS. This appointment was Tony's way of letting Joe and me know about it. We were shocked. We'd had no idea that he was ill because, living away from home, he'd been able to keep it a closely guarded secret.

Later, when we were home alone, Joe and I broke down and cried together, devastated in this already cruelest of years that the plague of AIDS, for which there was no treatment in 1987, had precious Tony in its deadly clutches.

As it happened, that year Joe had made significant headway in negotiating a much-desired 99-year lease for the Public Theater with the City's Department of Cultural Affairs. At last the city was ready to approach the closing of the arrangement when Diane Coffey, a new interim commissioner of cultural affairs, came into office and it was claimed that all previous negotiations were no longer valid, including the duration of the lease. Despite the thorough groundwork that had been laid by Associate Producer Jason Steven Cohen, the new interim commissioner took the position that a 99-year lease could no longer be considered and put forward an insulting offer of a ten-year lease.

This took place shortly after Joe's diagnosis, the deaths of our colleagues in the theater, and Tony's diagnosis. To be suddenly confronted now with a threat to the future of the Public Theater was a provocation Joe couldn't deal with in a rational manner, and there was a flareup of tempers during his meeting with Interim Commissioner Coffey, after which he stormed out of her office.

He said, "I thought it wasn't fair or proper after all these productive years, and the money we have spent—not to mention the money the City has spent—to put the Public Theater's future in jeopardy."

But he'd run into an administrative brick wall, so Joe decided to appeal to Mayor Edward Koch.

Dear Ed,
    You and I have both been around for a while (and hopefully for longer), and I would appreciate your intervention at this juncture so we can amiably settle what has become an irritating dispute. I'm sure you have been kept informed of these developments, but I want you to hear my own voice in this matter. May I hear from you?

                                                        All the best, Joe

His appeal was heard. And so, in the long saga of finding, saving, buying, selling, converting, restoring, producing in, and holding on to the Public The-ater building, Joe finally obtained a 99-year lease with the city of New York securing its physical premises for a century. All was well that ended well . . . at least until 2089.

It would seem trivial for me to mention that on top of the catastrophic events that had seared our minds and broken our hearts in 1987, the two Park productions that Joe stepped in to direct at the last minute, due to the sudden death and the fatal illness of their respective directors, received bad reviews were it not that they prompted him to reflect on the Central Park audiences' striking independence of the critics' opinions.

In a note to himself, Joe wrote, "The nay-sayers' comments seemed to have little effect on attendance for the two Shakespeare plays. Decent weather brought out close to capacity houses night after night. Even threatened rain did not deter a hardy 300-500 people from making their way through Central Park to the Delacorte Theater, hoping, sometimes against hope, that the dark cloud will pass (as sometimes it does) and reveal a starlit sky or a moonlit night."

That phrase—"Hoping, sometimes against hope"—was what we had to hold onto now.

54

The Coach's View

I was surprised to see Joe looking at a heavily marked up copy of *Don Quixote* which he had spread open on our dining table at home. His underlines and marginal notes in the book dated to an idea he'd once had for a film roughly based on Miguel de Cervantes' novel that would merge the eccentric adventures of Don Quixote with the real-life vicissitudes of Cervantes.

I remembered Joe telling me, "The film will open with a rowdy dinner party at which Cervantes, who is impersonating Don Quixote, regales his guests with the stories of his fantastic escapades."

Joe had been interested in shooting it in Andalusia with Kevin Kline as Cervantes-Quixote. He had gone to Spain twice in pursuit of the idea, but the financing hadn't materialized and he'd put the project on hold and his marked-up copy of the classic novel back on the shelf.

"Listen to this!" Joe now exclaimed, saying that he'd just re-read Carlos Fuentes' Introduction to *Don Quixote* and there was something in it he wanted to share with me.

"Okay," I said. "I'm listening."

Assuming the manner of a raconteur telling a hugely amusing story, Joe read two sentences from the introduction: "It so happens that there is this rogue who is writing a book about his own life and Don Quixote asks him 'Is the book finished?' And the rogue answers him: 'How can it be, if my life isn't over yet?'"

I laughed, but later when I looked at the open book on the table, I saw that Joe had underlined *"if my life isn't over yet"* with a red pencil.

During that harrowing year of 1987, Joe had initiated a major project with Bantam Books to publish the complete works of Shakespeare in a set of paperbacks illustrated with photographs from the Festival's productions and with introductions by Joe to each play. The boxed paperback collection, edited by the Shakespeare scholar David Bevington, was also to have a companion volume called *Shakespeare ALIVE!* chronicling the everyday life of people in Shakespeare's London. The talented Rhodes scholar and writer Betsy Kirkland came on board as Joe's collaborator, and the two of them worked feverishly throughout the year both on the introductions to the plays and the companion volume.

It wasn't until September, after Joe had finished the all-consuming tasks of directing *Richard II* and *Henry IV, Part 1* in Central Park, that he began to discuss something that would have been unimaginable to us at the beginning of the year: Who he might approach about taking over the Public Theater if he should no longer be able to run it. Although Joe was still feeling fine, he nevertheless knew he had to start dealing with this difficult issue. In keeping with the uniquely personal nature of the Public Theater, he never conceived of the choice of a successor as an initiative for a Search Committee to take, but rather as a personal responsibility on his part for which he would later seek the board's approval.

"There are very few people who could handle an organization of this size," Joe said to me at home. "I learned as I went, but it's not like starting over again. It's very very hard."

I nodded, trying to seem normally engaged as I always was whenever Joe spearheaded the discussion of an important subject this way.

"It needs a commonsense, hard-minded kind of person who has love for the theater," he went on. "The fundamental questions will be, Are they bright? Are they intelligent? Do they have a social conscience? Are they familiar with the theater? Do they have good resources? Do they have a good mind? Can they raise money? Do they have this kind of capacity?"

I nodded again. *Was I sane? Was I alive? Could we really be "discussing" the qualifications of someone to succeed Joe on the presumption that he might soon be dead?*

Joe had privately told a few friends about his illness, but we had decided against a public announcement of it, convinced that this would cast a pall over the Public Theater and adversely impact his ability to do his job effectively. We were aware of the rumors circulating that he was ill, but when asked about them in interviews, Joe parried the question.

"I'm producing ten plays this season and planning the next six years," he told one reporter. "Are these the actions of a sick man? Do I look sick to you?"

His argument was plausible because to all appearances he was his usual vigorous and audacious self operating at full tilt. What was one to make of this? Was there any hope in it? Joe's resolute and thrustful energy was so persuasive that at times even I felt reassured by it. He still did offbeat things, like a Bloomingdale's ad that consisted of a wrinkled snapshot of himself at the age of fourteen, to which he added a handwritten caption.

A year after my Bar Mitzvah and deep in the throes of memorizing Marc Antony's speech from Shakespeare's Julius Caesar (soon to be released on a small metal disc in a store on 14th St, price 10 cents—included use of background music, Stravinsky's "Firebird Suite") Photograph courtesy of adjacent photo-booth—price, one nickle. year 1935.

Joseph (Yussel) Papp

At the bottom of the ad, a line of copy said, "For one hundred years, Bloomingdale's has seen the fortunes of young men turn on how well they spend their nickels." For Joe, of course, the ad had nothing to do with nickels but with his connection to a more hopeful time in his youth.

Papp Estate

I marveled at his dominant, future-oriented stance that fall when he announced the "Shakespeare Marathon"—his ambitious pledge to produce all of Shakespeare's plays at the rate of six per year over the next six years. The first one, *A Midsummer Night's Dream*, was to open at the Public Theater that December with F. Murray Abraham, the Oscar-Award winning actor in *Amadeus*, as Bottom and Elizabeth McGovern, later famous for her role in *Downton Abbey*, as Helena.

As I passed the door to Joe's sunny office one day, he motioned me to come in.

"I want you to look at this," he said, indicating the printer's proof of an invitation spread out on his desk. "I'm inviting all of the Charter Subscribers of the Marathon to join us for a champagne toast when we complete it."

As I leaned over to look at the proof, I immediately spotted the date that Joe had chosen for his Marathon toast. It said:

"Wednesday, September 15th, 1993"

That was six years in the future—an uncertain horizon of time that Joe might have left and that we could hope for in our life together. But he was promising to be there, with a glass of champagne in hand.

After the Marathon was launched in December, Joe and I rented a beach house on Captiva Island off the west coast of Florida, arriving there with a large suitcase packed with enough plays and books to last us the two weeks that we had allotted for a much-needed break from working day and night throughout such a stressful year.

As soon as we hit the beach at Captiva, Joe opened the copy of *Cymbeline* that he'd brought with him for the purpose of reading it aloud to me.

Just before he began, I spotted a lightning whelk in the sand and slipped it in my pocket planning to restore its color and reticulated surface later with olive oil.

"*Cymbeline* is a fairy tale of a play," Joe explained as I settled on the beach blanket, "with an appealing element of the supernatural. It has a god who descends from the heavens sitting on an eagle while thunder and lightning are going on all around him, and then he throws a thunder-bolt at earth."

Listening to Joe's voice with the occasional squawk of a seabird in the distance, I was struck by Shakespeare's boldness in dramatizing such a dark and whimsical story, and by the pluckiness of a young and inexperienced Joe in choosing to direct it as his first play by Shakespeare in the 1950s. Reading it out loud to me now helped to refresh his memory of *Cymbeline*, which he'd recently suggested to director JoAnne Akalaitis as *her* first Shakespeare during the Marathon's 1989 season at the Public Theater.

I had once read the play and remembered the famous song to which Joe now intoned the inexpressibly sad lyrics:

> Fear no more the heat o' the sun,
> Nor the furious winter's rages.
> Thou thy worldly task hast done,
> Home art gone, and ta'en thy wages . . .

"I have a question," I said, interrupting Joe's recital for a moment. "It's a beautiful song—but Shakespeare gives it to this man in the scene who has just *beheaded* another person."

"That's right," Joe said.

"Good grief," I said, awed by the load of gruesome elements that a fairy tale is able to bear.

Tony, whose symptoms were in a manageable phase, flew down to join us for a few days in Captiva and Joe's daughter Barbara and her family drove from their home in Tampa to visit. Joe himself was doing incredibly well. Life seemed almost back to normal.

And "normal" soon included renewed skirmishes with certain members of the critical establishment that had always seemed to dog Joe's footsteps in the theater. So perhaps it was inevitable that a *Times* critic would seize upon the first six productions of the Shakespeare Marathon as fertile ground about which to write an ostensible "think piece." The resulting article aired critic Frank Rich's dissatisfaction with the productions in the Marathon, along with his skepticism about its motivation. He enumerated what he called the "sins" of the Marathon—the primary one being the lack "of a unifying principle, other than the rubric 'Joseph Papp Presents.'"

He put forward the provocative question, "Why, promotional expediency aside, is there a need for a Shakespeare Marathon?"

Joe replied with a vigorous rebuttal, dismissing the critic's insinuation of "promotional expediency" on his part: "Come on. Even the middle class needs a lift these days. The Marathon is an act of cultural affirmation. It proclaims Shakespeare alive . . . It is causing lots of people to read and reread the plays of Shakespeare. There is a destination, a road to follow, and thousands of people are on it. Is there a need for a Marathon? What a question!"

In all fairness, what the critic couldn't have known is that Joe—far from being motivated by promotional expediency—was seeking in the Marathon an affirmative path for the immediate future of the Public Theater. Be that as it may, Frank Rich's think piece provoked one of Joe's best ripostes, full of irreverent truths about the way that theater sometimes actually works. I include it here for the reader's entertainment.

"The Shakespeare Marathon: The Coach's View"
by Joseph Papp
New York Times, Sunday, February 19, 1989

An answer to "Peaks and Valleys in Papp's Marathon" by Frank Rich, *New York Times*, Sunday, February 9, 1989

"The Shakespeare Marathon, the New York Shakespeare Festival's 36-play undertaking launched in 1987, has been characterized in The New York Times as an enterprise lacking a unifying vision and having no unifying principle other than 'Joseph Papp presents.' Needless to say, I consider such charges baseless and I resent them.

"Our critic admits that the Marathon has produced, at the least, two unreservedly fine stagings. Yet the beginnings of one of them, *Coriolanus*, did not augur well at all. In fact, that production so lacked one of the musts laid down by our critic for a successful undertaking—to wit 'mating a play with a director who has a real passion for it'—that he would no doubt have vetoed this ill-born venture from the start.

"Although our critic wrote that this director 'would have such passion for *Coriolanus* was no surprise to anyone'—in fact, Steven Berkoff, our director, had absolutely no outstanding passion for *Coriolanus*. It was I, having seen his work in London and in the States over the years, who felt that Steven was the man for the job, but he remained uncertain and later revealed to me that he had made numerous inquiries amongst his friends as to his being the right director for the project. After Steven's colleagues and I overwhelmingly reassured him, he grudgingly accepted the assignment, although not until we had fought over the terms. At one stage, we nearly reached the deal-breaking point.

"Complicating our critic's passion theory even more is the fact that Mr. Berkoff was performing in London and was unable to come to the United States to cast the play. With the assistance of Rosemarie Tichler, our casting director, I passionately set out to second-guess Maestro Berkoff, putting Christopher Walken, Irene Worth, Keith David and Paul Hecht in the leading roles.

"Even the first week of rehearsals was so lacking in anything resembling passion that the concept of a set had yet to be found. There were, I admit, some passionate disagreements along the way, which caused the temporary departure of one of the leading actors, the costumer and the lighting designer.

"To an outsider, it would have appeared that *Coriolanus* was heading for a fiasco of unprecedented proportions, and one must assume that our critic, had he the authority, would have called it quits at this impossible juncture. But the producer, trained through years of experience to discern any signs of life, in what appears to be an irreversible catastrophe, was able to keep faith with the spark of Berkoff's genius, a spark that finally caught fire in a production of unusual style and interest.

"Over a thirty-five year period, we have had many instances in which plays, approached with the greatest care, have failed to receive unanimous approval. On the other hand, we have literally thrown shows together that happen to have the right writer, director and actors, all of whom combine to create a harmony and a chemistry that all the deliberate preparation in the world could not achieve. I'm not in favor of these situations, but the truth is, you cannot plan or predict them.

"Nobody knows what will finally make a show work until it does."

Four months later, JoAnne Akalaitis' *Cymbeline* opened at the Public Theater. The production bore the distinctive signature of her postmodern sensibility, which the Royal Shakespeare Company saw fit to commend in its survey of *Cymbeline*'s stage history from 1609 to the present, noting that Akalaitis had "celebrated the play's heterogeneous styles, aided by the full gamut of technical wizardry. The result was a visual extravaganza . . . framed . . . by a *surrealist* delight in the incongruous."

This British praise, however, was in stark contrast to the review of *Cymbeline* in the *New York Times* where chief critic Frank Rich belabored his complaint about the production's nontraditional casting.

"In casting a Black actor as Cloten, doesn't credibility (and coherence for a hard-pressed audience) demand that his mother also be Black? . . . It's productions like this, which practice arbitrary tokenism rather than complete and consistent integration, that mock the dignified demands of the nontraditional casting movement."

The criticism was surprising. After all, it was well-known that the Public Theater had a thirty-five-year history of colorblind—later called nontraditional—casting, and from its inception Joe had personified the policy in word and deed. Twenty years earlier he'd written: "Black actors, Hispanic actors, Asian actors, know that we're not going to twit them around and cast them in any kind of symbolic manner, that we give parts to good actors. I don't do it because I'm a liberal, because I'm not. I do it because I think it's the right thing. New York is a multiracial community and should be represented on the stage that way."

Joe's answer now to the critic's complaint about *Cymbeline*'s casting was a piece he titled "An Open Appeal to the NY Times Critic for Guidance," which ended, "You accuse our production of representing 'arbitrary tokenism.' If by that word you mean 'casting without regard for color in family roles,' then, yes, we are that word."

But Joe never sent it. I'm not sure of his reason, but I guessed that Joe simply didn't want to revive this moribund issue by replying to the critic.

With the launch of the Marathon and its strong focus on actors, Joe simultaneously began to approach directors whom he hoped to involve in these future productions.

He invited Stuart Vaughan, the New York Shakespeare Festival's first artistic director, to join the Public Theater as its resident director and to establish an educational unit.

Joe persuaded Gerald Freedman, the Public Theater's first artistic director, who was then in charge of the Cleveland Playhouse (and would later head the theater program at the top-ranked North Carolina School of the Arts), to direct *Love's Labor's Lost* in the coming season. He also talked with George C. Wolfe about a permanent in-house role at the Public as both writer and director. And he asked JoAnne Akalaitis to re-enter the lists of the Marathon with *Henry IV, Parts 1 and 2*.

At that time these overtures struck me as the first impulses of Joe's idea for a major reorganization of the Public Theater—each move that he made in this direction becoming a dominant or recessive thread in the larger narrative of his succession that now began to unfold.

55

Across Space and Time

Looking and feeling good on our return from Captiva Island in January 1988, Joe wore a snappy Oxford suit in Annie Leibovitz's portrait of him for a Barney's Department Store ad. Both he and Tony were natural clotheshorses in that just about everything they wore looked terrific on them and they had posed together for a men's fashion ad in *GQ Magazine*.

Because Joe had such good taste, I relied on his advice about what I should wear on the few formal occasions that we went to. As always, I'd choose a little black dress. Eyeing me in it, Joe would say, "It's okay, it's fine, but you need something to *contradict* it."

"How about orange socks?" I'd joke.

"No, but a scarf, perhaps, or a belt. What have you got?" and he'd help me select something.

It was a relief to attend a birthday party that choreographer-director Martha Clarke invited us to in the field adjoining her home in Connecticut, not only because I could wear overalls and wander about with other casually attired guests, but also because I had a chance to admire the elephant on her premises who was to appear the next year in Martha's *Endangered Species* at the Brooklyn Academy of Music.

At this time Florida State University had created the first endowed Chair in Theater in the United States and invited Joe to be its first occupant. A necessary condition of his acceptance was to conduct a graduate seminar in acting

Joe and me at Martha Clarke's party in the country in 1987.
Papp Estate

during the spring semester at the FSU campus in Tallahassee. Joe organized it as a workshop of scenes from *King Lear* with our friend, the idealistically ebullient and gifted actor Raúl Juliá, joining him to play Lear in radically different modes—including a "jovial" Lear—as Joe tossed student actors playing the other parts into different scenes on short notice, charged with making coherent acting adjustments to Raúl's performance.

Raúl had a great time doing this. Joe had always valued his rich linguistic facility in Shakespeare and other roles, delighting in Raúl's blustering Petruchio opposite Meryl Streep's defiant Kate in *The Taming of the Shrew* at the Delacorte, as well as the cynically seductive Mac the Knife that he portrayed in the Public's acclaimed *Threepenny Opera*. Raúl's intentional changeability as Lear now challenged the FSU acting students, its purpose being to sharpen their responses in scene work. Although Joe's approach in conducting the seminar this way ruffled an academic feather or two, it was the kind of unfettered experience that put into action his vast practical knowledge of Shakespeare. Later, as he'd always done with independently earned stipends, Joe donated his large five-figure Chair money to the Public Theater.

Poster by Paul Davis for *The Mystery of Edwin Drood*, the Tony Award–winning musical by Rupert Holmes which began at the Delacorte Theater in 1985.
© Paul Davis

Logo by Paul Davis for *The Normal Heart*, Larry Kramer's powerful play about the AIDS crisis in 1985. Its revival on Broadway in 2011 won a Tony Award.
© Paul Davis

Actor-playwright Wallace Shawn performing in his play *Aunt Dan and Lemon* at the Public Theater in 1985. Joe praised his "inexorable, irrefutable logic. It's the human mind at its best—a body of ideas that are structured so well that they become a potent force."

Martha Swope/Billy Rose Theatre Division, The New York Public Library

Kevin Kline as *Henry V* at the Delacorte Theater in 1985.

Martha Swope/Billy Rose Theatre Division, The New York Public Library

Alfre Woodard as a left-wing journalist, and Roshan Seth as a right-wing expatriate Indian novelist, in a scene from David Hare's brilliant *A Map of the World* at the Public Theater in 1985.

Martha Swope/Billy Rose Theatre Division, The New York Public Library

Joe and Academy Award–winning actress Estelle Parsons celebrating *The Belasco Project* in 1986. Parsons directed free Shakespeare for student audiences at the Belasco Theater on Broadway where the productions ran for almost a year.
AP Photo/Martha Swope

Joe before an outdoor staging of Federico García Lorca's *Bodas de Sangre* (Blood Wedding) performed by Mexico's El Laboratorio de Teatro Campesino e Indígena in Oxoloteca, Tabasco, in 1989. He said, "Most of it was done by 136 people on horseback."
Papp Estate

Scenic designer Santo Loquasto on his set for Hy Kraft's *Café Crown*, the Second Avenue hangout for the play's characters in the Yiddish theater at the Public Theater in 1988.

Martha Swope/Billy Rose Theatre Division, The New York Public Library

Al Pacino as Marc Antony in *Julius Caesar* at the Public Theater in 1988, a performance that rivaled Marlon Brando's portrayal in the 1953 film.

Martha Swope/Billy Rose Theatre Division, The New York Public Library

Christopher Walken (R) as the complex and opaque Roman general
Coriolanus with Irene Worth as Volumnia, his haughty mother, and Keith
David as Aufidias, an ally turned enemy, at the Public Theater in 1988.
Martha Swope/Billy Rose Theatre Division, The New York Public Library

Rehearsing *Twelfth Night* for the Delacorte Theater in 1989, Michelle
Pfeiffer (L) who played Olivia to Mary Elizabeth Mastrantonio's Viola.
Martha Swope/Billy Rose Theatre Division, The New York Public Library

JoAnne Akalaitis, co-founder of the Mabou Mines artist collective, on the stage of the Public's Newman Theater in 1991 where she directed *Henry IV, Parts 1 and 2.*

Joe commissioned this poster by Paul Davis when playwright Václav Havel became President of Czechoslovakia in 1989 after its Communist regime was defeated in a nonviolent "Velvet Revolution."

Playwright-director-filmmaker Bill Gunn, author of *Black Picture Show* (1975) and *The Forbidden City* (1989) which were produced by the Public Theater. His important work resisted classification, leading him to say, "There are times when the white critic must sit down and listen. If he cannot listen and learn, then he must not concern himself with Black creativity."

Playwright Caryl Churchill, author of *Top Girls* and *Serious Money*. Joe began producing her plays in the 1980s because of the unique experimental lens she brought to contemporary life and the virtuoso range of her language.

Martha Swope/Billy Rose Theatre Division, The New York Public Library

Playwright-director George C. Wolfe rehearsing the story-telling wizardry of his adaptation of *Spunk: Three Tales* by Zora Neale Hurston with (L–R) Reggie Montgomery, Ann Duquesnay, and K. Todd Freeman at the Public Theater in 1990.

Martha Swope/Billy Rose Theatre Division, The New York Public Library

(Far L–Far R) Cecilia Vega and Oscar Ciccone, the founders of Festival Latino de Nueva York, visiting El Morro in 1990, San Juan's spectacular fortress overlooking the Atlantic Ocean, as the possible site for a production of *Othello* with Raúl Juliá. (Center) Joe, me, and lighting designer Jules Fisher.

Papp Estate

On the porch of our cottage in the country.
Papp Estate

While we were in Florida I was invited to speak to an undergraduate class in playwriting. I had never taught anything before and when I entered the classroom and saw rows of desks and expectant faces trained on me and the blackboard, I had no idea what I was going to say to them. Luckily, however, my Play Department experience triggered an impulse to go around the room to find out what each student was working on and then ask them if they had any questions about it. That more than took care of the hour.

I was moved by a question from a Latino playwriting student who said he'd been advised to change his name. I mentioned some of the theater artists I knew—Miguel Piñero, Miriam Colón, Pedro Pietri, José Rivera, Eduardo Gallardo, Charles Gomez, Graciela Daniele, Jose Yglesias— none of whom had changed their names. I said he would undoubtedly get good advice from Raúl Juliá, doing the Lear workshop on another floor in the same building, and encouraged him to drop a note to Raúl there at the end of the class.

No sooner had Joe and I returned from the stint at Florida State University than we flew to Caracas where Joe was to receive the Presidential Order of Andrés Bello from Venezuela's Minister of Culture (this was long before the maladministration of the country's subsequent leaders). It caused a bit of a stir because this was the first time that Venezuela's presidential medal had ever been awarded to someone from the United States. El Nacional ran a front-page article about it with a large photograph of Joe under the headline: "Joseph Papp: 'Robin Hood' de los Festivales." The story, which I read aloud to Joe, referred to him as "Un norteamericano quien aprecia la importancia de la cultura Hispanoamericana" (An American who appreciates the importance of Hispanic American culture).

Throughout the 1980s Joe had raised the money to present an International Latino Festival each August showcasing worldwide music and theater in Spanish on the stages of the Public Theater and in Central Park. Administratively based at the Public Theater, the Latino Festival was an essential part of the Public's artistic mission and had become well-known throughout Latin and South America. As a result, when Joe visited countries in that hemisphere, he was sometimes greeted as an unofficial cultural emissary by their ambassadors and Ministers of Culture.

The renowned playwright John Guare—who had been a resident artist at the Public Theater when it had produced three of his plays and a musical—unwittingly alluded to this emissary effect when he was interviewed in the late 1980s:

> A couple of years ago I was in Peru, and I was just walking down a crowded street in Cusco, and I couldn't believe it—it's still so mysterious—because there was this picture of Joe in the window of a postcard store in Cusco, Peru. I have a photograph of me standing by it. That, in a sense, is Joe. You don't know why he is in the window of a postcard store in Peru. I have no idea, and that's as good an explanation of Joe as I can imagine. (From an unpublished excerpt in his interview with Kenneth Turan for *Free for All*)

The mysterious reason for the picture of Joe in the window of a Peruvian postcard store was undoubtedly because he had presented Peru's great singer Tania Libertad, a "Comendadora" of her country, in a concert during the Latino Festival in New York.

The kind of bewilderment that Guare so wittily expressed also beset people trying to make sense of some of the plays that Joe offered at the Public Theater. Although his choices were generally assumed to have programmatic coherence due to Joe's backing of them as their producer, it wasn't well understood just how wide-ranging his taste and interests actually were. Therefore, few people understood why he had produced a play that consisted only of talking light bulbs on the stage. (It was a first play written by an architect intrigued with the unseen mystery in a room.)

The use of language was often at the heart of Joe's interest, and it was language that propelled us to a YM-YWHA theater in the Bronx to see a "nouveau Yiddish" muşical called *Songs of Paradise (Lieder fun Gan Eyden)*. A freshly humorous take on stories from the Book of Genesis, this musical was the inspired collaboration of three remarkable women. Its co-authors were Miriam Hoffman, a columnist for the *Jewish Forward*, and later a distinguished professor of Yiddish Literature at Columbia University, and Rena Berkowicz Borow, a translator of Isaac Bashevis Singer and librarian for the Jewish Theological Seminary. Its composer was the award-winning singer-songwriter and cantorial soloist, Rosalie Gerut. The cast included the multi-talented theater artist Eleanor Reissa and the versatile Avi Hoffman, Miriam Hoffman's son, who was also its nimble director.

Later Joe said, "I didn't think I'd ever bring them to the Public, but I saw the play and I loved it, and I thought it belonged there."

In June 1988, the death of Artistic Director Wilford Leach from AIDS was a terrible personal and professional loss for Joe and me. Until recently Joe had regarded Wil as the person who would most likely succeed him. After Wil died, Joe paid tribute to him in his introduction to *Poets for Life*, writing, "Ah, dear friend whose radiant humanity touched all who had the good fortune of knowing you, how I miss the wonder of you. My fallen comrade. Dear, dear friend."

Joe now began to look in earnest for a successor. He approached the directors Jerry Zaks, Mike Nichols, and James Lapine, as well as actress Meryl Streep. All were moved and surprised that Joe had asked them. The three directors declined because they weren't interested in shouldering the responsibilities of running an institutional theater. Meryl declined because she couldn't shoulder those responsibilities with the young children she had at that time.

In retrospect, I'm not sure when Joe began to gauge his remaining capacity for travel, but it had seemed undiminished in September 1988 when we went to Athens for the first time. On the way we stopped in London to see a young Kenneth Branagh as a wonderful Touchstone in *As You Like It* and to check in with Steven Berkoff, the noted actor and playwright, about his directing *Coriolanus* at the Public. Then it was on to Greece.

We were there because in his early Actors' Lab days in California Joe had known the actor-director Jules Dassin, who later married the Greek actress Melina Mercouri, who became internationally famous for her portrayal of a free-spirited prostitute in the film *Never on Sunday*. She was now the Greek government's Minister of Culture, and Joe had accepted an invitation from her to attend a United Nations Symposium Against Apartheid.

After the Symposium in Athens we took a two-hour taxi ride into the mountains north of Athens to visit the site of the Delphic Oracle. On arriving there, Joe and I trudged up a statue-lined promenade leading to the Oracle's vast religious complex that had been built in 800 B.C.E. athwart the summit of Mount Parnassus.

Being on our own and not on a tour, we were free to walk around the site and examine its amphitheater in a leisurely manner, recalling when we'd each learned about the Greek roots of Western theater. For me it had been at NYU; for Joe at the Actors' Lab. I told him that I was excited by some recent discoveries about women's lives in classical Greece and Rome.

"There are these two feminist scholars," I said, "who've gone around the world translating inscriptions about Greek and Roman women. They find the inscriptions on shards in old museum drawers that no one has ever bothered to look at."

Snapping pictures along the way, I wanted to get a long shot of Joe in front of Delphi's amphitheater. As I backed off to frame the picture, I continued my latest hot news about women in the ancient world, shouting to him across the field, "CONTRARY TO THE HISTORY BOOKS, THERE SEEMS TO BE NEW EVIDENCE THAT SOME WOMEN *HAD* BEEN PERFORMERS IN THE MISOGYNISTIC CLASSICAL WORLD!"

Click. I wasn't sure whether Joe had heard me, but in any case he waved enthusiastically with both arms, and it made a nice picture.

We returned to Athens that evening and were back in New York City the next afternoon—an airborne redeployment of consciousness and bodily existence across space and time that has never ceased to amaze me.

56

A Playwright's Final Curtain Call

In January 1989 the "nouveau Yiddish" musical that we had seen the previous summer became an instant hit at the Public Theater, promptly selling out the 99-seat Shiva Theater and attracting new audiences of all ages who loved Yiddish regardless of whether they spoke it or not. It got a happy boost in the *New York Times* from critic Richard F. Shepard who wrote, "There is surely nothing now onstage in New York that is more sprightly in any of our city's many tongues than *Songs of Paradise*."

Joe, whose first language had been Yiddish, clued me on the words, and by the end of the show's long run, I had gotten to know its writers, women of serious accomplishment and inexhaustibly droll humor, forming friendships that last to this day.

***

Joe and I had been pleasantly surprised in 1984 when playwright Bill Gunn dropped by the Public Theater. Although it had been nearly a decade since we had seen him, he was still the soft-spoken man with a mustache and elegant manners that I remembered from the 1970s when Joe had produced *Black Picture Show*—Gunn's elliptically haunting play about a Black screenwriter's experience in Hollywood—on the main stage at Lincoln Center Theater.

That production in 1975 had coincided with the release of Bill Gunn's film *Ganja & Hess*, a Black vampire movie hailed by the *New York Times* as "a landmark in the history of African-American cinema and one of the most important films of the 1970s." Bill had received a standing ovation at the Cannes Film Festival for his screenplay and direction of the film.

Bill's relationship with Joe had become strained during the rehearsals of *Black Picture Show*, which Bill directed. I remembered that he'd called Joe from a telephone booth threatening to kill himself over some disagreement they'd had about the play. Nevertheless Joe always paid unstinting tribute to him as "One of the great Black writers. He understands the kind of psychological relationship of Blacks to whites more than anybody. He sort of knows both sides of the story in an emotional way."

Now, nine years after *Black Picture Show*, Bill had suddenly appeared bringing Joe the first draft of his new play called *The Forbidden City*. Set in the 1930s in Philadelphia where Bill had grown up, it chronicled the collapse of relationships in a Black family, particularly between a mother and son.

Joe wanted to produce it and we had a reading of it with Bill at our apartment in December 1984. Understanding that he was working on rewrites, Joe waited for the next version of the play, which he saw when Bill reappeared with the script in 1988. However, there was an unexpected condition now attached to the play, which was that Bill wouldn't let *The Forbidden City* be done at the Public unless Joe directed it. It seemed that, for whatever reason, he trusted him, and only him, to recognize a larger dimension in the psychological complexity of his characters and the Depression era they lived in.

This put Joe in an awkward position because since his diagnosis the previous year, he had given up any notion of directing again.

"I shouldn't direct Bill's play," he said to me at home. "I feel okay for now, but I don't know how much time or working energy I have left. It's going to take everything I've got just to see the next period of time through, whatever it is."

Bill was unhappy about Joe's reluctance to direct *The Forbidden City*. Knowing nothing about Joe's illness, he became more insistent about the matter, leaving Joe with the unsettling impression that Bill regarded him as the only hope of ever seeing this deeply personal play produced. Joe began to reconsider.

"If I do direct it, I'll have to rely on a close collaboration with Bill to get the current version of his script in shape," Joe told me, "and my experience with Bill as a writer has been that he'll only start to pull things together when he's facing the pressure of a production deadline." At the back of Joe's mind was the thought that since Bill was a younger man and an accomplished director in his own right, he'd be able to take over the direction of *The Forbidden City* if Joe became too ill to continue. So he finally said yes.

We drove up to Bill's home in Tappan, New York, for a preliminary discussion. His house, which overlooked the Hudson River, was a marvelous rookery that had been leased by Ben Hecht in the 1930s as the place to write his screenplay for the 1939 movie version of *Wuthering Heights*. When we entered Bill's living room, Joe and I were careful to step around a large tiger skin rug splayed on the floor with the tiger's head still attached to it. As we did so, two Siamese cats leaped onto the back of a sofa and howled at us. Bill cast a debonairly reproving look in their direction. Apologizing for the discourteous behavior of his pets, he welcomed us into his home which he shared with his partner, the composer and lyricist Sam Waymon, the brother of singer Nina Simone.

Joe had known Bill as an actor since 1963 when he'd cast him as Eros in a Central Park production that Joe directed of *Antony and Cleopatra*, Eros being the friend who stabs himself rather than help Antony commit suicide. The next play had been *The Winter's Tale*, directed by Gladys Vaughan, with Bill Gunn playing Archidamus, a lord of Bohemia, in a company that included Roscoe Lee Browne, Charles Durning, and James Earl Jones.

Bill and Joe discussed the cast and future schedule of *The Forbidden City*. Its title had resonant meanings. There was, of course, the tourist attraction of the Forbidden City in Beijing, a 178-acre palace complex built for China's emperors in the fifteenth century, which became a notorious vortex of intrigue from which they ruled for the next five hundred years. In the 1930s San Francisco's popular version of Harlem's Cotton Club had been named after it. And then there was the house in Philadelphia in 1936 in Bill Gunn's play, occupied by a middle-class Black family whose relationships are being torn apart under the influence of an imperially indifferent mother.

When rehearsals of *The Forbidden City* began in March 1989, Joe learned that Bill had been hospitalized in Nyack with a serious illness. He was frustrated that he couldn't leave rehearsals to go see him, but when he spoke to Bill on the phone, he was relieved to find him responsive and very eager to discuss the play. From then on Joe would call him every day to report on the production's progress, which became a substitute for the in-person collaboration with Bill that he had previously anticipated. On these daily calls he would share thoughts about the play that were on his mind as its director, as well as questions that had been raised by the cast, which featured Gloria Foster as the mother, Frankie R. Faison as her husband, and Akili Prince as their teenage son. Joe told me that Bill was fully engaged and articulate in these conversations.

"I find them helpful," he said, though of course he missed the kind of working partnership with Bill that he'd initially counted on, especially when he understood that Bill was going to be in the hospital a while longer. No one had told Joe anything about Bill's medical condition, and our worry about the exact nature of his illness intensified. We wondered if it could be AIDS, which had already affected so many people we knew in the theater.

We were still in the dark about this when Joe told me one day that during the course of recent phone calls he'd noticed "Bill's voice getting a little hoarse." The once smoothly engaging sound of that sharply intelligent voice then grew so faint that Joe said he could hardly make out what Bill was saying. Finally it simply became inaudible. The soundtrack had stopped. Realizing by now that Bill was dying, Joe established to his satisfaction that even though Bill could no longer speak, he was still able to hear. So Joe continued to call him every day with updates about the rehearsals, even though all that greeted him now was a kind of breathing silence at the other end of the line.

Bill Gunn died of encephalitis and complications of AIDS on April 6, 1989. *The Forbidden City* opened at the Public Theater two days later on April 8, 1989. The *New York Times* ran its theater review headed "A Mother Only a Son Could Love," alongside Bill Gunn's obituary, headed "Dies on Eve of Play Premiere"—a diabolical coincidence worthy of Bill's own invention. The tone of the review by Mel Gussow was inexcusably peevish and unforgivably dismissive on grounds that he'd disliked the play's characters because they were unsympathetic. He did say that Gloria Foster as the mother gave a "fire-breathing performance," but it wasn't meant as a compliment.

Thank God Bill never saw it. If he had, he would no doubt have replied as he'd done before by suggesting that the *Times* take a look at its "unchecked racist standards." In his 1973 article "To Be a Black Artist" he'd written, "There are times when the white critic must sit down and listen. If he cannot listen and learn, then he must not concern himself with Black creativity."

"Dies on Eve of Play Premiere" made for an unforgettable curtain call for this exceptional artist whose imagination sought to capture authenticity on a larger scale, defying the reduction of its complexity to racial stereotypes.

Joe had never told Bill about his own illness, and Bill had initially withheld full disclosure of his. Joe's unwavering steadfastness in such a difficult situation was what anyone who knew him would have predicted. Personally, I believe it must also have been what Bill Gunn himself had counted on from the beginning.

57

The Idea of Continuity

Over a period of weeks at the beginning of 1990, I often saw Joe glued to the red landline phone on our dining table engaged in lengthy conversations with Kevin Kline about him doing *Hamlet* a second time. They had both been dissatisfied with the direction of the previous production of *Hamlet* in 1986, and Joe was trying to persuade Kevin to do it again and also to direct the play himself this time.

The idea was concurrent with Joe's desire to encourage new directors. With a pivotal eye on the future, he had been making a point of seeing their work. After viewing young Michael Greif's production of *Machinal*, a 1928 feminist play by journalist Sophie Treadwell, Joe had invited him to direct a play at the Public the following season. He'd also invited Melia Bensussen, a director and Spanish translator who had been working in the Latino Festival and Play Department, to be in charge of a former sound studio on our new floor at 419 Lafayette Street, and under her direction the defunct space had been transformed into a home for semi-staged plays of uncommon interest.

What Joe saw in Greif and Bensussen were two young people with the directorial talent, producing skills, and purposeful energy to sustain a substantial future career in the theater. His interest in them at this time reminded me of one of my earliest impressions of Joe—"a man singularly skillful in discerning talent yet in the bud and also much disposed to nourish and advance it" (with thanks to Plutarch for this graceful and succinct way of saying it).

In May 1990 the *New York Times* spotlighted Joe's focus on new directors in an exclusive story headed "Papp Reorganizes Shakespeare Festival. An associate and three directors are brought in as new 'creative blood.'" In it Joe announced that he had named JoAnne Akalaitis as his artistic associate at the Public Theater and had turned the running of three of its stages over to directors George C. Wolfe, Michael Greif, and David Greenspan, an innovative off-off-Broadway director-writer-actor.

Joe said, "I've been looking for people to come in and begin to absorb some of the artistic shape of this organization and maybe totally reshape it. My objective is that hopefully their ideas have some connection with people who don't go to the theater today . . . I'll operate this institution as long as I possibly can, but I'm going to give everybody a chance to shape it internally."

He also announced the coming summer season in Central Park, with Morgan Freeman and Tracey Ullman in A. J. Antoon's Wild West version of *The Taming of the Shrew* and Denzel Washington in *Richard III*.

The story briefly noted (in one sentence) Joe's recent refusal "of a grant from the National Endowment for the Arts because of his concern over censorship" and quoted JoAnne Akalaitis saying, "I think the very existence of the theater is endangered in a way it has never been before by forces from the right."

At this time Joe was grappling not only with the survivability and future leadership of the Public Theater, so inextricably linked to his own mortality, but also with a serious threat to the National Endowment which had become embroiled in a faux issue whipped up by South Carolina Senator Jesse Helms about the NEA supposedly sponsoring "obscenity in the arts."

Helms had legislation pending in the Senate that would require recipients of NEA grants to sign a form pledging that their work complied with the obscenity restrictions Helms had enumerated in it. The bill had fervent right-wing supporters who wanted to get rid of the NEA.

Joe had penciled a note about "the zealots who have been rallied to attack the NEA as a conduit of immorality. These Americans are victims of an opportunistic leadership, both in and out of Congress, examples of which have been shown to have less of an interest in god than in their own greed."

In April he had written NEA Chairman John Frohmayer, stating his opposition to the Helms legislation, which the *New York Times* published as an op ed piece titled, "I'm a Producer, Not a Censor."

In July the *Los Angeles Times* published Joe's article "Once More Unto the Breach," in which he wrote,

> There always will be people who look askance at artists and decry their work for being offensive. It happened to Leonardo da Vinci and Oscar Wilde in their days. It even happened to Shakespeare in ours, in fundamentalist areas of the country where some have declared sections of his work obscene and have excised the offending passages in textbooks.
>
> The linking of art with pornography is a contrivance, a tactic by certain politicians to win elections. People applying for a grant from the NEA are not pornographers. Pornographers do not need government help . . . Pornography today is a multi-million-dollar industry that has nothing to do with museums, theaters, symphonies, opera companies, ballet companies and individual artists.
>
> It would be tragic if the politics of our time put a chill on today's artists. Long after all political battles have fallen by the wayside, a book, a piece of music, a ballet, a painting, a play will tell you about the time in which we are living.

That August in the midst of this NEA fracas and the lurking subject of his succession at the Public Theater, Joe experienced an onset of pains that neither of us had anticipated. To Joe it felt like the beginning of the end. However Dr. Garnick in Boston encouraged us to think of them as limited "brush fires" that could be put out with radiation, so we went up there for Joe's first course of treatment.

We rented an apartment in East Cambridge, a short daily commute to the hospital, so that Joe could continue to lobby, by fax and phone, senators and representatives in the House against the Helms legislation—it having become attached now to a five-year NEA re-authorization bill encumbered with no less than twenty-six restrictive amendments! Joe's efforts while receiving radiation were the kind of barnstorming of an issue, coupled with targeted one-on-one persuasion, that I had seen him do at other times. Fortunately, his treatment was successful, but the measures subsequently taken in Congress were mixed.

In October a compromise bill extending the existence of the NEA passed both houses after endless wrangling. It had no obscenity restrictions but required the NEA to take "into consideration general standards of decency."

"It's a trap," Joe said. "No one knows what decency is . . . There has been so much poison let loose . . . I don't consider this a victory. There are so many things that have entered the picture that it now needs a very elaborate explanation on how an arts institution relates to the NEA, or if it relates at all."

***

That fall Joe's son Tony was diagnosed with cytomegalovirus, an opportunistic disease of AIDS that affects the eyes. After he was hospitalized and partially lost sight in one eye, he gave up his apartment and artware gallery and moved back to live with us in the room where he'd once held sway as a mischievous twelve-year-old with twelve birds.

He was joined by his friend and lover Rosemary Jordan, a girl with a cheerful personality and a smile that was like healing sunshine. Although Tony was gay and she a lesbian, they were a sweet and loving couple who were deeply devoted to each other. Despite the unhappy circumstances that dogged all of our lives, it was wonderful to have them living with us, and our apartment seemed full of life again.

We were deeply sorry at this time for Joe's younger brother, Phillip Martel (he had changed his name from Murray Papirofsky in the 1940s), who was utterly bereft due to the loss of his high-spirited British wife after a long

Tony Papp and Rosemary Jordan at our place in the
country in 1987. Joe (L) is in the kitchen.
Gail Papp

illness. However, Phil grew closer to Joe and went to Joe's synagogue with him on Yom Kippur, the first time they'd done that together since they were children.

In September an inquisitive reporter for the *Village Voice* had asked Joe, "Everyone wants to know what is the story of your health?" to which he had answered bluntly, "You see me here." Then he added, "But you can't run a theater forever. I began to think really seriously when I turned fifty. How does this continue? Or does it continue?"

***

The following month, if you happened to be walking down Lafayette Street in New York City on October 14, 1990, and passed in front of the Public Theater, you'd have found yourself engulfed in symphonic music thundering up from its sidewalk grates. The music caused astonished pedestrians to stop in their tracks. Some of them recognized the orchestral suites from *West Side Story* and *Candide*. Others who looked up saw the huge banners flapping from the Public Theater's three flag poles, each one bearing the tall letters "LB." The music and flags were Joe's tribute to Leonard Bernstein who had died that day. During their brief two days of exposure on Lafayette Street, the only people aware of them were the accidental passersby in front of the Public Theater.

Joe, who had never done anything like this before, said nothing to me about it, and I didn't ask him. Although Leonard Bernstein had attended some of the shows at the Public Theater and lent his name to committees for the preservation of Free Shakespeare in Central Park, Joe had never had a close professional relationship with him. However I sensed that the music and flags signified Joe's recognition of the unique American achievement of an artistic *lantzman* of his own generation, in whose passing Joe had undoubtedly seen a foreshadowing of his own.

The next month a full-page article about "Joe Papp's four protégés" appeared in the *Daily News* with a picture of the four directors sitting around a restaurant table. Joe used the story to introduce a reason for his reorganization of the Public Theater beyond the infusion of "fresh creative blood" that had been cited in previous articles, saying to the reporter, "I'm trying to find a way to make an institution work way past the time when I or the next person is here. This idea of continuity is the beginning of the process."

58

The Crucible of Memory

Joe said he wanted to build a $35 million fund whose income would help to assure the future of the Public Theater. Privately he put the figure at $52 million. Asked by a reporter if it would be possible to get all the money necessary, Joe said, "I have to think so. Yes. We are undercapitalized for an institution of our size." Asked where he'd get the money, he replied, "I don't know."

At the end of December 1990, we spent a weekend at our country cottage where a light dusting of snow had covered the ground. I hung bars of soap in the lower branches of our evergreen trees to keep the deer from nibbling them and took a picture of Joe repairing a bird feeder outdoors through our kitchen window.

At the beginning of the new year he wore his grey tweed suit to a *New York Times* leadership lunch in publisher Arthur Sulzberger Jr.'s office. We still went to the office every day, and on the evening of February 14, 1991, Joe put on his tux to present a Justice in Action Award to actor BD Wong (*M. Butterfly*) at the Silver Palace in Chinatown.

Right after that his "brush fire" pain flared up again, but he resumed radiation treatments in New York City rather than Boston so that he could continue to mentor the first season of JoAnne and the three directors at the Public.

By March, however, it was a heartbreaking seesaw at home with Joe and Tony incapacitated at the same time by their treatments, lying on sofas

Gail Papp

opposite each other in our living room. Bemused by the fact that both he and his father had terminal illnesses, Tony said to Joe one day, "Who knows? Maybe we'll die together."

Nobody knew how sick they were. The press maintained the illusion, or believed that Joe was still on the scene at the Public Theater since articles about the Public's reorganization were based on phone interviews with Joe, accompanied by one of his former smiling photographs and a captioned quote such as, "If my theater isn't being criticized for being extreme, there's something wrong."

The stories suggested that a considered process was going on. The *London Times* interviewed Joe by phone about the Public's upcoming season with the four directors. In the article Joe is quoted saying, "Artistically I couldn't ask for more. I have freed myself from the obligation of my own taste . . . It takes a while to let go, but it's most gratifying to give up power to a new generation."

The next month, however, Joe told a reporter, "I won't retire. I'll have to be killed off."

When *USA Today* gave credence to "rumors of health problems," Joe brusquely told the reporter on the phone, "If I'm dying, you'll know it." A wonderful photo of him taken the previous year appeared with the story.

For a while he couldn't walk, but then learned to walk again. Although he'd lost an appalling amount of weight, his face seemed younger. Some people even thought he looked healthy. Joe was aware of this, and the illusion set in that his physical condition wasn't as severe as in fact it was. I think only Emmett Foster and I really understood this. My full understanding came in silent epiphanies such as when I realized one day that Joe wouldn't be wearing his suits anymore.

After periods of pain, Joe's old self would unexpectedly emerge again with an episode of better health. That's when he wrote poems, ordered a wedding ring for himself, a duplicate of mine, and would get on the phone if he felt I needed something.

When Tony's condition grew worse, we stayed in the country so that our apartment could be devoted to the twenty-four-hour high-tech nursing and medical care that his illness required and that we'd promised him. He'd told us that he didn't want to die in a hospital.

I had to tell my colleagues in the Play Department that I would be on an indefinite sabbatical and asked them to carry on as if we were still there.

Driven in from the country by Emmett to see Tony one day, we found our apartment filled with equipment and boxes of medical supplies. Tony was in a hospital bed in his room. He couldn't talk but he could squeeze our fingers. We'd brought him a recording of Mendelssohn's Violin Concerto, which we knew he loved, and played it—an unbearably tender moment during which Joe stood up from his wheelchair to hug Tony, forgetting that he was still too weak to stand, and collapsed back in it.

Bernie and Cora Gersten now generously offered us the use of their apartment so that we could stay in the city and be near Tony, however Joe's condition had grown worse and by the time we arrived at the Gerstens' empty apartment, he couldn't get out of bed. I sprinted across town to our own apartment where Tony, who had become unconscious, was being tended around the clock by a high-tech critical care nurse. Stricken by the sight of his helplessness, I asked his male nurse for reassurance that Tony would never be in pain. After he reassured me, I kissed Tony's forehead before returning to taking care of Joe in bed at the Gerstens' apartment.

On June 1 Tony's nurse called me. Tony had just died at 9:10 p.m., he said. Joe was lying in bed. Our friend Celia Mitchell was holding his hand. When I whispered that Tony was gone, Joe cried out, "Oh, my son!" He was too ill to attend the funeral or the memorial reception for Tony in the Gerstens' living room. A week later, after all the medical equipment and the hospital bed had been removed, we returned to our apartment.

Back in familiar surroundings, Joe's spirits improved and he decided to call a senior staff meeting at home. His purpose was to review the current and upcoming seasons, which he had previously planned. We were aware of the outstanding work that everyone had done during Joe's absence from the office. George C. Wolfe had adapted tales by Zora Neale Hurston, and Thulani Davis had adapted Brecht's *Caucasian Chalk Circle*, both of which George directed in memorable productions that had further enhanced his growing directorial reputation.

Michael Grief had restaged *Machinal* at the Public and revived Tony Kushner's *A Bright Room Called Day*, a haunting play that contrasts 1930s Berlin with 1980s America.

David Greenspan had tweaked everyone's thinking cap with two seventeenth-century plays from England and Japan.

JoAnne Akalaitis, currently identified as Joe's associate in the reorganization articles, was about to reprise her striking production of *'Tis Pity She's a Whore*, which Joe and I had seen at the Goodman Theater in Chicago the year before.

Kevin Kline had directed and starred in a superb production of *Hamlet*, which was filmed for public television.

Wallace Shawn had appeared in *The Fever*, his own ferocious monologue about the "contradictions and compromises of the urban liberal." Before its run at the Public Theater, Wally had tried it out in our living room.

At the Delacorte this coming summer there would be Raúl Juliá in *Othello* with Christopher Walken as Iago and a carnival-inspired *Midsummer Night's Dream (Sonho de uma Noite de Verão)* staged by the Brazilian director Cacá Rosset, whose work Joe and I had seen in São Paulo.

Before the staff meeting, Joe positioned himself in our rented stratolounger wearing a shirt with long sleeves that covered his skinny arms. Everyone knew he'd been ill, but he didn't look so bad. His face was tanned from the country, thin, but youthful and handsome. About the rest of him you couldn't't really tell because his clothes were loose and baggy. He seemed much better than in fact he was, with just enough energy for an hour-and-a-half meeting.

Once the ten senior staff members had arrived, Joe was reminded of the serious problems he'd had to leave behind a few months earlier. He very briefly acknowledged the lapse in time since he'd last seen them, but left unstated the burden of sudden responsibilities that had been thrust upon them by the unforeseen developments of his illness.

Never moving from the stratolounger, Joe conducted the meeting with his old authority and verve—precisely formulating present and future concerns as he saw them, pitching key questions, bridling at bad ideas, reinforcing good ones, and taking in the dynamics of the room.

After the meeting, however, Joe was worried. He told me that while the theater's leadership had artistic and managerial strengths, he felt it wasn't solid enough in the producing area. And in Joe's practical bricks-and-mortar habit of dealing with problems, he came up with something to do about it.

Vetting it first with three officers on the board, he proposed the idea of a troika structure at the theater with a person of broad producing experience to support the roles of the artistic director and managing director. The person he wanted to recruit was Robert Marx, who was then head of the Library for the Performing Arts at Lincoln Center. He was widely admired, experienced, and knew the theater. Joe felt he had a mindset compatible with the Public's mission, and a personality that would not compete with but complement the Public's nominal future Artistic Director JoAnne Akalaitis and Managing Director Jason Steven Cohen. But these two, unprepared for and offended by Joe's proposal, both immediately threatened to quit, although Steve Cohen promised to stay on until Joe died.

Realizing he hadn't had the strength to properly lay the groundwork for the idea, Joe withdrew it, but his worry about the producing muscle of the organization continued to bother him.

We had been looking for a doctor in New York to oversee Joe's treatment, and after a vexing interim at last found the remarkable Dr. Larry Norton at Mount Sinai. When Dr. Norton asked Joe to keep a medical diary, Joe obliged enthusiastically, setting down medical notes along with his constantly streaming thoughts about the future of the Public Theater. Interspersed throughout were brief entries about the day's events.

One of them was on August 11, 1991, when Joe made a superhuman effort to see the Brazilian company's *A Midsummer Night's Dream* at the Delacorte.

"8/11/91 Sunday," he wrote. "Delacorte Theater closing—go!go!— Returned from the Delacorte. Wonderful people, show and magic of the night. Gail with me protecting my back from over-zealous Brazilians who want to squeeze my ribs. Then a magic ritual in large circle."

The last picture taken of Joe was in that magic circle the Brazilian company had formed around him as he blew kisses to them. That same week he agreed to give an exclusive story to the *New York Times* during which he planned to announce JoAnne Akalaitis as the new head of the Public Theater. The interview was scheduled for Friday, August 16, 1991.

Before Alex Witchel, then the *Times* "On Stage and Off" columnist, arrived at our apartment that morning, Joe put on a long-sleeved shirt and sat himself in a regular chair rather than the stratolounger. When Ms. Witchel rang our bell punctually at 10:30 a.m., I showed her into the living room, then left her and Joe alone there, thinking to myself with aching disbelief, "My god, he's about to give up the Public Theater."

Joe's only diary note about the interview was "Lasted one hour—mostly sympathetic and informational. Now what is the next step?"

Later that day he wrote a poem "dedicated to Gail & close friends & to Children everywhere" that would become like a personal anthem to me in future years:

> Life is everywhere
> There is no end
> What we have sown, we reap
> Nothing disappears but is retained
> in the crucible of memory:
> Of extensions practices—
> children's talents lie the remnants,
> great and small,
> all having their own importance
> to one or to a million—
> Birds carry the message on their wings,
> In their songs,

In the flutter of their feathered tails.
<u>Pointing & rounding the Compass of</u>—
past, the present
and the oncoming future—
life in perpet-u-um,
swiftly moving toward & away
whamming in,
whisking out
uplifted by winds of time
and of space—
<u>never say never</u>—dear ones,
the key word
is <u>always</u>, always <u>will</u> be—
<u>ever</u>.

Five days later the interview with Joe appeared in the *Times*.

The New York Times

Papp Names Akalaitis to Step In As Shakespeare Festival Head
By Alex Witchel
Wednesday, August 21, 1991

"Joseph Papp, the founder of the New York Shakespeare Festival and its sole artistic leader for 37 years, has appointed JoAnne Akalaitis to succeed him, effective immediately."

Besides Joe's appointment of JoAnne Akalaitis as artistic director, the article mentioned his promotions of Jason Steven Cohen to managing director and Rosemarie Tichler to artistic associate (later artistic producer). "Mr. Papp will retain the title of Producer."

The story also reviewed the Public Theater's many recent reversals of fortune: A cut of $3 million in its operating budget . . . Forty-three staff members laid off due to the closing of the Public's four in-house production shops . . . A 33 percent cut in funds from New York City . . . A 60 percent cut in funds from New York State . . . A shift in foundation support away from the arts . . .

A drop in corporate support due to the recession . . . The end of profits from the Broadway production of *A Chorus Line* after its closing the year before.

Although the article was clearly sympathetic to Joe, the effect of this litany of unfavorable circumstances was depressing (who in their right mind would want to take on such problems?) and it left a troubled impression of the Public Theater's survivability.

For his part, Joe had a fierce personal reaction to seeing it in print. He wrote:

8/21 Wed. KING LEAR ON A RAMPAGE. NY TIMES ARTICLE—OUT TODAY. I'M FURIOUS AT HAVING TO BEG FOR SOMETHING THAT HAS BEEN MINE OVER MANY YEARS—MY FLESH AND BLOOD—MY MIND . . . I'm angry, I'm hurt, I'm coming through the dirt. My mouth is dry, my arms are clotted with straw.

By the next day, however, Joe had converted his feelings of King Lear on a rampage into the calm stance of Fortinbras at the end of *Hamlet* or the Duke of Albany at the end of *Lear*.

"8/22 Thurs.—11:45am office—See staff & do letters & calls."

I don't know that such connections were in Joe's thoughts, but when you see, act, or direct a lot of Shakespeare, it does tend to color the way you frame your own experiences, and these connections were certainly in my thoughts when we went to the Public Theater on Thursday, August 22, for the first time in several months so that Joe could spend a few hours at his desk saying goodbye to people on the staff.

I remembered what he'd written just three years ago about endings being essential to the integrity of Shakespeare's plays:

Shakespeare has Fortinbras (the Prince of Norway) observe Hamlet's passing with appropriate ceremony and remind us that life goes on. Even *King Lear* does not end abruptly with this old man's tragic death, which would produce a feeling of emptiness in the audience. This is not Shakespeare's objective. Instead he knows that we need a chance to breathe and to wonder, along with loyal Kent, that Lear "hath endured so long." As Nym remarks philosophically to Bardolph in *Henry V*, "There must be conclusions."

Later that day Emmett Foster drove us to the country, where Joe wrote:

3:00—Walked around grounds—uphill, saw the oncoming of fall on the trees, the vines—the stillness of the place, the light & shadows of fall with its mystery of half-asleep, half-awake. Remnants of the hurricane & some debris remain, weeds, brush, bushes. A few strong birds keeping the vigil, ready to spend the winter up North. Felt the wonder of change. A spotted fawn at the left-over of the saltlick. Gail & I hand to hand following the erratic design of nature's handiwork.

And at night, the night birds calling, the crickets chirping their song of songs—answering millennia which call upon these insects of the evening & early night to send their melodic instrumentation, their whistle of presence announced—their statement of the country-side.

The *Times* story, of course, was picked up by other media, and end-of-life farewells and features started to appear everywhere. After reading some of them, Joe joked, "I'm probably the only person who's had a chance to read his own obituary."

But not even this, or the soreness of his ribs, or the accompanying difficulties in walking and breathing could thwart his overwhelming lust for living and creating.

8/27—7:30am—The ambivalence of "here I am," a warm-blooded animal with normal needs, beset with the abnormality of a bird that lay stunned on the porch after trying to pass through what it imagined was open space and finding instead a hard-surfaced transparent glass, dropping it to the deck, bewildered—almost dead of trauma & utter surprise.

Back in the city and officially "divorced" from the Public Theater, Joe wrote:

Fri. Aug. 30 10:30am—I have thoughts that cry out for expression. I have a world of unfulfilled ideas poised in a runner's position . . . Is one great chance all? . . . Isn't that more than anyone can ask for? I don't want to think so. I cannot think so without abject surrender to forces demanding that I give up . . . My resistance to this concept is powerful and exceedingly painful as it requires the most fundamental struggle—life vs. surrender, death.

He stopped writing after that. A period of hospitalizations followed in September. I slept on a cot next to his hospital bed to head off the risk of his falling when he hallucinated at night. Eventually we were able to return home.

We learned that Czech President Václav Havel was in town and had tried to see Joe at the hospital and then at our apartment, but neither place had cleared the necessary security requirements. So Havel finally called Joe at home and spoke to him on the phone. Joe was deeply moved when he heard his voice.

On October 29 Kevin Kline and Phoebe Cates stopped by with their two-week old son, Owen Joseph. As they held the tiny baby up for him to see, Joe commented, "Actor. *Comedian.*"

The next day Joe said to me, "My mind is teeming with ideas." He wondered if he was going to die. He asked, "Do you still love me?" He knew very well how much I did and I kissed him.

When he died in my arms at 2 a.m. that night, I didn't realize what had happened at first, and Emmett Foster and Mrs. Morris, a home aide, who were with us in the room, had to tell me that he was gone. It was October 31, 1991.

59

A Globe Theater Birdhouse

After the fine speeches about Joe at his memorial service held the next day at the Public Theater and his burial near his parents at the Baron Hirsch Cemetery on Staten Island, I sat shiva for a week. This is the traditional time for family and friends to mourn together and to begin the process of healing. Having visitors at home during the day was somewhat comforting to me, but being alone at night was hard. Before going to bed I would recite the Mourner's Kaddish which I had memorized in Aramaic (the ancient spoken language of Biblical Jews) after I'd learned the correct pronunciation from audio cassettes that Mandy Patinkin and Jackie Mason (the comedian and former rabbi, who had done a show at the Public) thoughtfully sent me. During sleepless nights its cadences seemed to be synchronized to my own heartbeat—"*Yitgadal v'yit*kadash . . . *v'im*ru: a*men*."

When the week of sitting shiva was over, I went outdoors for the first time to do an errand. As I reached the sidewalk in front of our building, a very strange thing happened. I became aware that a *phantom leg* had somehow taken the place of my real leg, which was gone. The sensation was completely and absolutely real, and I could not for the life of me shake it. Of course in my rational mind I reasoned that the loss of a leg would be equivalent to losing *part of oneself*. Like the loss of a loved one. But my rational analysis didn't make the phantom limb go away and it took a little while for the bizarre sensation to subside.

I couldn't cry after Joe was gone. Instead I had dreams in which I longed for him to appear but he was present in them only by virtue of his baffling *absence* in them. It wasn't like him not to be there, I dream-reasoned. It bothered me. "Where did you go? Why haven't you been in touch?" I asked. Sometimes there was a ghostly trace of Joe in a dream where I'd dream-think that I had seen him in the distance wearing his grey tweed suit. But he didn't come close or talk to me, and my distant sighting of him would vanish. Then one night as I wandered in this troubled dreamscape, I heard Joe singing in brilliant quadraphonic stereo. It was the most alive and thrillingly present sound I'd ever heard. Although I still couldn't see him, I exclaimed, "You must be back!"

Later that month, having decided to resume some of my familiar activities, I went by myself to the opening of Michael Greif's production of *Pericles* at the Public Theater on November 25.

Pericles is the name of a young prince who is grieving for his wife Thaisa, whom he thinks has died and been buried at sea. (He was played by Campbell Scott, the son of George C. Scott and Colleen Dewhurst, Joe's colleagues in the Public's early days.) In Act III the coffin of Pericles' wife has been washed ashore and was visible in this production on the stage of the Newman Theater in the same place where Joe's casket had rested only twenty-four days before.

My heart jumped. The sight of the coffin startled me—as did the astonishing return to life in the play of the supposedly dead spouse of Pericles that it contained. Moved beyond anything I ever could have imagined, at my seat in the theater I wept silently and uncontrollably.

***

It was only a couple of years before this performance of *Pericles* that Joe and I had been sipping chilled white wine on the sun deck of our cottage in upstate New York, listening to the traveling caws of unseen crows in the dense summer foliage as we watched a black-capped chickadee land on the wood railing near us where I had sprinkled some seeds.

"Listen to this," Joe said in that eager voice of his that always commanded my attention. "I've just thought of it: a bird sanctuary that's a nesting house in the spring and a refuge in the winter. It could have removable panels so that in the summer it becomes a feeder, and so forth. You combine the functions with separate sections for different uses and kinds of birds."

Setting his wine glass on the deck, he reached for the landline phone at his feet that I had rigged on a long extension cord from a jack in the living room and called our friend, scenic designer Robin Wagner, to ask for his help in designing an open-air bird sanctuary.

I loved the idea they came up with for it: a replica of Shakespeare's Globe Theater.

"We'll want to see it here from the deck," Joe had said to me, "so I think we should install it up there on the hill above the house, don't you?" He pointed to the steep rise in our land where yellow forsythia bushes bloomed in the spring.

"Yes," I said, "that's the perfect place."

Phil Katz, a local contractor who was writing a book called *Imperator: The Life of Gaius Julius Caesar*, took on the task of creating the huge eighty-pound replica of the Globe Theater that Robin Wagner had designed. At his country workshop he began to build the Elizabethan stage, balconies, railings, and columns specified in Robin's blueprint, and to hand-carve one hundred cedar shingles with copper flashing for the roof of the birdhouse.

Although our Elizabethan aviary was supposed to be ready by the following summer, its painstaking fabrication required more time, so the summer passed, fall came, and winter folded into another year before it was finished. When the massive Globe Theater Birdhouse was finally installed in the spring of 1992 on a ten-foot-high post at the top of the hill that Joe had designated, it towered over a sweeping view of our cottage and its meadow.

During the day all kinds of birds alighted on the aviary's thrust stage and perched on its railings and shingled roof. Silhouetted on the hill at night, the Globe Theater Birdhouse looked magically expectant in the moonlight, as if waiting for a play to begin. All that was missing, I thought, was an Aida trumpet fanfare to bring on the players, and a flag on its roof to signal a performance as in Shakespeare's time.

Its absence there brought to mind the festive flags that I used to see waving on the ramparts of the theater in Central Park—where Joe, with an eagle eye trained on the stage from his seat in the darkened bleachers, had once whispered in my ear, "Tell Pandarus to say his lines out front. *To the audience.*"

60

Epilogue, or, The Continuation

It would be a daunting challenge for anyone to follow in the footsteps of a charismatic founder like Joe and take charge of a complex institution like the Public Theater. And yet, he has been succeeded by three artistic directors who have each built on his legacy in their own uniquely gifted ways with the result that the Public Theater remains at the top of its form in the twenty-first century.

JoAnne Akalaitis, the Public's Artistic Director from 1991 to 1993, is the person who courageously stepped up to the challenge when Joe asked her to be his successor. Her relationship with him began when Mabou Mines, the renowned experimental company that she co-founded, was in residence at the Public Theater in the 1970s–1980s. As a director she created an outstanding body of work at the Public that included provocative plays like *Dead End Kids: The Story of Nuclear Power* as well as exciting stagings of Beckett and Shakespeare, and, after she became the Public's artistic director, John Ford's seventeenth-century classic *'Tis a Pity She's a Whore*. All of her productions were distinguished by the iconoclastic artistry and social consciousness that won Joe's admiration of her as the kind of creative force he wanted to follow him at the Public Theater.

George C. Wolfe, the Public's Producer from 1993 to 2004, became involved with the Public when Joe produced his audaciously satirical play *The Colored Museum* in 1986. In 1989 he had been one of four directors to whom

Joe handed over the artistic administration of the Public Theater. Later, during his bold and innovative tenure as the Public's Producer, George C. Wolfe directed Suzan-Lori Parks' Pulitzer Prize–winning *Topdog/Underdog* and the unforgettable *Bring In Da Noise/Bring in Da Funk* with choreographer-performer Savion Glover, for which he won the 1996 Tony Award as director. He also directed the premiere of Tony Kushner and Jeanine Tesori's extraordinary musical *Caroline, or Change*, and directed and collaborated on the book of *The Wild Party* with composer Michael John LaChiusa.

Under separate auspices on Broadway, George C. Wolfe directed, with Joel Grey, the Tony Award 2011 revival of Larry Kramer's *The Normal Heart*, which had been developed by and premiered at the Public Theater in 1985. In 1998, he launched and named the hugely popular Joe's Pub, which is still going strong. His viewpoint was always original and complex.

As the Public's producer, George dramatically enriched and increased the diversity of the Public Theater's artistic representation and staff in the course of a splendid decade distinguished by brilliant, socially driven productions that won many major awards and that established an important legacy of his own alongside that of Joe's from a different era. He said, "I tried to make the Public look like the America that I live in . . . My ambition was not to exclude anybody but to expand the definition."

Oskar Eustis, the Public's Artistic Director since 2005, had previously served as the artistic director of Trinity Repertory Theater in Providence and as associate artistic director of the Mark Taper Forum in Los Angeles, where he staged the premiere of Tony Kushner's *Angels in America*, which he had commissioned.

Within his first decade it was widely recognized that Oskar Eustis's farsighted leadership had brought the Public Theater to another peak of artistic excellence and social relevance, with its productions having an almost continuous presence on Broadway and in national tours and foreign productions. He had spearheaded a major renovation that enhanced the physical beauty and utility of the Public's landmark building, created the handsome new Public Studios for artists across the street from it, and put into motion a sprucing up of the sixty-year-old Delacorte Theater in Central Park. He'd also reinvented the substance and spirit of the Public's Mobile Unit and established Public Works, which invites community members to join in the creation of participatory theater.

Many theater artists have flourished under his auspices, winning numerous awards for their outstanding work in all categories, including *Hamilton*, the ground-breaking, Pulitzer Prize–winning musical by Lin-Manuel Miranda.

After the world changed in 2020 with the onset of the Covid-19 pandemic and the police murder of George Floyd, Oskar guided the Public Theater through the difficult years that ensued when the necessary halt in performances for health reasons converged with the nationwide movement for racial reckoning. He has successfully brought artists, workers, and audiences back to the stages of the Public Theater with plays like *Fat Ham*, James Ijames' Pulitzer Prize–winning riff on Hamlet, and musicals like Shaina Taub's *Suffs*, whose suffragist story eerily coincided with the Supreme Court's overturning of a woman's constitutional protection under *Roe vs. Wade*. He also reopened Shakespeare in the Park with Associate Artistic Director Saheem Ali's triumphant production of *The Merry Wives of Windsor* in a dazzling adaptation by Jocelyn Bioh.

Oskar says, "Our job is trying to hold up a mirror to America that shows not only who all of us are as individuals, but that welds us back into the community that we need to be. That's what the theater is supposed to do."

Appendix

Featured Actors, Choreographers, Composers, Directors, and Playwrights/ Lyricists/ Translators at the New York Shakespeare Festival and Public Theater, 1956 to 1991

FEATURED ACTORS (1956–1991)

Abraham, F. Murray
Adams, Mason
Adu, Frank
Aidman, Charles
Ailey, Alvin
Aldredge, Thomas
Alexander, C. K.
Alexander, Jane
Allen, Debbie
Allen, Joan
Allen, Jonelle
Allen, Penelope
Allen, Phillip Richard
Allen, Rae
Allen-Jones, Augusta
Alvarado, Trini
Ambrose, Amanda
Amidon, Priscilla

Amos, John
Anderman, Maureen
Anderson, Dion
Aniston, Jennifer
Antonacci, Greg
Arndt, Denis
Arnott, Mark
Arostegui, Diana
Atherton, William
Atienza, Edward
Auberjonois, Rene
Azito, Tony
Baker, Henry
Baker, Lenny
Baker, Mark-Linn
Balaban, Bob
Baldwin, Alec
Bamman, Gerry

Baranski, Christine
Barnett, Brigitte
Barr, Joseph
Barry, Raymond J.
Bartenieff, George
Bassett, Angela
Batson, Susan
Beane, Hilary Jean
Beckel, Graham
Belgrave, Cynthia
Benczak, Margaret
Benjamin, Paul
Benjamin, Richard
Bennion, Peggy
Beverley, Trazana
Bimbo
Birney, David
Birney, Reed

Drefuss, Richard
Drischell, Ralph
Duell, William
Duff-Griffin, William
Dukakis, Olympia
Dukes, David
Dunn, Michael
Durang, Christopher
Durning, Charles
Dussault, Nancy
Dworkin, Stan
Dysart, Richard A.
Dzundza, George
Eberling, George
Ehrenreich, Jake
Eikenberry, Jill
Eisenberg, Deborah
Elias, Alix
Elias, Hector
Elizondo, Hector
Elkins, Flora
Elliott, Patricia
Elliott, Shawn
Elliott, Stephen
Epstein, Pierre
Esperson, Patricia
Esterman, Laura
Evans, Karen
Faber, Ron
Fargas, Antonio
Ferraro, John
Fibich, Felix
Fields, Joe
Figueroa, Eduardo
Fitzgerald, Geraldine
Ford, Clebert
Forsythe, Henderson
Foster, Gloria
Fraser, Alison

Freeman, Morgan
French, Arthur
Frey, Leonard
Fuller, Penny
Fundación Rajatabla,
　Caracas, Venezuela
Gammel, Robin
Gaines, Sonny Jim
Galloway, Leata
Garfield, John, Jr.
Garrey, Colin
Gates, Larry
Gatton, Paul
George, Nathan
Gere, Richard
Gerringer, Robert
Gerut, Rosalie
Getz, John
Gibb, Andy
Gibbs, Sheila
Gibson, Thomas
Gien, Pamela
Gilbert, Lou
Gill, Ray
Gim, Asa
Giovanni, Nikki
Glaser, Paul Michael
Glen, Pamela
Glover, John
Glover, Savion
Goldblum, Jeff
Gómez, José Felix
Goodman, John
Goodman, Robyn
Goodwin, James
Gordon, Ruth
Gorman, Mari
Goslar, Lotte
Goya, Tito

Grassle, Karen
Greenberg, Sid
Greene, Ellen
Greist, Kim
Grey, Joel
Grey, Penelope
Grifasi, Joe
Grody, Kathryn
Group X, Stage Division
　of the Juilliard School
Grupo LaMama
Guidall, George
Guillaume, Robert
Gunn, Bill
Gunn, Moses
Gunton, Bob
Gwynne, Fred
Hagedorn, Jessica
Hagen, Uta
Hall, Albert
Hamilton, Lisa Gay
Hanan, Stephen
Handler, Evan
Harewood, Dorian
Harris, Jared
Harris, Joan
Harris, Julie
Harris, Neil
Harris, Rosemary
Hartley, Mariette
Hayes, Ben
Haynes, Jayne
Heard, John
Hearn, George
Hecht, Paul
Heckart, Eileen
Hedaya, Dan
Heffernan, John
Heflin, Marta

Mardirosian, Tom
Markle, Stephen
Marshall, Larry
Marshall, William
Martin, Ethel
Martin, George N.
Martin, Nan
Martinez, Nathalia
Mascolo, Joseph
Mason, Jackie
Mason, Marsha
Mastrantonio, Mary
  Elizabeth
Matlock, Norman
Maxwell, Roberta
Maxwell, Roberta
Mayer, Jerry
McArthur, Susan
McCarty, Conan
McCauley, Robbie
McClure, Spike
McElduff, Ellen
McGillin, Howard
McGinn, Walter
McGonagill, Gerald E.
McGovern, Elizabeth
McGovern, Maureen
McGuire, Michel
McKechnie, Donna
McKenna, Siobhan
McKenzie, Richard
McKinney, Chris
McManus, Don R.
McMartin, John
McMillan, Kenneth
Meara, Anne
Meat Loaf
Meisle, Kathryn
Mercado, Hector

Merin, Eda Reiss
Meyers, Bruce
Meyers, Marilyn
Miller, Betty
Miller, Harold
Miller, Jason
Miller, Linda
Moffat, Donald
Mokae, Zakes
Montgomery, Reggie
Moor, Bill
Moreno, Gigi
Moreno, Rene
Morgan, Cass
Moriarty, Michael
Morris, Garrett
Morris, Gary
Morris, Jonathan
Morton, Joe
Moss, Paula
Mulgrew, Kate
Mullins, Melinda
Murch, Robert
Murphy, Donna
Murray, Brian
National Theater Work-
  shop of Venezuela
National Youth Theater
  of Venezuela
Naughton, James
Nelligan, Kate
Nelson, Novella
Neumann, Frederick
Nixon, Cynthia
Noble, James
O'Brien, Erin J.
O'Connor, Kevin
Offner, Deborah
Ohama, Natsuko

O'Neal, Ron
O'Neill, Margaret
O'Shea, Milo
Oreskes, Daniel
Owens, Geoffrey
Pabon, Ramon
Pacino, Al
Page, Geraldine
Pankow, John
Parry, William
Parsons, Estelle
Pashalinski, Lola
Patinkin, Mandy
Patton, Will
Peacock, Chiara
Pearthree, Pippa
Perez, Jose
Pfeiffer, Michelle
Pichette, Joe
Pickles, Christina
Pierce, David Hyde
Pietropinto, Angela
Pine, Larry
Pinza, Carla
Pitchford, Dean
Pittsburg Factory
  Theater
Plimpton, Martha
Plimpton, Shelley
Plummer, Amanda
Plummer, Christopher
Plumley, Donald
Pogson, Kathryn
Pompeo, Augusto
Prado, Francisco
Pregones Group Theater
Prentiss, Paula
Primus, Barry
Procaccino, John

Taliaferro, Clay
Tandy, Jessica
Tarso, Ignacio Lopez
Tate, Dennis
Taylor, Clarice
Taylor, Lili
Taylor, Regina
Teatro del 60, Puerto Rico
Teatro do Ornitorrinco, São Paulo, Brazil
Tejera, Jose
Testa, Mary
Theater for a New Audience
Theater for the New City
The Manhattan Project
Thomas, Richard
Thompson, Sada
Tomei, Concetta
Torn, Rip
Toussaint, Lorraine
Tricerri, Christiane
Tripplehorn, Jeanne
Triska, Jan
Tsoutsouvas, Sam
Tsukayama, Masane
Tucci, Maria
Tucker, Forest
Tupou, Manu
Turner, Stephen
Turturro, John

Ullman, Tracey
Ullmann, Liv
Valdes, Ching
Vance, Courtney B.
Vance, Danitra
Van Tieghem, David
Vestoff, Virginia
Vickery, John
Vietnam Veterans Ensemble Theater Co.
Vigoda, Abe
Vinovich, Stephen
von Bargen, Daniel
Voskovec, George
Waite, Ralph
Walken, Christopher
Walken, Glenn
Walsh, Kenneth
Warren, Joseph
Warriner, Frederic
Washington, Denzel
Washington, Sharon
Waterston, Sam
Watson, Douglass
Watson, John
Waymon, Sam
Weaver, Sigourney
Weber, Jake
Weiss, Jeff
Weller, Peter
Westenberg, Robert
White, Jane

White, Lillias
Whitton, Margaret
Widdoes, Kathleen
Wiest, Diane
Wikes, Michael
Wildpret, Erich
Williams, Clarence, III
Williams, Dick Anthony
Williams, Sammy
Williams, Treat
Wilson, Elizabeth
Windom, William
Winfield, Paul
Winkler, Mel
Winston, Hattie
Wiseman, Joseph
Wolfe, Wendy
Wong, Victor
Woodard, Alfre
Woodard, Charlayne
Worth, Irene
Wright, Max
Wright, Samuel E.
Yarbrough, Camille
Young, Burt
Yulin, Harris
Zakkai, Jamil
Zang, Edward
Zaslow, Michael
Zeigler, Joseph
Zorich, Louis
Zwick, Joel

CHOREOGRAPHERS (1956–1991)

Adler, Diane
Ailey, Alvin
Allen, Debbie
Anthony, Mary
Avian, Bob
Barry, B. H.
Bayes, Sammy Dallas
Bennett, Michael
Bibble, Susan
Blanc, Marsha
Breuer, Lee
Broome, John
Cahan, Cora
Castellino, Bill
Clarke, Hope
Cobb, Caitlin
Cohen, Za-eva
Conrad, Gail
Cunningham, James
D'Cruz, Marion
Daniele, Graciela
Del Barrio, Raymond G.
DeLuca, John
Dodge, Marcia Milgram
Elice, Eric
Erdman, Jean
Fagan, Garth
Faison, George
Feld, Eliot
Figueroa, Willie

Fitzgerald, Ara
Folly, Val
Godreau, Miguel
Gordon, Marvin
Goslar, Lotte
Green, Alice
Griffin, Robert
Hanayagi, Kinnosuke
Hennum, Nels
Hidalgo, Allen
Hightower, Loren
Joffrey, Robert
Johnson, Louis
Jonsen, Tommy
Kaegi, Adriana
Keen, Elizabeth
Kirpich, Billy
Lampert, Rachel
Lee, Baayork
Lone, John
Maddox, Matt
Martel, Diane
Martin, Ethel
Martin, George
McIntyre, Diane
McKayle, Donald
Minns, Albert
Monk, Meredith
Moss, Paula
Muller, Jennifer

Murphy, Eddie, Jr.
Nahat, Dennis
Nels, Peter
Nikolais, Alwin
Overlie, Mary
Oyama, David
Pappas, Ted
Paul, Tina
Payson, Herta
Pistone, Martino N.
Posin, Kathryn
Rogers, Poli
Saddler, Donald
Salaam, Abdel
Salid, Otis
Salmon, Scott
Smallwood, Tucker
Smith, Michael
Streep III, Harry
Taylor-Corbett, Lynne
Theodore, Lee Becker
Tosti, Kenneth
Trisler, Joyce
Turner, Gail
Vazquez, Eddy
Weber, Anthony
Weber, Lynne
Wolshonak, Derek

COMPOSERS (1956–1991)

Abajian, Chris
Agyapon, Kweyao
Amram, David
Applebaum, Louis
Barron, David
Barron, John
Bayeza, Ifa
Benary, Barbara
Bicât, Nick
Bienstock, Arthur
Blades, Rubén
Blanco, Juan Marcos
Boone, Jobriath
Bostio, Kysia
Burg, Brad
Byers, Bill
Carroll, Baikida
Cavalli, Francesco
Cave, Claude, II
Chic Street Man
Coates, Keith
Colon, Willie
Corigliano, John
Coughlin, Bruce
Cox, Ronny
Danoff, Bill
Darnell, August
Davis, Larry
Del Negro, John
Dennis, Robert
Donizetti, Gaetano
Durkee, Norman
Dyer, Doug
Elliott, William
Fabián, Rafael Matías
Fabián, Salvatore Matías
Feldman, Bob
Finn, William

Fleming, Leopoldo
Ford, Nancy
Foreman, Richard
Fox, Patrick
Gates, Keith
Gerut, Rosalie
Glass, Philip
Goizueta, Adrián
Golub, Peter
Goya, Tito
Gross, Charles
Guare, John
Guilmartin, Ken
Hamlisch, Marvin
Hardwick, Cheryl
Harper, Wally
Henley, Leroy
Hernandez, Andy
Hoiby, Lee
Holmes, Rupert
Hwong, Lucia
Jaffe, Jill
Jans, Alaric
Johnson, Tom
Justice, Jimmy
Kagan, Sergius
Kaz, Fred
Kay, Hershy
Keen, Elizabeth
Kernochan, Sarah
Kievman, Carson
Killian, Scott
Laplante, Skip
Leempoor, Xantheus Ruh
Legrand, Michel
Lewis, John
Link, Peter
Lone, John

MacDermot, Galt
MacDonald, Catherine
Maloney, David
Mandell, Tom
Mann, Harry
Margoshes, Steven
Masterson, John
McAnuff, Des
McLean, Jackie
Mendez, Felix
Meyers, Nicholas
Modestti, Mirelsa
Monk, Meredith
Montgomery, Robert
Morris, Butch
Morris, John
Mozart, Wolfgang
  Amadeus
Murray, David
Nietzche, Jack
Nivert, Taffy
Nunez, Juan Carlos
Nurock, Kim
Odland, Bruce
O'Riada, Sean
Partch, Harry
Patterson, David
Peaslee, Richard
Penn, William
Pennington, Mark
Pine, Margaret
Puccini, Giacomo
Purcell, Henry
Ramírez, Ramiro (Ray)
Robins, Kenneth
Roswn, Louis
Ross, Randy Lee
Rundgren, Todd

Sahl, Michael
Salzman, Eric
Schierhorn, Paul
Schlosser, Peter
Schneider, Jana
Schreier, Daniel Moses
Shawn, Allen
Shepard, Sam
Sherman, Kim D.
Shioles, John
Shire, David
Silverman, Stanley
Smyrl, David Langston

Sperling, Ted
Spivak, Larry
Starobin, Michael
Stavrou, Alexander
Steinman, Jim
Steward, Ron
Sullivan, Sir Arthur
  Seymour
Swados, Elizabeth
Tanker, Andre
Tate, Neal
Telson, Bob
Tiranoff, Louise M.

Toledo, Pedro Rivera
Tosti, Kenneth
Trujillo, Marc Allen
Tunick, Jonathan
Vargas, Arturo Cornejo
Vasconcelos, Naná
Ward, Michael
Waymon, Sam
Weill, Kurt
Weinstock, Richard
Welch, David
White, Claude
Wood, Haydn

DIRECTORS (1956–1991)

Aaron, Jules
Ackerman, Robert Allan
Adell, Ilunga
Akalaitis, JoAnne
Alasa, Michael
Albino, Ramon
Alden, Christopher
Alden, David
Aldredge, Tom
Aleandro, Norma
Alfaro, Emilio
Algarín, Miguel
Allen, Billie
Allen, Rae
Antoon, A. J.
Araña, Reinaldo
Ardolino, Emile
Armando, Eddy
Athayde, Roberto
Baker, Mark-Linn
Baker, Word
Balaban, Bob
Barton, John
Bennett, Michael

Bensussen, Melia
Berg, Peter Von
Berghof, Herbert
Berkeley, Edward
Berkoff, Steven
Bernhardt, Melvin
Bey, Rafic
Blackwell, Sam
Blahnik, Jeremy
Bleckner, Jeff
Bonney, Jo
Brandoni, Luis
Brass, Tinto
Braswell, John
Breuer, Lee
Browne, Roscoe Lee
Bullard, Thomas
Bushnell, William H., Jr.
Cabrera, Pablo
Cacaci, Joe
Call, Edward Payson
Camillo, Marvin Felix
Carballido, Emilio
Carrasco, Carlos

Casas, Myrna
Castel, Sonia
Castellano, Bill
Castillo, Juan
Castro, Vicente
Catania, Alfredo
Chaikin, Joseph
Chambers, David
Charnin, Martin
Childress, Alice
Ciccone, Oscar
Ciulei, Liviu
Clarke, Martha
Clarke, Maureen
Clingerman, John
Coleman, Kevin
Coonrod, Karin
Cornell, Ted
Crinkley, Richmond
Curtis, Simon
Cynkutis, Zbigniew
d'Amboise, Jacques
Daniele, Graciela
Davey, Mark-Wing

DiFusco, John
DiGirolamo, Claudio
Dowling, Joe
Downey, Robert, Sr.
Duke, Bill
Dyer, Doug
Echols, Paul C.
Edelstein, Barry
Egan, Robert
Elliott, Kenneth
Ernotte, André
Fergusson, Honora
Field, Crystal
Figueroa, Eduardo
Fitzgerald, Geraldine
Fraad, Eric
Fraser, Jon
Freedman, Gerald
Friedman, Joel
Friedman, Kim
Funes, Filander
Gaines, Sonny Jim
Galban, Magarita
García, Anthony J.
García, Santiago
Gelber, Jack
George, Nathan
Gertsen, Bernard
Gile, Bill
Gill, Peter
Gillotte, Tony
Giménez, Carlos
Godreau, Miguel
Goldby, Derek
Goslar, Lotte
Grant, Lee
Greenspan, David
Gregg, Susan
Gregory, André

Greif, Michael
Grosbard, Ulu
Guilmartin, Ken
Gunn, Bill
Guskin, Harold
Guzman, Delfina
Hall, Adrian
Hare, David
Hart, Bill
Havinga, Nick
Hedley, Robert
Hoffman, Avi
Hofsiss, Jack
Holmes, John Pynchon
Hooks, Robert
Horwitz, Murray
Howell, Jane
Hughes, Douglas
Innaurato, Albert
Irby, Dean
Jenkin, Len
Johnston, Ernestine
Jones, James Earl
Jones, Richard
Jones, Walter
Jordan, Richard A.
Kahn, Michael
Keiser, Kris
Kellman, Barnet
Kenny, Sean
Kent, Steven
Kenyatta, Damon
Kievman, Carson
King, Woodie, Jr.
Kinney, Mary Lisa
Kline, Kevin
Krausnick, Dennis
Kulick, Brian
Langham, Michael

Larangeira, Crispin
Larry, Sheldon
Lathan, Bill
Leach, Wilfred
Ledesma, Inda
Lerena, Duman
Lespier, Alvan Colon
Lessac, Michael
Leveaux, David
Leventon, Annabel
Lieu, Ron Van
Life, Regge
Lindsay-Hogg, Michael
Lipton, Jame
Livingston, Robert H.
Lone, John
Lopez, Abel
Louis, Murray
Lowry, Mary
Macbeth, Robert
Mack, Ron
Madden, John
Maggio, Michael
Mako
Maldonado, Adal
    Alberto
Maleczech, Ruth
Maloney, Peter
Maltby, Richard, Jr.
Margulies, David
Markle, Christopher J.
Marlin-Jones, Davey
Marshall, Barry
Martin, George & Ethel
Martin, Manuel, Jr.
Matschullat, Kay
Meadow, Lynne
Meckler, Nancy
Medrano, Hugo

Medrano, María Alicia
  Martínez
Mee, Charles L., Jr.
Mee, Erin B.
Meyer, Michael
Milton, James
Mingus, Charles, Jr.
Monk, Meredith
Moses, Gilbert
Near, Timothy
Nelson, Novella
Nelson, Richard
Neumann, Frederick
Nichols, Mike
Nikolais, Alwin
Ninagawa, Yukio
O'Horgan, Tom
Oman, Timothy
Packer, Tina
Papp, Joseph
Pareja, Ramon
Parsons, Estelle
Pasquin, John
Patterson, David
Paul, Kent
Penn, Arthur
Pennington, Mark
Penuela, Fernando
Peters, William
Phillips, Robin
Phippin, Jackson
Pierce, Paula Kay
Pilgrim, Geraldine
Pomare, Eleo
Raffle, Shelly
Rame, Franca
Raymond, William
Redgrave, Vanessa
Reissa, Eleanor

Rene, Norman
Renfield, Elinor
Ribalow, Meir Zvi
Richards, Lloyd
Richardson, L. Kenneth
Riofrancos, Osvaldo
Rivera, Valli Marie
Robbins, Tim
Robins, Kenneth
Robinson, Andre, Jr.
Rogers, Poli
Rolf, Frederick
Rombola, Ed
Ronan, Robert
Rosset, Cacá
Rudman, Michael
Sameth, Jack
Sanchez, Francisco
Sanchez, Juan
Sanchez, Luis Rafael
Sanchez, Mario Ernesto
Sanders, Donald
Santaliz, Pedro
Santander, Felipe
Schachter, Steven
Schneider, Alan
Schneider, Paul
Schultz, Michael
Schumann, Peter
Schweizer, David
Scott, Oz
Serban, Andrei
Shange, Ntozake
Shanley, John Patrick
Shapiro, Leonardo
Shapiro, Mel
Sharim, Nissum
Sherin, Edward
Sherman, George

Shyre, Paul
Sills, Paul
Simon, Cyril
Simon, Roger Hendricks
Skagestad, Tormod
Skurski, Gloria
Small, Robert Graham
Sokolow, Anna
Solis, Giselle
Southern, Richard
Stafford-Clark, Max
Stekelman, Ana Maria
Stewart, Gordon
Storer, Jeff
Sullivan, Daniel
Swados, Elizabeth
Sydow, Jack
Tabakov, Oleg P.
Tate, Dennis
Tavora, Salvador
Tavorachis, Salvador
Taylor, Carl "Rafic"
Teodoro, Jose Antonio
Tillinger, John
Torn, Rip
Turner, Charles
Vaughan, Gladys
Vaughan, Stuart
Vela, Julia
von Berg, Peter
Vos, Richard
Walcott, Derek
Warren, David
Waters, Les
Weill, Claudia
Wheeler, David
Wilson, Lisle
Wolfe, George C.
Woodruff, Robert

Worsley, Dale
Wright, Garland
Zaks, Jerry

Zapata, Miguel Rubio
Zimmer, Steve
Zizka, Jiri

Zollo, Frederick
Zwick, Joe

PLAYWRIGHTS, LYRICISTS, AND TRANSLATORS (1956–1991)

Abbensetts, Michael
Abujamra, Marcia
Acaz, Mba
Adell, Ilunga
Aeschylus
Agueros, Jack
Akalaitis, JoAnne
Alasa, Michael
Albee, Edward
Aleandro, Norma
Aleichem, Sholem
Alexander, C. K.
Algarin, Miguel
Aloma, Rene R.
Anderson, Robert
Ansky, S.
Antonacci, Greg
Antoon, A. J.
Artaud, Antonin
Athayde, Roberto
Augenlicht, J. C.
Auletta, Robert
Avellaneda, Martha
Babe, Thomas
Baker, Mark-Linn
Baraotti, Sergio
Baumann, Michael
"Bommi"
Beckett, Samuel
Bensussen, Melia
Bermel, Albert
Black, Lewis
Blackwell, Vera
Bogosian, Eric

Bond, Edward
Bonfigli, Barbara
Boone, Jobriath
Borow, Rena Berkowicz
Bread & Puppet Theater
Brecht, Bertolt
Breuer, Lee
Broad, Jay
Brown, Gerald
Buber, Martin
Buchner, Georg
Bulgakov, Mikhail
Bullins, Ed
Burr, Anne
Burr, Charles
Burroughs, William
Burton, C. L.
Cabrera, Pablo
Cacaci, Joe
Cacoyannis, Michael
Cale, David
Carroll, Lewis
Casas, Myrna
Catania, Carlos
Cea, Jose Roberto
Cerda, Carlos
Chaikin, Joe
Chekhov, Anton
Childress, Alice
Chioles, John
Churchill, Caryl
Clarke, Martha
Cohen, Marvin
Colette

Colon, Rosalba
Colon, Willie
Congdon, Constance
Congreve, William
Corradi, Pedro
Corwin, Walter
Courtney, C. C.
Courtney, Ragan
Covington, Julie
Crinkley, Richmond
Cryer, Gretchen
Dalton, Roque
d'Amboise, Jacques
Dante, Nicholas
Darnell, August
Dávila, Jesús Gonzáles
Davis, Thulani
Dean, Phillip Hayes
DeCecco, Sergio
de la Parra, Marco
Antonio
Demy, Jacques
Diaz, Jorge
Dickens, Charles
DiFusco, John
Director, Roger
Doctorow, E. L.
Dostoevsky, Fyodor
Downey, Roger
Dumaresq, William
Dunnigan, Ann
Durang, Christopher
D'Urfey, Thomas
Dyer, Doug

Larangeira, Crispin
Lardner, Ring
Laviera, Jesus Abraham
Layton, Susan
Le Candeleria Company
Ledesma, Inda
Lee, James
Legrand, Michel
Leivick, H.
Leonard, Hugh
Lerici, Roberto
Lind, Jakov
Link, Peter
Linn-Baker, Mark
Little, Anastazia
Llosa, Mario Vargas
Lorca, Federico García
Mabou Mines
MacGowran, Jack
Machiavelli, Niccolo
Mailer, Norman
Maldonado, Adal Alberto
Maleczech, Ruth
Maltz, Albert
Mamet, David
Manger, Itsik
Mannheim, Ralph
Margulies, Donald
Mark, Charles C.
Mark, Claude C.
Márquez, Gabriel García
Martin, Manuel, Jr.
Marzán, Julio
Mason, Jackie
Mayer, Jerry
McAnuff, Des
McCall, Tulis
McGonagle, Susan
McGrath, Russell

McGuire, Michael
Mednick, Murray
Mee, Charles L., Jr.
Meléndez, Jesus Papolito
Meyer, Marlane
Meyer, Michael
Middleton, Thomas
Miles, Cherrilyn
Miller, Jason
Miller, Marilyn Suzanne
Miller, Nina
Miller, Susan
Miller, Terry
Milner, Ron
Mingus, Charles L., Jr.
Modestti, Mirelsa
Molière
Monk, Meredith
Montgomery, Robert
Monzaemon, Chikamatsu
Moody, Michael Dorn
Moran, Michael
Moriarty, Michael
Morner, Palaemona
Morton, Carlos
Nabokov, Vladimir
Nathan, Robert
Nelson, Naomi
Nelson, Richard
Neruda, Pablo
Neumann, Frederick
Nichols, Robert
Noonan, John Ford
Ntshona, Winston
O'Brien, Edna
O'Neill, Eugene
Orkeny, Istvan
Orton, Joe
Osorio, Pepon

Osorio, Raul
Oyamo
Page, Louise
Palmer, John
Parnell, Peter
Partch, Harry
Paul, Christina
Pena, Edilio
Penuela, Fernando
Perez, Silverio
Perez, Silvio
Pesutic, Mauricio
Peters, William
Peyton, Caroline
Pierce, Paula Kay
Pietri, Pedro
Pinero, Arthur Wing
Piñero, Miguel
Pinter, Harold
PITS (Playwriting in the
    Schools)
Ponzi, Joe
Povod, Reinaldo
Price, Tim Rose
Prokofieva, Sofia
Rabe, David
Rado, James
Rafalowicz, Mira
Ragni, Gerome
Rahman, Aishah
Rame, Franca
Ramirez, Ramiro (Ray)
Raymond, William
Reardon, Dennis
Reddin, Keith
Reding, Rodney
Rial, José Antonio
Rivera, José
Robbins, Tim

Bibliography

Bain, Douglas. "CLOSE UP. JOE PAPP," *Daily News*, July 30, 1985

Balfour, Katherine. Forward, WEVD Radio, April 28, 1981

Barnes, Clive. "A Tremendous *A Chorus Line* Arrives," *New York Times*, May 22, 1975

Barnes, Clive. "Slings and Arrows of Outrageous Papp: Director Throws Bard to the Philistines," *New York Times*, December 2, 1967

Bosworth, Patricia. "Arts & Entertainment. Gail Merrifield: New York Theater World's Best Kept Secret," *Working Woman Magazine*, November 1985

Bradley, Adam. "Building a New Canon of Black Literature," *The New York Times Style Magazine*, March 3, 2023

Brady, James. "IN STEP WITH: Joseph Papp," *Parade Magazine*, April 20, 1986

Burke, Edward C. "Papp Doth Win Battle of Public Theater," *New York Times*, March 26, 1971

Byron, Stuart. "ARTBEAT. The Politics of Culture. He's Getting His Act Together and Taking It to L.A." *Village Voice*, April 9, 1978

Caro, Robert A. *The Power Broker: Robert Moses and the Fall of New York*, Vintage Books, 1975

Carroll, Maurice. "Papp Walks Out on City Talks About Buying Festival Theater," *New York Times*, March 12, 1971

Chira, Susan with Jessica Bassett, "The Workplace, Then and Now," *New York Times*, October 1, 2018

Darrach, Brad. "Impresario Joe Papp Is America's Premier Theater Man," *People Magazine*, July 28, 1975

Davis, Charles T. *Black Is the Color of Cosmos: Essays on Afro-American Literature and Culture, 1942–1981*, edited by Henry Louis Gates Jr. Garland Publishing Company, 1982

Dewhurst, Colleen, with Tom Viola. *Colleen Dewhurst: Her Autobiography*. A Lisa Drew Book/Scribner, 1997

DeWitt, Karen. "New Fiscal Year Ends Anti-Obscenity Pledge," *New York Times*, October 31, 1990

Egan, Cy. "Papp Theater: To Be or Not To Be?" *New York Post*, March 12, 1972

Epstein, Helen. *Joe Papp: An American Life*. Little, Brown and Company, 1994

FitzGerald, Frances. Blackwood Productions. Taped interview with Joseph Papp, 1982

Foster, Emmett. Taped interview with Gail Papp about *The Normal Heart*, 1995

Franklin, Ruth. Night Talk, WOR Radio, August 25, 1980

Gates, Henry Louis, Jr. "Charles Twitchell Davis: The Seminal Scholar of the African-American Literary Tradition," *Journal of Blacks in Higher Education*, 2008

Gelb, Arthur. "City Room," A Marian Wood Book published by G.P. Putnam's Sons, 2003

Hamburger, Phillip. Phillip Hamburger Papers 1931–1991, New York Public Library, Manuscript and Archives Section

Hare, David. "No Ordinary Joe," The *Guardian*, February 6, 2006

Hart, Bill. Taped interview with Gail Papp about *The Normal Heart*, 1995

Havel, Václav. *Letters to Olga: June 1979–September 1982*. Translated from the Czech with an introduction by Paul Wilson. Faber and Faber, 1990

Horn, Barbara Lee. *Joseph Papp: A Bio-Bibliography*, Greenwood Press, 1992

Hutcheson, Stuart. Performance Today, NPR, March 19, 1971

Jefferson, Margo. "REVISIONS; Reading a Play Demands Reading Between the Lines," *New York Times*, December 11, 2000

Jefferson, Margo. *Negroland, A Memoir*. Pantheon Books, 2015

Jefferson, Margo. *Constructing a Nervous System*. Pantheon Books, 2022

Kauffmann, Stanley. "Theater: The Stages of Joseph Papp," *The American Scholar*, vol. 44, no. 1 (Winter 1974–75)

King, Christine E. and Brenda Coven. *Joseph Papp and the New York Shakespeare Festival: An Annotated Bibliography*. Garland Publishing, Inc., 1988

King, Larry. *The Larry King Show*, WOR Radio, February 25, 1982

Kramer, Larry. *The Normal Heart*. Dutton and Plume Paperback, 1985

Lefkowitz, Mary R. and Maureen B. Fant. *Women's Life in Greece and Rome: A Source Book in Translation*. Johns Hopkins University Press, 1982

Lipson, Karin. "On Arts Funding. Few Fans for NEA Compromise," *Newsday*, October 31, 1990

Little, Stuart W. *Enter Joseph Papp: In Search of a New American Theater*. Coward McCann & Geoghegan, Inc., 1974

Martinson Cabaret Stories: *Daily News, New York Post, New York Times, Playbill, Variety*, 1977

Michener, Charles. "Joe Papp's Universal Theater," *Newsweek*, July 3, 1972

New York Post, "Papp Moving to Lincoln Center," March 1973

Papp, Joseph. "The Price of This Ticket Is Responsibility," *New York Herald-Tribune*, March 18, 1958

Papp, Joseph, assisted by Ted Cornell. *William Shakespeare's "Naked" Hamlet: A Production Handbook*. The Macmillan Company, 1969

Papp, Joseph. Letter to Mayor John V. Lindsay, March 16, 1973

Papp, Joseph. Speech, National Press Club, Washington, D.C., September 16, 1980

Papp, Joseph. Re George C. Scott. Studs Terkel, WMFT, 1980

Papp, Joseph. Comments about the demolition of the Morosco Theater, March 22, 1982, on WOR News, WCBS News, WNBC

Papp, Joseph. "Speaking for Everyman: Ian McKellen Celebrates Shakespeare's Birthday," interview on National Public Radio, October 20, 1987

Papp, Joseph. Foreword to *The Bantam Shakespeare: The Complete Works of William Shakespeare*. Edited by David Bevington, Bantam Books, 1988

Papp, Joseph. Letter to Frank Stanton, President, CBS, July 19, 1989

Papp, Joseph. Foreword to *Poets for Life: Seventy-Six Poets Respond to AIDS*. Edited with an Introduction by Michael Klein. Crown Publishers, Persea Books, New York, 1989

Papp, Joseph. "I'm a Producer, Not a Censor," *New York Times*, April 14, 1990

Papp, Joseph. "NEA: Once More Unto the Breach," *Los Angeles Times*, July 2, 1990

Papp, Joseph, and Kenneth Turan. *Free for All: Joe Papp, The Public, and the Greatest Theater Story Ever Told*. Doubleday, 2009

Rich, Frank. "Fantasy *Cymbeline* Set Long After Shakespeare," *New York Times*, June 1, 1989

Rich, Frank. "Peaks and Valleys in Papp's Marathon," *New York Times*, February 6, 1989

Rosenbens & Fitz Show, WNEW-AM, NY, April 17, 1990

Rothstein, Mervyn. "Papp, Seeking Aid, Resists Signing Pledge on Obscenity," *New York Times*, April 19, 1990

Rothstein, Mervyn. "Papp Reorganizes Shakespeare Festival," *New York Times*, May 29, 1990

Russell, Roberta. "Prime Movers," *Wall Street Journal* interview, November 21, 1978

Sheen, Martin. "Oral History of the NY Shakespeare Festival," 1987

Shmulewitz, Yitzakh. "The Teacher Moshe's Grandson," *Jewish Daily Forward*,
    January 14, 1977. Translated from Yiddish by Susan Levin

Stockwell, Anne. "Wolfe's New Direction: Out Director George C. Wolfe Talks
    about Moving from Theater to Film with HBO's Lackawanna Blues," The
    Advocate, February 1, 2005

Swados, Elizabeth. "Upfront: Broadway Baby," *Vogue*, December 2000

Terkel, Studs. WMFT Radio, Chicago, 1980

Theatre Talk, NYU School of Education, June 22, 1966. Edited by Dr. Leroy Paves
    and Barbara James

Turan, Kenneth, and Joseph Papp. *Free for All: Joe Papp, The Public, and the
    Greatest Theater Story Ever Told.* Doubleday, 2009

Valladares, Carlos. "Cosmic Freeze Frames: A Poetics of Bill Gunn," *Gagosian
    Quarterly*, Spring 2021

Voutas, Martha. "The Business of Dressing for Business: Women Who Succeeded in
    Business without Really Trying to Dress for It," *Working Woman Magazine*, April
    1978

Weiss, Rep. Theodore. Congressional Record, 1991

Winfrey, Carey. "Papp Quits Lincoln Center, Citing Artistic-Fiscal 'Trap'," *New
    York Times*, June 10, 1977

Witchel, Alex. "Papp Successor Chosen: JoAnne Akalaitis Has Succeeded Joseph
    Papp as Head of the New York Shakespeare Festival," *New York Times*, August
    22, 1991

Acknowledgments

This is my first book undertaken later in life. I'm therefore exceedingly grateful to my friends and theater colleagues, as well as people I didn't previously know, for their support during my work on *Public/Private*. I will start with friends and colleagues.

For the book's genesis I'm indebted to Celia Mitchell (1911–2008), a psychotherapist (not my own) and former supervisor at the Jewish Family Service who was a dear personal friend to Joe and myself. I have dedicated the book to her because it was Celia's original suggestion that I write about my life with Joe and thanks to her steadfast belief in my ability to do it, she caused it to happen.

I'm deeply grateful for the support of Rosemarie Tichler, the former artistic producer of the Public Theater, whose invaluable feedback and unflagging personal encouragement helped me to believe that my task was worthy of Joe's legacy.

I've been deeply moved by the support I've received from Oskar Eustis, the artistic director of the Public Theater. Although I enjoy the reassuring warmth of his bear hugs, I have always been keenly aware of his brilliant analytic mind and have tried to adhere to that high standard in my writing and recollections, just as I would if Joe himself was looking over my shoulder.

Heartfelt thanks to actor-playwright Kathryn Grody for her creative thoughts about the early drafts of my book and for recommending the sanctuary of The Writers Room, and to her and actor-singer Mandy Patinkin for introducing me to Developmental Editor Arielle Eckstut, whose expertise was most helpful at just the right time.

The book's stunning Appendix of Featured Actors, Choreographers, Composers, Directors, and Playwrights at the Public Theater from 1956 to 1991 was compiled from the amazing records generously shared with me by the Public Theater's current Casting Directors Jordan Thaler and Heidi Griffiths.

I'm indebted to writer-performer and Public Staff Assistant Emmett Foster (1947–2023) for the time he spent regaling me with his vivid recollections about playwright Larry Kramer (1935–2020), which I've incorporated verbatim in my chapter about *The Normal Heart*. I'm similarly indebted to Public Theater Literary Manager Bill Hart (1937–2008) for sharing with me his luminous insights about this important play.

I'm greatly beholden to Kenneth Turan, former film critic at the *Los Angeles Times* and the co-author with Joe of *Free for All: Joe Papp, The Public, and the Greatest Theater Story Ever Told* (Doubleday, 2009). He sent me nineteen cartons of the transcripts of his 161 interviews for *An Oral History of the New York Shakespeare Festival* commissioned by the Public Theater in 1987, which later served as the basis of *Free for All*. His interview transcripts fill 6,688 pages, and Kenny has been incredibly gracious about my use of several unpublished quotes from them.

Of crucial importance: This book owes its physical existence today due to the fact that a few years ago I met Kate Gyllenhaal, a member of the theatrical Gyllenhaal clan, who is an extraordinary fitness coach/choreographer and the Co-Founder of CREA Interactivity. Kate's advocacy and encouragement truly changed my life when she put me in touch with her sister-in-law Phyllis Azar, a former book publishing executive at Macmillan Publishers, who recommended another key person in this book's unpredictable journey—Bridget Marmion, president of Bridget Marmion Book Marketing. Bridget has been a generous and astute professional advisor who, with the expert assistance of her company's tech-savvy vice president, Rich Kelly, has given me an education in the strategic art of bringing a book to the attention of its potential readers.

I also owe Bridget thanks from the bottom of my heart for introducing me to my agent Philip Turner, of Philip Turner Book Productions. He is not only someone superbly attuned to the publishing market for books about theater, but who also brought his formidable skills as an editor to my manuscript, for which I am eternally grateful.

It was due to Philip Turner's improvement and presentation of my memoir that it found a home at Applause Theatre and Cinema Books, an imprint of Globe Pequot, America's foremost publisher of theater, cinema, and TV books, where I have received wonderful support from Acquisitions Editor John Cerullo and his accomplished staff.

I'm especially grateful to Barbara Claire, Editorial Assistant at Rowman & Littlefield/Globe Pequot, for her unflagging help with the photo sections, and to Ashleigh Cooke, Production Editor at Rowman & Littlefield Publishing Company, for overseeing the final Page and Photospread Proofs.

The expertise of Photo Researcher Nicole DiMella of Lemon Snap Image Services has been absolutely indispensable in finding the wonderful images that appear in the book. Jeremy Megraw, photograph librarian at the New York Public Library's Billy Rose Theater Division, was also essential in that painstaking work. I owe thanks to Jeffrey Kane of LTI/Lightside Photographic Services for the restoration of personal snapshots, and to Public Theater Intern Caroline Mabee for her help copying photos and documents in the Public Theater's archives. I'm also grateful to Joe Peng, managing director of Mac Concierge, Inc., for the excellent photographic design and maintenance of my website https://gailpapp.com.

I want to thank Barbara Carroll, Joe Papp's singular chief of staff, for keeping me in touch with colleagues from our era and for providing me with a towering stack of many years of Joe's daily appointments, which made it possible to fact-check myself.

Many thanks to Lynn Holst, former associate director of the Public Theater's Play Department and later vice president of Entertainment at RHI Hallmark, for her close reading of the manuscript and sustained interest. I'm grateful for the encouragement I received from Jason Steven Cohen, former associate producer of the Public Theater, as well as from Iris Fodor, Professor Emerita at NYU Steinhardt, Sebastian Zimmermann, the author and photographer of *Fifty Shrinks*, and my friend actor/psychotherapist Ellen Feinstein, whose witty empathy was most welcome during the challenging task of writing a first book.

I'm indebted to Helen Epstein, the distinguished author of *Children of the Holocaust: Conversations with Sons and Daughters of Survivors* and many other books, for her generous and patient help at the beginning of my writing process.

I was lucky indeed to meet Kelly Caldwell, my instructor in Memoir Writing at the Gotham Writers' Workshop. Her judicious comments and friendly advocacy inspired my steady improvement over the course of two hugely rewarding terms in her classes. A lovely boost came from *Writer's Digest* editorial reader Carolyn Walker with her sensitive early response to the book, and I later benefited from author/editor Louise Bernikow's professional critique of the manuscript.

A compilation of Joe's writing, which supports his quotes that I've used in the book, was made possible with the expert assistance of freelance editors Charlotte Carter, Mark Evan Chimsky, and the indefatigable Christine Chamberlain, the founding principal of Camden Writers.

On a personal note, I must express my love and deepest thanks to Joe's five children—Susan Lippman, Barbara Mosser, Michael Faulkner, Miranda Adani, and the late Tony Papp—for their wonderful presence in my life.

My everlasting gratitude and love includes Rosemary Didi Jordan, my live-in daughter-in-law and a practitioner of Wise Earth Aryuveda, for her discerning ear, excellent judgment, and sunny companionship at home.

Finally, I'm forever beholden to the memory of my gifted and unusual parents—Gladys Bovard Merrifield and Richard Forrester Merrifield, who would have been please to know that, like them, I wrote a book.

Index

About the Author

GAIL MERRIFIELD PAPP was born in San Francisco into a family with a deep theater lineage. After joining Joseph Papp's New York Shakespeare Festival in 1965, she became director of New Works Development for the Public Theater and was responsible for some of its best-remembered productions. These include *The Normal Heart*, Larry Kramer's Tony Award–winning play about the AIDS crisis, for which she received the Human Rights Campaign Arts and Communication Award, and Rupert Holmes' Tony Award–winning Best Musical *The Mystery of Edwin Drood*. Gail Merrifield and Joseph Papp were married in 1976.

Gail Papp has served as editorial advisor to two books about her husband: *Joe Papp: An American Life* by Helen Epstein (Little, Brown & Company, 1994) and *Free for All: Joe Papp, The Public, and the Greatest Theater Story Ever Told* by Kenneth Turan and Joseph Papp (Doubleday, 2009).

Producer-Director **JOSEPH PAPP** (1921–1991) founded the New York Shakespeare Festival which since 1954 has produced free Shakespeare in New York City. He also founded the Public Theater as a home for new American work, which opened in 1967 with the original production of *Hair*. He produced six hundred plays and musicals that won more than 200 stage, film, and television awards.

Called "the most important force in the English-speaking theater" in the twentieth century, Joe Papp was also an outspoken champion of human rights and the First Amendment who, in the words of the *Congressional Record*, "struggled to make New York City and our country a more livable place, to uplift our spirits, to challenge our minds, and see us through to another day."

Of course, Joe could have chosen from dozens of speeches that he knew by heart, but he offered instead a single line from *King Lear*, explaining that he had just seen Laurence Olivier's film of it with President Reagan at the White House, which, of course, impressed our conservative hosts and their special guest.

"It's the line when the Earl of Gloucester meets King Lear on the heath," Joe said to Roy Cohn, who leaned forward now in rapt attention.

"Gloucester wants to kiss Lear's hand," Joe went on, "but the mad king withdraws it, saying, 'Let me wipe it first; it smells of mortality.'"